KT-551-895

JAMES MOTTRAM

STOCK NO.

TD | 35

PUBLIC ENEMIES: THE GANGSTER MOVIE A-Z

© James Mottram 1998

All rights reserved. No part of this publication may be reproduced, in any
form or by any means, without permission from the publisher

Printed in Hong Kong by Colorcraft Ltd.

for the publishers
BT Batsford
583 Fulham Road
London
SW6 5BY

ISBN 0 7134 8276 1

A catalogue record for this book is available from the British Library

Pictures: courtesy of Gary Parfitt and the British Film Institute

To Jami, for the love, strength and inspiration you have given me.

Technical abbreviations used in this book:

Dir. - Director, **Prod.** - Producer, **Exec. Prod.** - Executive Producer, **Scr.** - Screenwriter,
DOP - Director of Photography, **Ed.** - Editor, **Art Dir.** - Art Director, **Prod. Des.** - Production Designer,
Vis. Cons. - Visual Consultant, **Music.** - Music Composer, **Music Ed.** - Music Editor,
Music Sup. - Music Supervisor

ACKNOWLEDGEMENTS

I would like to thank the following for their assistance in the preparation of this book.

To my editor Richard Reynolds, without whom this book would just be a pipe-dream; to Robert Tanitch for his
objective advice, and to my parents, for taping the Humphrey Bogart season a decade ago.

For their generous supply of library tapes, I am indebted to Channel 4 and Hayden Williams. Thanks also
must go to the informative assistants of both Star Video and Flicks n' Pix, and to David Snell for his tireless
accedence to my demands. I would also like to thank the BFI library, without whose resources I would have
been lost. I also send my heartfelt thanks to Debra McMahon, for our head-to-heads on *The Godfather*, and to
Rose, James, Alex and Amy – those who never took to life in the 'village' – thank you for suffering.

Special thanks also to the Teran family for accommodating my erratic needs during the summer of '97.

J - DEC 2000

CONTENTS

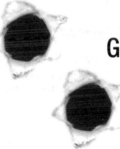

CHECKED   JUN 2008

INTRODUCTION

'At bottom, the gangster is doomed because he is under the obligation to succeed, not because the means he employs are unlawful... This is our intolerable dilemma: that failure is a kind of death and success is evil and dangerous, is – ultimately – impossible. The effect of the gangster film is to embody this dilemma and resolve it by his death.'

(Robert Warshow, 'The Gangster as Tragic Hero', *The Immediate Experience*, 1948)

The gangster film has remained the most perennial of generic entertainments, since its early grounding in works like D.W. Griffith's *The Musketeers of Pig Alley*. Unlike the western, the horror or science fiction film, all of which have fallen from favour for prolonged periods resurfacing only as either Hollywood fads, post-modern exercises or revisionist works, the chameleonic gangster film has instinctually survived audiences' fickle tastes. As Warshow suggests, the gangster's experience is ours, his rise and fall mirrors the potential and possibilities for our own lives, though we vicariously enjoy his sadistic adventures. We may never have met one, and we may not indulge in criminal activity, but his existence in the modern world 'as an experience of art' is universal. His is not the folklore of the frontier, but grounded in historical events that cinemagoers had undergone, a figure of both city and country. Be it Prohibition, World War II, the Cuban missile crisis or Vietnam, the success of the gangster film thrived on real-life source material.

From the genre's conception was a desire to create works gleaned from 'Today's Headlines'. Writers such as *Chicago Tribune* journalist Ben Hecht (screenwriter of *Scarface* and *Kiss of Death*) were glancing back only a few years to events that shaped America. European and Asian attempts at emulating the genre have also drawn from their own histories, prompting the idea that the genre is a cipher for narcissistic self re-evaluation. Indeed, historians of the next millennium could do worse than examine the genre as an accurate reflection of social and political history. Consistently re-inventing itself, the history of the gangster film, and its gangsters, parallels that of its country of origin. For

the US, the 1930s saw films like *Scarface* reflect the heyday of Prohibition, highlighting the desire for and dilemma of social mobility. Prior to the enforcement of the Hays Code, which stipulated guidelines for potentially amoral screen material, the gangster film hit its peak; with most produced by Warner Brothers studios, hedonistic classics such as *The Public Enemy* and *Little Caesar* were made. The late thirties, with what may be regarded as the second cycle, saw other studios (Fox, MGM) try their hand at the genre, while Warners' efforts like *The Roaring Twenties* and *The Last Gangster* omitted the violence in place of nostalgia for the era. Post-World War II, and from the gangster film flourished the pessimistic tone of *film noir*, with films like *Out of the Past*, inspired by nationwide disillusionment. Here, the gangster was no longer the city wide boy but a loner up against almost unseen forces. The nuclear shadow hanging over the States, the Cold War and the McCarthy era led to films like *On the Waterfront* and *White Heat*, while the Kefauver investigations led to a spate of documentary-like examinations of syndicate crime in the early fifties. The gangster had become the businessman, covering his activities with respectability; this then transmuted into nostalgia in the late part of the decade – leading to a re-examination of real gangsters who had assumed mythic status. One may argue that the mid-sixties was the one blip in the genre's history, Arthur Penn's *Bonnie and Clyde* coming to the rescue with its graphic violence in the late part of the decade. Considered almost dead, it was this – together with Francis Ford Coppola's *The Godfather* series (inextricably linking gangsters to politics and industry) – that spawned a host of imitations, spin-offs and sub-genres. Both were

SOLIHULL S.F.C.
LIBRARY

nostalgic, presenting their figures in some ways as innocents. But from that moment on the longevity of the genre was secured, sparking increasingly violent works in the hope of verisimilitude.

Two questions require answers: what is a gangster and what constitutes a gangster film? By definition, a gangster is one who belongs to a gang of criminals. This implies organisation and hierarchy, with a disciplined aim. While goals for each gang may be different – a one-off heist, or a gradual conquering of territory, and not just racketeering as many would imagine – collaboration is vital. Bank robbers, like John Dillinger or Bonnie and Clyde, also fall into this category, rarely working alone. In the strictest sense, a gangster is someone who works in tandem with the law. Rather than conceal the crime, as a murderer might, a gangster will often use his network of connections – including those in the judicial system – to circumvent the law, often preferring their own methods of punishment when necessary. In the case of Dillinger or Bonnie and Clyde, while reverting to outlaws in the mould of Robin Hood, with gangsters there is a perverse desire to nurture their reputations amongst the public.

In cinematic terms, the gangster film relies upon a set of conventions rigid enough almost to allow for elements to remain interchangeable, as does any genre. The ambitions of Little Caesar are much the same as Tom Powers or Tony Camonte. The audience expects, and is satisfied by the predictable experience. Of course, individual films break the mould – Raoul Walsh's *White Heat*, for example – but succeed partly through being offset against the guidelines we all know. Traditionally, the film shifts from childhood (indicating an underprivileged background) to adulthood, in which the mobster has scaled the heights of his profession. His downfall is precipitated by a number of actions: greed, betrayal, or jealously all lead to an increased alienation. Naturally, certain scenes and images became standard. Rotating newspapers, indicating the passage of time and the relevance to the day; car chases, highlighting the increasing automation of the world and the final shoot-out, the gangster now a tragic lone figure facing the forces of society – all are deemed necessary. Reference to family – the matriarch in particular – alongside the extended criminal family is also vital, as is the theme of honour. Those that fit these tailor-made requirements are what one might regard as strict gangster films.

The question is made more complex when one considers that the gangster film has launched a number of sub-genres, the best examples of which are covered in this work. These include: the heist, the prison movie, the hit-man movie, the yakuza, the semi-doc biopic, the lovers-on-the-run, blaxploitation and gangsta rap. Such offshoots follow their own rules, while adhering to certain umbrella points governing all. The heist movie, for example, features a gang of criminals pursuing one goal, a diamond store robbery in the case of *Reservoir Dogs*. It will often follow each individual gang member's path separately before, during and after the robbery. But Tarantino's film also draws from its father genre: language, cultural reference and motivations all occur. The prison movie, such as *Each Dawn I Die*, will feature an examination of appalling conditions, leading to a climactic riot sequence. But within this environment gangsters, albeit restrained, are able to create mini-power structures, ruling what little territory they have. In the case of yakuza or gangsta films like *Menace II Society* they feed into their own sub-cultures. The Hughes' Brothers film, a visceral social document, emanated from the music produced by anti-establishment rap musicians, a cry for change as films like *Dead End* were in the thirties. Yakuza films follow the codes of duty and humanity, the antithesis of the 1930s American gangster, and found their inspiration from the earlier samurai films. Yet their belief in the gangster as myth follows the pattern established by films based on real-life figures, like Bonnie and Clyde, whose personal history has become sentimentalised and absorbed into the popular consciousness. In its time, it has also has proved the most flexible and accommodating of genres, incorporating others to form unusual hybrids. The gangster-comedy (*Lady Killer, Brother Orchid*), horror (*Black Friday*), or western (*Last Man Standing*) or musical (*Love Me or Leave Me, A Pocketful of Miracles*) are interesting, if not entirely successful, experiments, attempting to anticipate audience demands.

Living and breathing, the gangster film is ever-evolving, yet subsequent to *The Godfather* the form has become dissipated. Film-makers have subsequently found no new blueprint to follow, no specific cycle to fall into. Although the gangster film has frequently been seen in some form on our screens in the last 25 years, providing even – as with *Goodfellas* – some of the finest additions to the genre, overall we have not seen a consistent pattern emerging. Not one trend has been universally followed, with the exception that post-*Bonnie and Clyde* film-makers have increased screen violence for the sake of titillation or authenticity. One may argue this lack of unity stems from the fortunate quelling of real mob violence; the newspapers are no longer ideal source fodder. More often, as film-making becomes a pursuit for wider groups of the social spectrum, indeed as our society becomes more fractured, so the genre follows suit.

To set the pattern for the 1990s, the heist movie, with works like *Face*, *Heat* and most importantly *Reservoir Dogs*, was back in vogue. Films such as *The Usual Suspects* combined sub-genre (heist), with myth and questioned our belief in truth, while *Pulp Fiction*, *Trigger Happy* and *Things To Do In Denver When You're Dead* relied on self-referential hip cultural references. The black gangster film emerged as a socially responsible document. The nostalgic gangster biopic, meanwhile – *Casino*, *Donnie Brasco*, *Bugsy* – also lived on. The increasing demands of Hollywood studio executives for profit-viable products, however, may be detrimental to the genre, as to the quality of any other film. Recent efforts such as *Hoodlum* and the remake of John Cassavetes' *Gloria* smell of commercialism; the gangster may approve, but an increased fragmenting of the genre can only lead to its disintegration.

For those who are unable to find mention of their favourite gangster film in this book, I can only offer the comforting thought that I no doubt agonised over dropping it. This selection is, of course, personal and meant to provide an introduction to the almost inexhaustive supply of movies relating to the genre on a worldwide basis. Films that have been excluded include those which pay little heed to generic requirements, and thus prove unenlightening as regards the history of the gangster film. The James Bond series, for instance, includes the use of the Mafia at various points: *Live and Let Die* and *Goldeneye* being two examples. Even SPECTRE, Bond's nemesis organisation, can be considered a reflection of mob rule, but the Bond films, inevitably, must fulfil their own set of regulations, disregarding mob convention.

To receive the most from this book, the reader is encouraged to liberally cross-reference, using the book's alphabetical structure. Under each appropriate entry a number of other films will be listed that relate to that item generically and are covered in this volume. Films are held under their most common title. *Brighton Rock*, known in the USA as *Young Scarface*, will be held under B, for example, and not Y, although a note in this section will be made directing the reader to the correct segment. Foreign language films likewise receive entries under their popularised name, be it in the original language or English. Space permits full entries for 200 of what I consider the most essential films from the genre, covering not only the USA but British film, French, Italian, Japanese, Chinese, Thai and Jamaican. Added to this, a large number of gangster-related works have been referenced and briefly analysed in connection with those under discussion. These can be found via the index, with the intention of inspiring the reader to pursue an interest in these important works also. For those who wish to understand the progression and transmutation of the genre from its birth to the present day, a chronology has also been provided, listing the quintessential works alongside their year of release. This also afforded the opportunity to note down key historical events in both the underworld and Hollywood that informed or hindered the films. While entries for films inspired by events or figures from the twentieth century will, of course, discuss such matters within each individual analysis, the brief history lesson is present to help provide a clear overview of the correlation between generic shifts and movements in the criminal fraternity. The result, I trust, will prove both enlightening and entertaining.

James Mottram, January 1998.

CHRONOLOGY OF KEY RELEASES AND RELATED HISTORICAL EVENTS:

NB: Titles in italics are films to be found in this volume, released in the year shown.

1912: *The Musketeers of Pig Alley*. The Kansas City Black Hand activities drastically increase with the arrival of master extortionist Joseph 'Scarface' DiGiovanni from Sicily. The Black Hand itself was an extortion racket practised on innocent citizens, initially in Italy, and then in the US.

1917: Charles 'Lucky' Luciano meets Vito Genovese; the pair actively bootleg during Prohibition, but also involve themselves in narcotics and prostitution.

1919: Black Sox Scandal. Arnold Rothstein bribes eight players on the Chicago White Sox team to throw the World Series. Rothstein forced to testify the following year, so intense was the scandal. **Al Capone arrives in Chicago, ordered to protect Johnny Torrio at all times. The first task is to murder Big Jim Colosimo, in order that Torrio may take over his financially rewarding rackets.** In Japan, Toyama Mitsuru founds the first national federation of gangsters – Dai Nippon Kokusui-kai, or the Great National Essence Society. A collection of 60,000 gangsters, labourers and ultra nationalists, they act as a massive strike-breaking force.

1920: 16 January. The Volstead Act becomes law, prohibiting the manufacture, distribution and sale of liquor. Over 200,000 speakeasies spring up, serving it illicitly thanks to a web of corrupt bureaucrats and law enforcers. Prohibition itself becomes the mother of organised crime; the Broadway Mob – controlled by Lucky Luciano, Meyer Lansky, Frank Costello and Bugsy Siegel – take $12 million a year from alcohol alone, while Al Capone is reported to have reaped some $60 million from bootlegging. Luciano meets Lanksy – already close friends with Siegel – and together they formulate the idea for the 'combination', pooling resources and ploughing profits back into further numbers rackets (an illegal betting system), with the idea that rivals will all eliminate each other in gang wars.

1924: Charles Dion O'Banion dies, gunned down in a flower shop. His North Side gang included the likes of George 'Bugs' Moran and Earl 'Hymie' Weiss. Earlier in the year, he had been celebrated at the 'Balshazzar Feast' (depicted in *Little Caesar*), but his rivalry with Johnny Torrio and Al Capone leads to his downfall. Setting up Torrio, O'Banion convinced him to pay $500,000 for a brewery, and subsequently organises the police on his payroll to arrest the gangster. Joseph Bonanno enters the US via Havana and begins to work for Al Capone. **J. Edgar Hoover becomes director of the Federal Bureau of Investigations, where he will remain until his death in 1972. The FBI itself is reorganised to include a national fingerprint file and crime laboratories.**

1925: Johnny Torrio, while with his wife, is gunned down by 'Bugs' Moran and Emmanuel Weiss, one of the most feared assassins of Murder, Inc, in revenge for the previous year. He survives, as Moran's gun empties before he can finish him. **Luciano and Genovese switch allegiance from working for Jacob 'Little Augie' Orgen and Arnold Rothstein to supporting Joseph 'Joe the Boss' Masseria.** Charles 'Pretty Boy' Floyd is imprisoned for four years for a payroll robbery.

1926: Earl 'Hymie' Weiss, rival to Al Capone, plus three bodyguards and his lawyer are slain entering a church.

1927: *Underworld*. **Motion Picture Producers and Distributors Association issue 11 'don'ts' for producers concerning lewdity, drugs etc in**

response to outcries concerning 'new immorality' in film. The Manhattan-based gangs of Owen 'Owney' Madden and Waxey Gordon begin to make war against each other. Arnold Rothstein arbitrates. Madden, originally in charge on the Gopher gang between 1911 and 1914, teams with Schultz to wage war against Gordon and 'Legs' Diamond for control of the liquor industry. Gordon, the epitome of the showy gangster in the twenties, ran rum-running in New York, but was never at ease with Lansky, Luciano and Buchalter – who finally supply Thomas E. Dewey with information that sends him down for income tax evasion. Luciano's income is now in excess of $1 million, as he controls over 5,000 prostitutes.

1927-8: *The Racket.* **Formation of the Seven Group, organised to bring peace to the profit-destructive bootlegging wars. Comprising of seven separate power groups, it includes Lucky Luciano and Frank Costello from Manhattan, Meyer Lansky and Bugsy Siegel as 'enforcers' and Johnny Torrio, out of retirement in an advisory role. Arnold Rothstein is credited with the conception, but – due to welching on a huge gambling debt – his death is brought about by the end of the year.** Eliot Ness appointed to head a special Prohibition Squad of nine officers in Chicago with the specific assignment of harassing the Capone gang. **The origins of Murder, Inc. begin; set up by notorious killer Albert Anastasia. The infamous organisation, later headed by Louis 'Lepke' Buchalter, developed its own language ('contract' meant a killing).** Lepke organises the death of 'Little Augie' Orgen, to assume control of the union rackets and garment industry. Orgen's gang of Irish, Italian and Jewish mobsters had included Waxey Gordon, Luciano and his deputy, Jack 'Legs' Diamond. **Johnny Lazia assumes control of the Kansas City Mob, backed by political powerhouse Tom Pendergast.** George 'Machine Gun' Kelly meets Kathryn Thorne, the woman responsible for perpetuating his myth.

1929: The St. Valentine's Day Massacre, ordered by Al Capone to kill Bugs Moran, the last major leader of Dion O'Banion's North Side Gang. Moran escapes and public opinion turns against Capone. He is later sentenced to **11 years in a federal prison in Atlanta for income tax evasion.** Atlantic City Conference occurs; the first summit of US crime bosses. In attendance are Johnny Torrio, Al Capone, Meyer Lansky, Dutch Schultz, 'Lucky' Luciano, Frank Costello, 'Louis 'Lepke' Buchalter and Albert Anastasia. Conference establishes nationwide gambling syndicate, but more importantly galvanizes the gangs of America into a powerful single unit. **Luciano beaten to a bloody pulp in October, presumably by the 'Legs' Diamond gang.** Lester Gillis, aka George 'Baby Face' Nelson, begins to work for Al Capone, eventually proving too violent even for him.

1930: *Little Caesar.* **Hays Office (run by Will Hays, head of the MPPDA) issue a new code, partly in response to the increasing popularity of gangster films. In particular, 'crime against the law' was not to be shown 'in such a way as to throw sympathy with the crime... or to inspire others.'** Frank Nash escapes from Leavenworth prison and robs banks through the Midwest, with 'Machine Gun' Kelly and the Barker Brothers.

1931: *City Streets, The Public Enemy, Quick Millions.* **Salvatore Maranzano and Joe 'The Boss' Masseria assassinated. Both had been embroiled against each other in the Castellammarese War, fighting over the bootlegging and gambling rackets of Manhattan. Bugsy Siegel kills the latter, ordered by Luciano, to appease the former. Luciano felt Masseria was a 'Moustache Pete', meaning he clung onto ancient ways of racketeering. Maranzano dictates a new structure, named the 'five family plan'. This hierarchical structure would be led by him, naming himself 'Boss of Bosses'. Although this is later adopted to some degree by the Mafia, Luciano – feeling slighted – orders Maranzano's execution also.** 'Legs' Diamond – who survived more bullet wounds than any other gangster – is finally killed by two unidentified men. The murder remains unsolved. **'Machine Gun' Kelly, together with Thorne and local hoodlum Albert Bates, spend the next two years robbing banks.**

1932: *Scarface.* Clyde Barrow meets Bonnie Parker; convicted and imprisoned on seven counts of burglary and car theft, he escapes using a handgun smuggled to him by Parker.

1933: Prohibition repealed by the 21st Amendment, following a Democrat victory in Congress a year earlier. 17 June. The Kansas City Massacre at the Union Station takes place. Charles 'Pretty Boy' Floyd identified by FBI Agent Melvin Purvis a year later as one of the killers, alongside local bank robber and ex-sheriff Verne Miller. The purpose was to free Frank 'Jelly' Nash, following his capture by the authorities. **Paroled from a ten-year sentence, John Dillinger begins a series of violent bank robberies in his native state of Indiana. He is eventually held responsible for 16 murders, while 'Machine Gun' Kelly, now known as 'Pop-gun Kelly', is arrested and awarded a life sentence.**

1934: *Lady Killer*. Al Capone transferred to Alcatraz. **Created to eliminate gang warfare, improve communications and maximize profits, the Syndicate is established as a nationally organised directorship. Charles 'Lucky' Luciano, Meyer Lansky and Johnny Torrio lead, bringing Louis 'Lepke' Buchalter, Frank Costello, Vito Genovese and Abner 'Longy' Zwillman together. Lansky organises structure, banking system and representatives of syndicate.** Johnny Lazia, boss of the Kansas City mob (backed by politician Tom Pendergast), assassinated. **Bonnie and Clyde are shot dead at a police roadblock in Louisiana, after almost two years on the run for bank robbery.** John Dillinger, now deemed Public Enemy No. 1, is shot dead upon leaving a Chicago movie theatre. **'Baby Face' Nelson, having united with Dillinger on two robberies, is himself killed by the FBI in a wild shootout.** 'Pretty Boy' Floyd is gunned down by agents while crossing a field.

1935: *G-Men, The Glass Key*. **Dutch Schultz assassinated by Charles 'the Bug' Workman at the Palace Chop House and Tavern, Newark, New Jersey, organised by Murder, Inc. A protégé of Arnold Rothstein, he took the name Schultz because 'it was short enough to fit in the headlines but is regarded with contempt by other mobsters for his shabby appearance. Running the beer trade in the Bronx, Schultz is the wild card of the syndicate; his desire to assassinate Special Prosecutor Thomas E.**

Dewey leads to the contract that killed him. Bo Weinberg also killed in this year, by Bugsy Siegel. Schultz's top lieutenant, Weinberg, is revealed as aiding Luciano in siphoning money from Schultz's rackets. **Luciano now emerges as the 'Boss of Bosses', but sentenced to 30 to 50 years at Clinton Prison, indicted on 90 counts of extortion.**

1936: *Bullets or Ballots, Marked Woman, Pépé le Moko, The Petrified Forest*. Meyer Lansky goes to Cuba, setting up an exclusive gambling franchise in Havana, with the co-operation of dictator Fulgenico Batista.

1937: *Dead End, Kid Galahad, The Last Gangster, Manhattan Melodrama*. **Lepke 'Buchalter' seized by paranoia; begins ordering the assassinations of any syndicate member he feels may inform on him. This includes George 'Whitey' Rudnick and Max Rubin.** Thomas E. Dewey elected New York district attorney. **Vito Genovese flees the country, upon being charged with the murder of Ferdinand Boccia.**

1938: *Angels with Dirty Faces, King of the Underworld*. Following the imprisonment of Luciano and Buchalter, Joseph Bonnano – who controlled gambling empires from Montreal to Haiti after the deaths of Masseria and Maranzano – flees to Sicily.

1939: *Each Dawn I Die, Invisible Stripes, The Roaring Twenties*. **Al Capone released from Alcatraz.** Gossip columnist Walter Winchell is trusted by underworld to handle the surrender of Louis 'Lepke' Buchalter to J. Edgar Hoover. **Johnny Torrio begins two-and-a-half-year sentence at Leavenworth Federal Prison for income tax evasion.**

1940: *Black Friday, Brother Orchid, Castle on the Hudson, Johnny Apollo*. Brooklyn District Attorney Burton B. Turkus discovers several members of Murder, Inc. willing to turn state's evidence, including Abe 'Kid Twist' Reles who will talk over a period of two years revealing minute details. **Albert Anastasia goes into hiding.** Lepke Buchalter is tried, convicted and sentenced to death for the murder of Joseph Rosen.

1941: *High Sierra*. **Torrio paroled; enters into semi-retirement.**

1942: *All Through the Night, The Glass Key, Johnny Eager*. Anastasia enlists in army to avoid deportation to Italy, avoid Turkus' investigations and perpetuate the myth that he was a war hero.

1943: Frank Nitti, legendary enforcer for Al Capone, blows his own brains out rather than face a term in prison, following an indictment for tax evasion. Sicilian bandit, Salvatore Giuliano, who petitioned President Harry Truman to make Sicily America's 49th state, shoots two carabinieri (state policeman) dead. Subsequently, he flees to the hills and begins collecting his guerrilla force together.

1944: Louis 'Lepke' Buchalter dies in the electric chair. Bugsy Siegel begins to develop his idea for a gambling casino in the small desert town of Las Vegas, using $5 million of syndicate money.

1945: *Dillinger*

1946: *The Killers.* **Charles 'Lucky' Luciano is released from his conviction, only to be deported to Italy. Meyer Lansky one of the few bosses to attend at the dockside.** Vito Genovese, according to Joe Valachi's testimony (see 1963) becomes the Mafia's 'Boss of Bosses'.

1947: *Body and Soul, Brighton Rock, Kiss of Death, Out of the Past.* **Al Capone dies, ravaged by syphilis.** Luciano leaves Rome, Italy, for Havana, Cuba, where he meets with Lansky, Costello and Siegel. At odds with Luciano over the loan taken to pay for his casino, Siegel is assassinated. Mickey Cohen supposedly inherits Siegel's criminal fiefdom in Los Angeles. **New York DA's office uncovers a number of abuses in boxing, handled by mob bosses.**

1948: *Criss Cross, Force of Evil, Key Largo, The Street With No Name, They Live by Night.* Over the last four years, the Sicilian town of Corleone has suffered as many as 53 Mafia murders.

1949: *Caged, White Heat.* **Salvatore Giuliano is shot dead by a former lieutenant Gaspare Pisciotta, coerced into the task by police upon his own capture. The murder, it is reported, is carried out with the agreement of former Giuliano backer and Sicilian Mafia overlord Don Calogero Vizzini, now unable to control the bandit.**

1950: *The Asphalt Jungle, Gun Crazy (Deadly is the Female), Kiss Tomorrow Goodbye.* Chaired by Senator Estes Kefauver, the Senate Special Committee to Investigate Crime in Interstate Commerce is empanelled. Broadcast on television, the nation watches over 600 witnesses testify against organised crime. Frank Costello loses composure on TV, storms out and subsequently loses favour with mob. Thomas E. Dewey is also unwilling to co-operate, after Luciano reveals that his release from prison cost an estimated $90,000 in contributions towards his campaign for the Presidency. **Senator Joseph McCarthy delivers a Lincoln's Day speech claiming the State Department in West Virginia is 'infested' with Communists. The following years would see a number of prominent Hollywood directors and actors called before the House of Un-American Activities Committee either to testify against colleagues or explain their beliefs.**

1951: *The Enforcer, The Racket.* Albert Anastasia, with the blessing of Luciano, orders the murder of Philip Mangano; his brother Vincent soon disappears. Anastasia now takes over. The brothers were overlords of the broad Brooklyn/Manhattan territories subsequent to Luciano's deportation. **Waxey Gordon arrested for peddling heroin and sentenced to 25 years in Alcatraz, where he dies a year later.**

1953: *The Big Heat*

1954: *On the Waterfront.* Pisciotta, who remained in prison after killing Giuliano despite government promises of freedom, is poisoned in his cell with strychnine. **'Machine Gun' Kelly dies in his cell.**

1955: *The Big Combo, The Desperate Hours, Guys and Dolls, The Ladykillers, Love Me or Leave Me.*

1956: *The Killing.* Ronnie Kray sentenced to three years in prison for assaulting Terry Martin with a bayonet. Kray and brother Reggie had spent the decade organising London's most feared 'protection' racket.

1957: Apalachin Conference is held at Joseph Barbara's New York mansion. Raided by the FBI, before the 60-odd underworld leaders can begin, it is a landmark in that it proves to the world the existence of organised crime. Speculation has it that the initial meeting is called by Vito Genovese as part of his ascendancy plans in the wake of Albert Anastasia's recent assassination. This is ordered by Genovese himself, for Anastasia authorising the failed attempt on the life of Frank Costello. The Anastasia murder is assigned by Carlo Gambino to Joseph Profaci,

who in turn chooses the Gallo Brothers (Joseph 'Crazy Joey', Albert 'Kid Blast' and Lawrence). 'Bugs' Moran dies at Leavenworth prison. Eliot Ness dies.

1958: *The Bonnie Parker Story, Machine Gun Kelly.* Tokyo police estimate 70,000 yakuza in Japan; five years later the figure grows to 184,000. **Kathryn Thorne paroled from the Cincinnati Work House.**

1959: *Al Capone, Some Like it Hot.* Vito Genovese is exposed by his own men, including Joe Valachi, following his escape from the Apalachin debâcle.

1960: *A Bout de Souffle, Ocean's Eleven, The Rise and Fall of Legs Diamond.*

1961: *Frightened City, The George Raft Story, Pocketful of Miracles, Underworld USA, King of the Roaring Twenties: the Story of Arnold Rothstein*

1962: *The Scarface Mob.* **Charles 'Lucky' Luciano dies, greeting a film producer at an airport.** Jimmy Hoffa brought to trial, through John F. Kennedy's exhaustive investigations, for misappropriating $1.7 million of union funds. Head of the powerful Teamsters union, his dealings with organised crime were well known. Convicted two years later. **Joseph Profaci dies of natural causes; Joseph Colombo Snr takes control of the family and refuses the Gallo Brothers autonomy in Brooklyn. A shooting war resumes between them.**

1963: Joe Valachi testifies before a Senate committee. One of the few Mafia members who violated the code of silence, he reveals, as much as a foot-soldier can, the inner-structure and power struggles of the Mafia. He introduces the East Coast euphemism for Mafia, the Cosa Nostra, into common vocabulary. John F. Kennedy assassinated.

1964: The Killers. Owney Madden dies; leaves an estimated $3 million behind. **Carmine Galante, boss of the Bonanno Family, enrages other mobsters by planning the systematic elimination of the governing leadership of the other families. This leads to the Banana War that ends in the ruination of his plans to install his son as successor.**

1965: *Young Dillinger.* Ronnie Kray kills George Cornell in the Blind Beggar pub in Bethnal Green.

1966: *Virginia Hill,* former lover of **Bugsy Siegel, takes on overdose of sleeping pills and** dies on the ski-slopes of Salzburg.

1967: *Bonnie and Clyde, Le Samourai, Point Blank, St. Valentine's Day Massacre.* UK's Richardson brothers, fraudsters and torturers, convicted. Eddie sentenced to ten years; Charley 25. **Reggie Kray, prompted by Ronnie to prove his worth, kills Jack 'the Hat' McVitie, who had insulted the Krays with repeated insults.**

1968: *The Brotherhood, Bullitt.* Ellsworth 'Bumpy' Johnson, millionaire intermediary between Harlem street gangs and the white organised Mafia, dies of a heart attack.

1969: *Bloody Mama, The Italian Job.* **Krays sentenced to life imprisonment for the murders of Cornell and McVitie.** Vito Genovese dies in his cell in Atlanta.

1970: *Borsalino, A Bullet For Pretty Boy, Performance.* **More than 100 people are shot dead in a wave of shootings on the French Riviera, following the jailing of crime leader 'Mimi' Guerini for his part in a gangland murder.** Meyer Lansky flees to Israel, on learning Federal agents were to charge him with income tax evasion. **New York City mayor John Lindsay empanels the Knapp Commission. Scores of policeman are implicated for taking bribes and participating in gambling.**

1971: *The Gang That Couldn't Shoot Straight, Get Carter, The Grissom Gang, Shaft, Villain.* Hoffa pardoned. **Joe Valachi dies of heart attack in Texas Federal Prison.** Thomas E. Dewey dies.

1972: *Black Gunn, Boxcar Bertha, The Godfather, The Harder They Come, Hit Man, Prime Cut, Superfly, The Valachi Papers.* **Crazy Joe Gallo assassinated.** Manny Gambino, nephew to the all-powerful Carlo Gambino, is kidnapped and murdered. The perpetrators are tracked down and assassinated by three men, one being John Gotti who is sent down for seven years. Upon release he is awarded with a top position in the Gambino crew.

1973: *Black Caesar, Black Hand, Charlie Varrick, Dillinger, Hell up in Harlem, Lucky Luciano, Mean Streets, The Outfit.* **Frank Costello dies.**

1974: *Big Bad Mama, Black Godfather, Borsalino & Co, The Godfather Part II, Lepke, The Taking of Pelham 123.* Ralph Capone, brother of Al, dies.

1975: *Capone, The Yakuza.* **Jimmy Hoffa disappears.**

1976: *Bugsy Malone, The Killing of a Chinese Bookie.*

Mickey Cohen dies. **Carlo Gambino dies of a heart attack; brother-in-law Paul Castellano serves as his successor.**

1978: *Corleone, The Driver.* Carmine Galante arrested by Federal Agents for violating parole (following a 12-year stretch for narcotics) by associating with known criminals. Following Gambino's death, Galante is considered the toughest mobster in the New York Families. A year later he is gunned down in a restaurant.

1980: *Gloria, The Long Good Friday.*

1981: **New Jersey State Police detective Robert Delaney, having penetrated the state mob's structure, claims he met members who had seen *The Godfather* at least ten times.**

1983: *Once Upon a Time in America, Scarface.* Meyer Lanksy dies of a heart attack, aged 81. **Anthony Cirillo elected president of the Genovese family.**

1984: *Broadway Danny Rose, The Cotton Club, The Hit, Johnny Dangerously, The Pope of Greenwich Village.* The Medellin drug cartel now controls roughly 80 percent of the cocaine in Columbia. Formed two years before, Pablo Escobar Gaviria – elected to the Colombian Congress – controls US distribution, laboratories, transportation and aircraft.

1985: *Prizzi's Honor.* **Following the death of Aniello Dellacroce, John Gotti assumes charge of the Gambino crew, which by now has lost much of its prestige. It was reported that Gotti engineered the deaths of many rivals to climb to this position.** Medellin Cartel in the next two years will assassinate 15 judges, including the Supreme Court Justice Hernando Baquero Borda. **Joseph Ferriola, known as Mr Clean, assumes the top position in the Chicago mob.**

1986: *At Close Range, A Better Tomorrow, Mona Lisa, Wise Guys.* Gotti begins to face a series of intensive federal prosecutions for racketeering.

1987: *A Better Tomorrow II, Big Bad Mama II, China Girl, City on Fire, Ganglands: the Verne Miller Story, The Sicilian, Stormy Monday, The Untouchables.*

1988: *Married to the Mob, I'm Gonna Git You, Sucka!* **Tommasso Buscetta testifies before the Senate Permanent Subcommittee on Investigations, identifying and updating the structural leadership of the Cosa Nostra. His statement indicates the change drugs has brought to the Mafia.**

1989: *A Better Tomorrow III, Black Rain, Cookie, The Cook, the Thief, His Wife, and Her Lover, Harlem Nights, The Killer, Violent Cop.* Delroy 'Uzi' Edwards, the first person believed to have ever sold crack cocaine, is sentenced to seven consecutive life imprisonments, plus 15 years in prison, and fined $1 million. **John Gotti arrested outside a restaurant in Little Italy; charged with conspiracy, the trial, eventually returning the verdict of not guilty, concerned over 28,000 taped conversations recorded between March 1985 and May 1986.** Over 250 tonnes of chemicals used to process cocaine are confiscated by the Colombian government. Drugs cartels in return declare war on the bureaucrats, beginning with the assassination of Judge Carlos Valencia Garcia.

1990: *Boiling Point, Desperate Hours, Dick Tracy, The Freshman, The Godfather Part III, Goodfellas, The Grifters, King of New York, The Krays, The Lost Capone, Men of Respect, Miller's Crossing, My Blue Heaven, State of Grace.* **John Gotti arrested again; this time convicted on 44 charges of racketeering, loan-sharking, obstruction of justice, bribery and murder. He is sent to the Federal Penitentiary in Marion, Illinois.**

1991: *Billy Bathgate, Bugsy, Dillinger, Mobsters: the evil empire, New Jack City, Reservoir Dogs*

1992: *Hard Boiled, Mad Dog and Glory, Ruby.*

1993: *Boiling Point, A Bronx Tale, Carlito's Way, La Scorta, Menace II Society, Romeo is Bleeding, Sonatine, The Young Americans.*

1994: *American Yakuza, Bullets over Broadway, Getting Gotti, Little Odessa, Pulp Fiction.* Pablo Escobar Gaviria gunned down. **Irish crimelord Martin Cahill assassinated by IRA.**

1995: *Casino, Clockers, Get Shorty, Heat, Kiss of Death, Leon, Shanghai Triad, The Usual Suspects.* Ronnie Kray dies.

1996: *American Yakuza II, Bound, Fallen Angels, The Funeral, Hard Men, Kansas City, Kids Return, Last Man Standing, Mulholland Falls, Original Gangstas, Things To Do In Denver When You're Dead, Trigger Happy.*

1997: *Donnie Brasco, Face, Hoodlum, Dang Bireley's and the Young Gangsters.*

1998: *Resurrection Man, Mojo, Face, Hoodlum, The General, Lock, Stock and Two Smoking Barrels.*

A

A Bout de Souffle (aka Breathless)

(France, Imperia/Société Nouvelle de Cinématographie, 1960, 90 mins)

Credits
Dir/Scr: Jean-Luc Godard
Prod: Georges de Beauregard
DOP: Raoul Coutard
Ed: Cecile Decugis
Music: Martial Solal
Art Dir: Claude Chabrol

Cast: Jean Seberg (Patricia Franchini), Jean-Paul Belmondo (Michel Poiccard), Daniel Boulanger (Inspector Vital), Jean-Pierre Melville (Parvulesco), Henri-Jacques Huet (Antonio Berrutti)

A small-time hoodlum kills a policeman and goes on the run with his lover.

Dedicated to Monogram pictures, production company of B-pictures including the likes of *Dillinger* (qv), Jean-Luc Godard's first feature cost just $90,000 (raised by Claude Chabrol) but launched the French Nouvelle Vague, which in turn exerted a key influence on sixties American cinema. Ironically more closely resembling PRC Picture's *Detour* than anything rival company Monogram ever produced, the film was based on a newspaper clipping shown to Godard by François Truffaut (who went on to direct his own homage to the American crime film, *Tirez sur le Pianiste*). Drawing from the likes of *Gun Crazy* and *They Live By Night* (qqv), the film utilizes the jump cut technique, where characters shift suddenly around the locales having changed clothing – suggestive of Michel's own erratic thought process. Recognised upon release but equally criticised for being short on profundity, it was seen as a film that promoted amoral nihilism as a legitimate reaction in contemporary society. This apart, Godard borrows (and stylistically exaggerates) elements of *film noir*, or as critic Steve Smith noted: 'does not so much imitate as enact the process of imitation through the story of a perilous and fatal attempt to imitate'. Low-life hood and Bogart fan Michel, who acquires a car and Patricia along the way (the necessary accessories of the genuine *noir* protagonist) takes on the mantle of American tough gangster hero. His death in the finale (a change from Truffaut's original ending) is in line with generic rules, just as Patricia is the femme fatale, turning him over to the police. But Godard plays with convention: Patricia sees Michel only as a diversion, not a vital fiscal means for survival; Michel's demise is humdrum and derisory, not dramatic.
By including a cameo from Jean-Pierre Melville, playing philosopher Parvulesco (interviewed at Orly airport by Patricia), Godard constructs an ironic spirit, questioning those (like Melville) who attempted to resuscitate French cinema through Hollywood. Melville had already used Belmondo in his gangster picture *Le Doulos* and would go on to use another *noir* classic *This Gun For Hire*, for *Le Samourai* (qqv), which in turn would influence Walter Hill's *The Driver* (qv). Likewise, Godard would go on to make *Bande A Part* (aka *Band of Outsiders*), which would in turn influence a whole wave of 'alienated youth' pictures.

* The film was explicitly remade in 1983, starring Richard Gere.

See also: *Borsalino*; *Borsalino & Co*

Al Capone

(US, Allied Artists, 1959, 105 mins)

Credits
Dir: Richard Wilson
Prod: Leonard J. Ackerman, John H. Burrows
Scr: Henry Greenberg, Marvin Wald
DOP: Lucien Ballard
Ed: Walter A. Hannermann
Music: David Raksln
Art Dir: Hilyard M. Brown

Cast: Rod Steiger (Al Capone), James Gregory (Schaefer), Martin Balsam (Keely), Hehemaih Persoff (Johnny Torrio), Fay Spain (Maureen), Murvyn Vye (Bugs Moran), Lewis Charles (Hymie Weiss), Robert Gist (O'Banion)

Biopic of the notorious Chicago gangster, from his rise as first lieutenant of local mobster Johnny Torrio through his bootlegging and protection rackets, as he outguns Weiss, Moran and O'Banion, to his ultimate fall at the hands of the IRS.

Al Capone: Rod Steiger as the legendary Al Capone

Al Capone combines the nostalgia for the Roaring Twenties, and the classic gangster films that followed a decade later, with the documentary techniques popularised in the film's own time. Produced at a time when gangster biographies were in vogue, spurred on by *The Untouchables* TV series, it followed the likes of Don Siegel's *Baby Face Nelson*, Herbert J. Leder's *Pretty Boy Floyd* and William Witney's *The Bonnie Parker Story (qv)*. Narrated by police sergeant (and later Captain) Schaefer (a composite, based on Chicago cop John Siege), he tells the tale for the relevance it has to the late fifties. As Capone moves from bootlegging to protection rackets, Schaefer says: 'The underworld invaded the business world. The black jack and Tommy gun now wore white collars and business suits. Al Capone set a frightening new pattern for crime in America that still exists today.' Released by 'B' picture factory Allied only two years after the Apalachin Conference, it was a time when America and J. Edgar Hoover had to face up to the reality that organised crime existed and masqueraded behind legitimate business. As Steiger's Capone says: 'I'm not a gangster, I'm a businessman... I serve the public.'

Rod Steiger's intense, volatile 'method' Capone, with a striking physical verisimilitude, ensures this remains one of the screen's finest portrayals of the man. Discounting Paul Muni's and Edward G. Robinson's characters in *Scarface* and *Little Caesar* (qqv) (both modelled on Capone), Steiger's work eclipses other biographical portraits from the likes of Neville Brand, Jason Robards and Ben Gazarra, with only the accomplished turn by Robert De Niro in *The Untouchables* (qv) likely to succeed Steiger's as definitive. Of importance, Schaefer's accusations to duplicitous newspaper man Keely (based on Jake Lingle) offers a part explanation for Capone's rise; along with corrupt politicians, Keely is a leech – one of 'the highest paid messenger boys in history' and it is the media's influence, alongside the public's clamour for illegal liquor that brought Capone to an unstoppable power.

Reaching a hysterical peak in the final three scenes (Capone's interrogation of Keely after his betrayal,

Schaefer's restaurant confrontation of Al, and his final demise in prison, beaten by bricks as he screams 'I'm Al Capone!'), the film's low-budget lighting, photography and montage sequences remain elegant descendants of the classics of the genre.

See also: *Capone*; *Gangland: the Verne Miller Story*; *George Raft Story, The*; *Lost Capone, The*; *St. Valentine's Day Massacre, The*; *Scarface Mob, The*; *Untouchables, The*.

All Through the Night

(US, Warner Brothers, 1942, 107 mins)

Credits
Dir: Vincent Sherman
Prod: Jerry Wald, Hal Wallis
Scr: Edwin Gilbert, Leonard Spigelgass
DOP: Sid Hickox
Ed: Rudi Fehr
Music: Adolph Deutsch
Art Dir: Max Parker

Cast: Humphrey Bogart (Gloves Donahue), Conrad Veidt (Hall Ebbing), Peter Lorre (Pepi), Karen Verne (Leda Hamilton), Barton MacLane (Marty Callahan)

Sports promoter stumbles on a Nazi spy-ring, after the baker of his favourite cheesecake is murdered.

A fine example, as was briefly shown in *The Roaring Twenties* (qv), of the gangster fighting for a cause nobler than personal aggrandisement. Unfortunately the coy dialogue (calling Hitler 'Whatshisname') and flippant tone ('Joe DiMaggio couldn't have done better', as a guy receives a club to the back of the head) sit uneasily with the serious subject matter. Humphrey Bogart's rousing speech to the Brooklyn gangsters, concerning the Nazis – 'These are no penny racketeers trying to muscle in. They want to move in wholesale. Take over the whole country' – gives little credit to the audience, sounding close to a public information film as he documents the 'unconstitutional' removal of freedom rights. What does arise that is of interest for our purpose is

twofold. The comment, in reference to Hitler, that 'One man, if he's inspired can change the world', parallels the gangster figure's desire for control and supremacy. But the 'God bless America' patriotism runs stronger. As one mobster says, on hearing of the Nazi's despicable schemes: 'It's against the law.' A belief in the Constitution, at first dismissed by the heavies that Bogart addresses, is clear. Hypocrisy, possibly, but also an indication that the screen gangster is someone who works in tandem with the law, and when it suits him will adhere to it. To emphasise this, Bogart's character – 'a promoter... not J. Edgar Hoover' – is not as ruthless as his previous roles. There is resistance to the Nazi/gangster comparison: 'I may not be Model Citizen No. 1, but I pay my taxes, stop at traffic lights and buy 24 tickets every year to the Policeman's Ball.' The script, then, ensures that citizens are united under one banner, differences forgotten.

American Yakuza

(US/Japan, NEO Motion Pictures, 1994, 91 mins)

Credits
Dir: Frank Cappello
Prod: Mike Leahy, Aki Komine
Scr: Max Strom, John Allen Nelson
DOP: Richard Clabaugh
Ed: Sonny Baskin

Cast: Viggo Mortensen (Nick Davis), Ryo Ishibashi (Shu), Michael Nouri, Robert Foster, Franklyn Ajaye, Cristina Lawson, Yuji Okumoto, John Fujioka

An undercover cop ingratiates himself with the yakuza, and learns their ways, after saving the life of one member, only to discover they are trading arms with the FBI.

American Yakuza 2: Back to Back

(US/Japan, NEO Motion Production, 1996, 87 mins)

Credits
Dir/Scr: Roger Nygard

Prod: W.K. Border, Aki Komine
Scr: Lloyd Keith
DOP: Mark W. Gray
Ed: Roger Nygard
Music: Walter Werzawa
Prod. Des: Anthony Stabley

Cast: Michael Rooker (Bob Maloney), Ryo Ishibashi (Koji), Danielle Harris (Chelsea), John Laughlin (Lt. Dussecq), Koh Takasugi (Hideo)

A father and daughter get caught in the crossfire of a deal between American gangsters and two yakuza representatives, one an Elvis fanatic.

The original, produced on a measly $4 million, offered a watered-down version of Sydney Pollack's superior *The Yakuza* (qv), complete with pat culture clash, already seen in versions from Pollack's film to Ridley Scott's *Black Rain* (qv), and pseudo-John Woo gunfights. Its only signs of authenticity: the use of Ishibashi, Japanese actor and rock star, along with renowned Japanese tattoo artist Ryoji Kasumi (drafted in to create authentic yakuza symbols on the actors). Full of honour and loyalty soundbites ('The yakuza is our family now. It gives us absolute loyalty and trust'), the most interesting aspect is how the Mafia use the FBI, sending pictures to them detailing yakuza killings, in order for them to dispatch a force the mob misunderstands and fears.

The sequel, apart from using Ishibashi again, bore little resemblance to the original. Despite the TV-style cutaways, the humour is as black as the contrivances are outrageous, moving as we do though the disposable sunny suburban landscape.

See also: *Black Rain*; *Boiling Point*; *Kids Return*; *Sonatine*; *Yakuza, The.*

Angels with Dirty Faces

(US, Warner Brothers, 1938, 97 mins)

Credits
Dir: Michael Curtiz
Prod: Sam Bischoff

Scr: Warren B. Duff, John Wexley
DOP: Sol Polito
Ed: Owen Marks
Music: Max Steiner
Art Dir: Robert M. Haas

Cast: James Cagney (William 'Rocky' Sullivan), Pat O'Brien (Father Jerome 'Jerry' Connolly), Humphrey Bogart (James Frazier), Ann Sheridan (Laury Ferguson), George Bancroft (Mac Keefer)

An idolized gangster is asked to lose face and fake cowardice as he goes to the electric chair.

The apex of the Warner Brothers gangster films, James Cagney was the first actor playing a gangster to be honoured in, according to *Today's Cinema*, the 'finest role of his career'. Although he was only nominated for Best Actor at the Academy Awards, losing out to Spencer Tracey's work in *Boys Town*, he won the New York Critics Circle award, a prize he would later take home (along with the Oscar) for *Yankee Doodle Dandy*. Reunited with director Curtiz, after gangster comedy *Jimmy the Gent*, Cagney's role would ultimately prove the definitive Cagney screen image: a tough but basically decent man from the wrong side of the tracks, who has slipped into crime (usually as a gangster), but is allowed some form of redemption before the final reel.

The ending was the only part to receive adverse criticism. One critic suggested if they were going to attempt serious problems, producers 'should be prepared to carry them through to their logical conclusions'. Yet it followed in step with the Environment vs. Innate Personality issue that characterised crime films of the period. Rocky, it is argued, is a product of Reform School, an angel whose face has been smeared with dirt by the world and, in death, is released from the earthly encumbrance, his body, and so the purity of his soul shines through. With the presence of a Catholic priest on the fringes of the film (in the shape of Rocky's friend, and one-time hoodlum, Father Jerry), such a reading has merit.

* Performances from the Dead End kids as the petty street gang who worship Rocky were also commendable. They had the previous year appeared in *Dead End* (qv), with Humphrey Bogart (here acting

Angels With Dirty Faces: Rocky Sullivan (Jimmy Cagney) goes to the chair, watched by Father Jerry (Pat O'Brien).

as Rocky's former henchman, turned double-crosser) and followed this film up with a sequel (*The Angels Wash Their Faces*), starring Ronald Reagan as the DA enlisted to help prove a gang member's innocence, after false accusations of arson.

Asphalt Jungle, The

(US, Loew's Inc., 1950, 112 mins)

Credits
Dir/Scr: John Huston
Prod: Arthur Hornblow Jr.
Scr: Ben Maddow, based on the original novel by W.R. Burnett
DOP: Harold Rosson
Ed: George Boemler
Music: Miklos Rozsa
Art Dir: Cedric Gibbons, Randall Duell

Cast: Sterling Hayden (Dix Handley), Louis Calhern (Alonzo D. Emmerich), Jean Hagen (Doll Conovan), James Whitmore (Gus Minissi), Sam Jaffe (Reimenschneider), Anthony Caruso (Louis Ciavelli)

Recently paroled criminal masterminds a million-dollar jewellery heist, drawing together various underworld figures.

An influence on Quentin Tarantino's *Reservoir Dogs* (*qv*), Huston again (as with *The Maltese Falcon* and *Treasure of the Sierre Madre*) focused on a group of people with conflicting motives, brought together, and eventually down, by greed. Such a sin, as mastermind Herr Reimenschneider readily admits to his 'hooligan' colleague Dix, had made him 'blind' towards crooked bankrupt lawyer Emmerich, the man who, in claiming he has a more profitable fence for the jewels, double-crosses his own gang. Unlike Stanley Kubrick's attempt to film the heist genre six years later with *The Killing* (*qv*), which also starred Sterling Hayden, Huston does not feel the need to document the crime in precise detail, preferring instead to analyse the human condition – 'like a soul in hell', as safecracker Ciavelli's wife comments. No idealisation or romanticism, the criminal world is as impersonal and functionary as the unnamed Mid-West city that hides it, or the manner in which Reimenschneider, a part which won Jaffe Best Actor at the Venice Film Festival, conducts his business. In a marvellously ambiguous sentence, 'Crime', as Emmerich states 'is just a left-handed form of human endeavour'. Huston and scriptwriter Ben Maddow, while de-glamorising the underworld, simultaneously celebrate it, drawing the criminal life in line with our own achievements. Unflinchingly realised, Louis B Mayer condemned his own studio's feature as 'full of nasty, ugly people doing nasty things. I wouldn't walk across a room to see a thing like that'. As the concluding speech suggests, the criminal is the predator, waiting to prey on the weak; it is a case of survival of the fittest, the law of both asphalt and tropical jungle, and our alertness to that, is what's called for.

* The film features an early bit-part for Marilyn Monroe, as the 'niece' of Emmerich.

See also: *Criss-Cross*; *Face*; *Heat*; *Taking of Pelham*

The Asphalt Jungle: Emmerich (Louis Calhern) divides the spoils with Herr Reimenschneider (Sam Jaffe).

123, The; Usual Suspects, The.

At Close Range

(US, Cinema '85, 1985, 115 mins)

'Performances are rooted in method-induced macho posturing, mostly captured in extreme close-up. (There is a great deal of pore examination. The camera is at far closer range than the emotional truth).'

(David McGillivray, *Films and Filming*)

Credits
Dir: James Foley
Prod: Elliott Lewitt, Don Guest
Scr: Nicholas Kazan
DOP: Juan Ruiz-Anchia
Ed: Howard Smith
Music: Patrick Leonard
Prod. Des: Peter Jamison

Cast: Sean Penn (Bradford Whitewood Jnr.), Christopher Walken (Bradford Whitewood Snr.), Mary Stuart Masterton (Terry), Chris Penn (Tommy Whitewood), Millie Perkins (Julie)

A son discovers his criminal father will stop at nothing – including raping the son's girl and killing his brother – to protect himself.

A glossy pop-promo of a film (featuring repeated strains of star Penn's then-wife Madonna singing *Live to Tell*), it was based on a story discovered by producer Lewitt in 1978 in *The Philadelphia Inquirer*. The film's inspiration is underworld boss Bruce Johnston Snr, who lured teenagers into his fold in rural Pennsylvania, trained them as criminals and, when they became a liability, executed them. Director Foley prefers the stylised, psychoanalytical approach. Dropping any thoughts of concentrating upon the theme of the criminal fraternity passing on skills to the next generation (Brad Jnr is told he is a born thief), Foley touches instead on family saga. Initially impressed by their estranged father's local tractor heisting activities, the two sons eventually crave a normal adolescence, and Bradford Snr's actions take loyalty to its extreme. 'I'm your blood, your family,' he says, having just killed his own son Tommy to prevent him giving evidence against him in court. In the scene, the boy's older brother, played by Sean Penn, brandishes the murder weapon at his father, what he calls 'the family gun'. Almost a lament for the demise of 'family values' (their step-father is equally cruel), Foley scales down the genre – to the extent that their ambitions become ridiculed. 'Everywhere I go, I see money,' says Walken. In the background, a game of Monopoly is being played. His desire to be a big-shot is no more realistic than the paper money on the board.

* The belief in the family generations extended to the casting. Apart from his ex-wife's singing talents being utilised, Sean Penn's brother Chris plays Tommy, and the pair's grandmother in the film is played by their mother.

B

Better Tomorrow, A

(Hong Kong, Film Workshop, 1986, 115 mins)

Credits
Dir: John Woo
Prod: Tsui Hark
Scr: Chan Hing Kai, Leung Suk Wah
DOP: Wong Wing Hang
Ed: Kam Ma
Music: Joseph Koo
Prod. Des: Bennie Lui

Cast: Chow Yun Fat (Mark Gor), Ti Lung (Sung Tse Ho), Leslie Cheung (Sung Tse Kit), Waise Lee (Tam Shing), Emily Chu (Jackie)

Ex-con, syndicate member (and older brother to a cop who's unable to achieve promotion due to his sibling's profession) attempts to leave the life, only to revenge himself upon those who usurp him.

Better Tomorrow 2, A

(Hong Kong, Film Workshop, 1987, 120 mins)

Credits
Dir/Scr: John Woo
Prod/Scr: Tsui Hark
DOP: Wong Wing Hang
Ed: Cinema City Editing Unit

Music: Joseph Koo
Prod. Des: Andy Li

Cast: Ti Lung (Sung Tse Ho), Chow Yun Fat (Ken Gor), Leslie Cheung (Sung Tse Kit), Dean Shek (Lung), Kwan Shan (Ko Ying Ping)

During Ho's prison sentence, Kit goes undercover to nail a counterfeiting operation, trailing the criminal to New York, where the brother of the deceased Mark runs a Chinese restaurant.

Reputedly the highest grossing film in Hong Kong history and the picture that made actor Chow Yun-Fat a household name. With *A Better Tomorrow* John Woo, moved away from light comedy to blend his now familiar form of melodrama with choreographed violence, here seen in its embryonic stage. A template in many ways for the superior *The Killer* (qv), *A Better Tomorrow* is a masculine cry for help by those facing uncertainty, uniting those set apart by traditional boundaries of good and evil. Mark, companion to Ho (the brother to cop Kit), laments that Hong Kong will vanish for good. Asked if he believes in God, he contests that he *is* God: 'A God is someone who controls their own destiny.' In regard to Hong Kong's 1997 release from British rule, it is the male figure – represented here as the corporate gangster – who has the most to lose, and appears the least in control over his own fate. As Mark says: 'If we don't watch out, we'll have nothing.'

Part II was rightly regarded as a highly overblown and commercial sequel, though not as confusing for viewers unfamiliar with the original as some had claimed. Outrageous and quirky, Woo briefly explores madness, as gangster Johnny is driven insane in an asylum, a theme put to far better use in his Vietnam film *Bullet in the Head*. Characterisation remains static from Part I, the film merely popularist fodder for the Cantonese gangster film market.

* A prequel to the two films, *A Better Tomorrow III* (aka *Love and Death in Saigon*), this time directed by Tsui Hark, took 'the series in a somewhat surprising direction', according to *Variety*, as Hark moved away from warring gangster clans. Set

between Hong Kong and Vietnam during the chaotic withdrawal of US troops in 1974, Chow Yun-Fat's original character Mark is resurrected as he becomes involved in currency smuggling, while trying to secure exit visas for his uncle and cousin. A recent fourth title, directed by Wong Jing and called *Return to a Better Tomorrow*, shamelessly borrows from its predecessors, careering between violence and sentimentality much in the Woo tradition. A family melodrama, it sees Michael Wong yearn to join a Triad outfit, only to simultaneously fall for a heroin addict and recoil at his own wife's cruelty to their child.

See also: *Hard Boiled*; *Violent Cop*.

Big Bad Mama

(US, New World, 1974, 83 mins)

Credits
Dir: Steve Carver
Prod: Roger Corman, Jon Davison
Scr: Frances Doel, William Norton
DOP: Bruce Logan
Ed: Tina Hirsch
Music: David Grisman
Art Dir: Peter Jamison

Cast: Angie Dickinson (Wilma McClatchie), Tom Skerritt (Fred Diller), William Shatner (William J. Baxter), Susan Sennett (Billie Jean), Robbie Lee (Polly)

A mother and her two daughters go on a bank-robbing spree in Depression-era Texas.

Big Bad Mama II

(US, Concorde, 1987, 85 mins)

Credits
Dir/Scr: Jim Wynorski
Prod: Roger Corman, Matt Leipzig
Scr: R.J. Robertson
DOP: Robert New
Ed: Noah Blough

Music: Chuck Cirino
Art Dir: Billie Greenbaum

Cast: Angie Dickinson (Wilma McClatchie), Danielle Brisebois (Billie Jean), Julie McCullough (Polly), Bruce Glover (Crawford), Robert Culp (Daryl Pearson)

The female trio return, intent upon revenging themselves on a corrupt politician by robbing his banks and kidnapping his son.

Two films, the first that followed the wake of the Corman's own *Bloody Mama* and Robert Aldrich's *The Grissom Gang* (*qqv*), the second a belated sequel. Both tow the exploitative, proto-feminist sub-genre line, with male oppression as much to blame as the economic depression (exemplified in the scene where the daughters start stripping to earn money). Unlike the influences, the father figure (rendered ineffectual in Corman and Aldrich's films) is actually absent, replaced instead by two lovers for Angie Dickinson's effervescent Ma. With delusions of grandeur for her children, she protests at her eldest's wedding that women's lives are 'nothing but dirty dishes... and being poor'. She aspires beyond the Bonnie and Clyde stakes (through their bootlegging, bank robbing and kidnapping) – wanting instead to be up with 'Ford, Rockafella, Capone and the rest of them'. And in sweet revenge she uses her pretty daughters and their innocent sexuality as 'bait' when they go a-raiding; a parallel to the way she keeps fellow robber Diller in check after he gets young Polly pregnant.

See also: *Bonnie and Clyde*; *Boxcar Bertha*.

Big Combo, The

(US, Security Pictures/Theodora Productions, 1955, 89 mins)

Credits
Dir: Joseph H. Lewis
Prod: Sidney Harmon
Scr: Philip Yordan
DOP: John Alton
Ed: Robert S. Eisen

Music: David Raksin
Prod Des: Rudi Feld

Cast: Cornel Wilde (Lt. Leonard Diamond), Richard Conte (Mr Brown), Brian Donlevy (Joe McClure), Jean Wallace (Susan Lowell), Robert Middleton (Capt. Peterson), Lee Van Cleef (Fante)

A Lieutenant becomes obsessed with bringing the head of a syndicate to justice.

Sharing much with Fritz Lang's *The Big Heat* (qv), made two years earlier (not least the titular use of 'Big', a trait common to at least 20 American films in the fifties), the film felt both contemporary to its peers and, with John Alton's low-key but distinguished photography, nostalgic for baroque stylisations of *noir*. While both Alton and director Lewis had already found success within the genre (*T-Men* and *Gun Crazy* [qv] respectively), *The Big Combo* was unrelenting in its darkness, matching its subject matter. Referring to the widely used euphemism for the Eastern Branch of the Mafia ('combo' meaning 'combination'), like Lang's work, the film set the rogue cop against the criminal syndicate, waging a one-man war against the leader – with a mink-clad mistress linking cop and gangster. Just as neither film offers any solutions to combating such widespread crime, so revenge with a gun is denied by the hero for the loss of a partner in the finale. *The Big Combo* deals less with police corruption and more with the mechanics of the 'combination'. Brown, the corporate-minded gangster, is seen as 'not a man, [but] an organisation', a person who 'doesn't kill to get what he wants – he buys'. Hiding his Italian roots, and by inference associations with first-generation gangsters, with a bland Anglicised surname (watch his knee-jerk reaction to the word 'Spaghetti' in the lie-detector test), he is referred to as a 'Book-keeper' or 'Accountant', ruthlessly running his legal and illegal activities by the maxim 'First is first, and second is nobody'.
Where Lewis's film differs from Lang's is in the sexual rapport between players. Cop Diamond is mystified by Brown's sexual mystique (he is informed that 'a woman doesn't care how a man makes his living, just how he makes love' by his own perfunctory partner), but he is determined to 'save' the gangster's girl, Susan Lowell. Her obsession with Brown (matched by Diamond's) emanates in the famous scene where he abuses her and then, kissing her, sinks his head below camera level, the girl left captivated by his aura. Winners, and criminals, are sexually attractive (and attracted). Diamond, the lone crusader against crime, spends his life as a lonely bachelor, his affair with the stripper torrid at best.

See also: *Big Heat, The*; *Frightened City*; *Force of Evil*; *Street With No Name, The*; *Underworld USA*.

Big Heat, The

(US, Columbia Pictures Corporation, 1953, 90 mins)

Credits
Dir: Fritz Lang
Prod: Robert Arthur
Scr: Sidney Boehm, based on the original novel by William P. McGivern
DOP: Charles Lang, Jr
Ed: Charles Nelson
Music: Daniele Amfitheatrof
Art Dir: Robert Peterson

Cast: Glen Ford (Dave Bannion), Gloria Grahame (Debby Marsh), Jocelyn Brando (Katie Bannion), Alexander Scourby (Mike Lagana), Lee Marvin (Vince Stone)

A web of racketeering is uncovered after the suicide of a corrupt police official.

Film noir without the black, Lang swapped the traditional use of shadowy locations for brightly lit studio sets and liberal close-ups but retained the corrosive mood of the genre, with additional violence so shocking for its time that the picture received an X certificate. Drawing on German symbolism, Lang creates the underworld milieu through an expressionistic unease. The Retreat nightclub with its gleaming row of glasses (where our hero draws a blank in his investigations), spells a reflective surface, designed to prevent the revelation of further corruption. As the bartender breathes to polish up his receptacles, we

SOLIHULL S.F.C.
LIBRARY

The Big Heat: Vincent Stone (Lee Marvin) is confronted by Debby Marsh (Gloria Grahame) and a face only a mother could love.

understand not only the work that has gone into achieving this cover-up, but that the deeper we look, the more we will see our own image. Forever economical, Lang presents the twin themes of violence and police corruption in the opening sequence – as the hand of police record's clerk Tom Duncan takes a gun to his head and commits suicide.

Glen Ford's Sgt. Dave Bannion, the avenging individual pitted against an all-powerful foe, is an example of the rogue cop, a 1950s creation to replace the G-Men (Hoover preferring his men to fight the visible desperadoes, Public Enemy No. 1, rather than the organised syndicates he denied even existed). This rebel against political and departmental bureaucracy was the alternative to the tenacious reporter or the crusading District Attorney, as shown by Humphrey Bogart in *The Enforcer* (qv). Given the lowly status of sergeant, he is the John Doe, the common man who enjoys the perfect marriage (as shown in the opening scenes) and the middle-class existence. His gangster peers represent an urgency to move away from their origins, a trait also found in Joseph H. Lewis' *The Big Combo* (qv).

Syndicate boss Lagana may be seen reclining between silk sheets in his white suburban villa, but his Prohibition activities, the portrait of his mother and his speech betray his immigrant roots. Similarly, second-in-command Stone lives in an apartment furnished by a laughably eclectic collection of Impressionist paintings, abstract sculptures and 1950s table-lamps. His penchant for sadistic violence (culminating in Gloria Grahame receiving a pot of hot coffee in the face) was also a modern trait, already seen in Richard Widmark's portrayal of Tommy Udo in *Kiss of Death* (qv). But as Bannion points out, his methods were 'old fashioned... Prohibition kind'. The characters live out a Lang theme; that of entrapment, in this case, in their own cinematic heritage.

See also: *Frightened City*; *Force of Evil*; *Street With No Name, The*; *Underworld USA*.

Billy Bathgate

(US, Touchstone Pictures, 1991, 107 mins)

*'This refined, intelligent drama about thugs
appeals considerably to the head but has little
impact in the gut, which is not exactly how it
should be with gangster films.'*

(Todd McCarthy, *Variety*)

Credits
Dir: Robert Benton
Prod: Arlene Donovan, Robert F. Colesberry
Scr: Tom Stoppard, based on the novel by E.L. Doctorow
DOP: Nestor Almendros
Ed: Alan Heim, Robert Reitano
Music: Mark Isham
Prod. Des: Dennis Bradford, Patrizia Von Brandenstein, Tim
Galvin, Bruce S. Pustin, Thomas A. Razzano, John Willett

Cast: Dustin Hoffman (Dutch Schultz), Nicole Kidman (Drew
Preston), Bruce Willis (Bo Weinberg), Steven Hill (Otto Berman),
Loren Dean (Billy Bathgate), Steve Buscemi (Irving)

**Young hustler becomes the confidant of New York
Mobster, Dutch Schultz.**

Universally criticised as a fascinating misfire, the
credibility of the piece is undermined through the
use of the subjective narrator, the young Bathgate,
who remains (almost) a wide-eyed innocent,
literally with Bible in hand, to the end. When
Dutch's lawyer Otto, the man who takes Billy under
his wing, fires the boy, he says: 'Now there goes a
kid with luck'. Billy's coming-of-age is over; he has
emerged unscathed and as if to emphasise this,
Lucky Luciano (Stanley Tucci), having despatched
Dutch and his mob, keeps him alive, adding: 'I'll be
looking in on you from time to time, just to see
how you're getting along.' Luciano becomes his
fairy Godfather, in this cautionary fable of the price
of ambition. The death of disloyal lieutenant Bo
Weinberg, opening the film and leading to the
confident 30-minute flashback of Billy's initial
introduction to Dutch, is example enough. 'Loyalty
is worth its weight in gold', Billy is told. This he
ignores to the extent of falling for Dutch's mistress
(and Weinberg's former girl) Drew Preston. But

Bathgate will walk away, his hands unsoiled.
A rites-of-passage gangster movie, then? Produced in
the age of Tarantino/Scorsese amorality, Benton's film
heralds an innocence, not unlike the spirit inside his
script for Arthur Penn's *Bonnie and Clyde* (*qv*) and
rather seems out of its time because of it. Again akin
to this earlier work, Benton prefers to mythologise
rather than document; Schultz's death originally at
the hands not of the admittedly more glamorous
Luciano but actually Charles 'the Bug' Workman. Not
so much a maturing for the genre, more a regression,
Benton treads water. With a $40 million budget
assisting towards some superlative production values,
we are left with a period drama and a trite moral.
Hoffman's Dutch (too old, with the actor – then 53 –
playing the part of a man 20 years younger) sways
between calculating businessman, using the Church
and financial system to boost his reputation, and
stubborn hot-head, ignoring tax demands and
erupting into unforeseen spasms of violence. At
times, he approaches Vic Morrow's definitive
portrayal of Schultz in *Portrait of a Mobster*, but
unlike his contemporary Robert De Niro, with his
take on Al Capone in *The Untouchables* (*qv*), is unable
to make the role his own.

See also: *Bugsy*; *Cotton Club, The*; *Hoodlum*;
Mobsters: the Evil Empire.

Black Caesar (UK title: The Godfather of Harlem)

(US, Larco, 1973, 87 mins)

Credits
Dir/Prod/Scr: Larry Cohen
DOP: Fenton Hamilton, James Signorelli
Ed: George Folsey
Music: Barry De Vorzon
Prod. Des: Larry Lurin

Cast: Fred Williamson (Tommy Gibbs), D'Urville Martin (Reverand
Rufus), Gloria Hendry (Helen), Art Lund (John McKinney), Val
Avery (Cardoza)

**A young black man, having worked for the Mafia, takes
control of Harlem, killing the mob book-keeper to capture
accounts and consolidate his power.**

Hell up in Harlem

(US, American International, 1973, 98 mins)

Credits
Dir/Prod/Scr: Larry Cohen
DOP: Fenton Hamilton
Ed: Franco Guerri, Peter Honess
Music: Fonce Mizell, Freddie Perren
Prod. Des: Larry Lurin

Cast: Fred Williamson (Tommy Gibbs), Julius Harris (Papa Gibbs), Gloria Hendry (Helen), Margaret Avery (Sister Jennifer), Gerald Gordon (Mr Di Angelo)

Surviving a police-organised assassination attempt, Harlem gangster joins up with his father to continue his reign.

Black Caesar: Tommy Gibbs (Fred Williamson) takes one in the gut.

Critically mauled at its time of release, 'the most wretched example so far of the most sickening kind of Blaxploitation' (Stuart Byron, *Village Voice*), Larry Cohen deliberately evoked the 1930s gangster movies, with *Little Caesar* (qv) an obvious role-model. Using the generic structure embodied by the likes of the Robinson film, Cohen depicts the rise and fall of 'a white nigger', or a 'black man trapped in white men's dreams', as *The Hollywood Reporter* (5/2/73) termed it. Only the appearance of Gibbs' long-lost father (to become more significant in the sequel), who left his family during the time of the Depression, links the film to its historical heritage.

The crucial difference between the two, apart from the deliberate lack of exhilarating violence in Cohen's work, becomes clear at the end. While both films adopt an ambivalence towards the gangster-protagonist, Cohen's is able to veer away from the imposed moralistic ending suffered by *Little Caesar*. Gibbs, by returning to his childhood slum to die, shows that nothing has been achieved; there is no re-establishment of traditional values, the key to the tragic form that Mervyn Le Roy's film took. *Black Caesar* is an assertion of Black Power (spurred on by a desire to help the black community), and the warning of corruption in its absolute form. Gibbs, as he gradually accumulates wealth, loses the desire to revenge himself upon the oppressive white world; rather, when he humiliates the policeman who beat him years before by shining his face black, he has become a traitor to his own race. 'All you wanted was money, cash to live in a white house', he is told. He becomes a Caesar among his people, a demigod who appropriates white culture into his lifestyle. While he may throw his former landlady's mink coats from the balcony of his new flat, he importantly does not destroy the property – merely adds it to his accumulating empire, no different from the Mafia before him.

The final 20-minute sequence, in particular, split critics. As Gibbs staggers wounded through the streets to escape a police assassination, the scene, clearly unrehearsed, allows for a *cinema vérité* feel to the action, as passers-by literally gape at actor and camera. Both brave and laughable, it typifies one's response to the film as a whole.

Hell up in Harlem takes some liberties with its predecessor. The final scene of *Black Caesar* (qv) originally (before being deleted) showed Gibbs beaten to death by a gang of young blacks. With this removed, the way was open for a sequel. Borrowing from *Caesar*'s footage and simultaneously rewriting its ending, with Gibbs still shot but now saved by his peers, Cohen does little with the headway he created with the Blaxploitation genre. Lurching from one fight sequence to the next, as Gibbs decides he wants 'to make New York a decent place to live', only the violence itself proved influential on other gangster films. Gibbs' elevated stance in his Beverley Hills apartment, as he guns down assailants, reminds one of Al Pacino's more famous sequence at the end of Brian De Palma's *Scarface* (qv) and the victim beaten and suffocated inside a plastic bag that fills with his own blood is repeated in Scorsese's *Casino* (qv). The final scene in *Hell*, with its 'We're going to start over' speech, indicated a third part – that never saw the light.

See also: *Black Godfather*; *Black Gunn*; *I'm Gonna Git You, Sucka*; *Original Gangstas*; *Shaft*.

Black Friday

(US, Universal, 1940, 69 mins)

Credits
Dir: Arthur Lubin
Prod: Burt Kelly
Scr: Curt Siodmak, Erick Taylor
DOP: Elwood Bredell
Ed: Phil Cahn
Music: Hans Salter
Art Dir: Jack Otterson

Cast: Boris Karloff (Dr Ernest Sovac), Bela Lugosi (Eric Marnay), Stanley Ridges (Red Cannon/Professor Kingsley), Anne Nagel (Sunny Rogers), Anne Gwynne (Jean Sovac)

A professor, injured during a gangland shootout, receives a gangster's brain in a transplant and begins to act on the memories and impulses that resurface from his new organ.

A rare merging of the horror and gangster genres, Universal Pictures made this under the working title of *Friday the 13th*, following the success of *Son of Frankenstein* the previous year, a front-runner of the studio's second cycle of horror films. Elements of this classic and *Dr Jekyll and Mr Hyde* were liberally borrowed to rake together the plot, as a mild-mannered English Professor repeatedly transforms into a gangster, with no later recollections at his violent actions. Originally

meant to appear together once more, in the end Lugosi and Karloff did not both appear in a scene. In fact, as the studio discovered, Karloff was miscast as the suave and gentle English Professor (unable to cope with changing into the crude gangster Red Cannon). Thus, Karloff took the role of Sovac, Lugosi (due for the Sovac role) was relegated to a supporting role as a gangster who double-crosses Cannon, and Ridges was brought in to play the dual role, outshining both in the process.

Far more accomplished in embracing the horror elements, even to the extent of using extracts of the *Son of Frankenstein* score, the gangster plot seems hashed, but provides one pertinent line. A police chief, asked if the gangland slayer on the rampage is a pal of Red's out for revenge after he was believed to have died, replies: 'A dead gangster has no friends.'

Black Godfather, The (aka Street War)

(US, Jef Films, 1974, 96 mins)

Credits
Dir/Prod./Scr: John Evans
DOP: Jack Steely
Ed: Jim Christopher
Music: Martin Yarbrough
Art Dir: Erik Nelson

Cast: Rod Perry (J.J.), Damu King (Diablo), Jimmy Witherspoon (Nate), Don Chastain (Tony Burton), Diane Somerfield (Yvonne), Duncan McLeod (Lt. Joe Sterling)

Black hoodlums attempt to keep their ghetto free of the heroin which is supplied by the white Mafia.

Despite Jimmy Witherspoon's Brando-esque diction, Robert Evans' film bears little resemblance to the film that shares part of its title. An ardently political addition to the Blaxploitation genre, the film, through a series of dialogues, the addition of a tender love scene, and a reduction in action sequences, provides a more serious examination of the situation facing the large majority of the targeted audience. Placing a different emphasis on the usual meaning of the generic term, it is an investigation of the exploitation of the black community. What keeps the film within the bounds of the genre is Evans' protagonists. The black gangsters, led by J.J. and Nate, are only one step above their oppressors, the white pushers, led by Burton. J.J., asked to unite with a militant action group against the drug problem, is even accused of being in it just for the money (backed up by the $350,000 he requests in exchange for the dope shipment that he hijacks).

Evans spares us from soapbox idealism. As J.J. himself says 'Corruption – always has been here and always will be. I've got what they've always wanted – money. Without it, you're nothing. Money buys you dignity. Poverty is a crime... that idealistic shit don't pay your rent.' Sharp enough to recognise that power lies within than hands of those who control the economy, the film is also perspicacious enough to note that, black or white, the cycle of corruption can still continue. Burton's control of the neighbourhood may end 'where he sees the first black face' but Diablo's closing rhetorical statement 'What the hell are we fighting for?' stresses that the ghettos are still awash with confusion and unguided values.

See also: *Black Caesar*; *Black Gunn*; *Hell Up In Harlem*; *I'm Gonna Git You, Sucka*; *Original Gangstas*; *Shaft*.

Black Gunn

(US, Columbia Pictures, 1972, 95 mins)

Credits
Dir: Robert Hartford-Davis
Prod: John Heyman, Norman Priggen
Scr: Franklin Coen, Robert Shearer
DOP: Richard H. Kline
Ed: Pat Somerset
Music: Tony Osborne
Art Dir: Jack DeShields

Cast: Jim Brown (Gunn), Martin Landau (Capelli), Brenda Sykes (Judith), Luciana Paluzzi (Toni), Vida Blue (Sam Green), Stephen McNally (Laurento)

A nightclub owner becomes entangled with the mob when his brother – involved in the Black Action Group – robs a betting shop for funds and steals ledgers belonging to the organisation.

Originally written for an English setting (and produced/directed by an Anglo team), it prompted *Variety* (27/12/72) pertinently to note: 'Most black gangster pix currently glutting the market are cheaply produced, either because this genre has a limited play-off or because film-makers share one major company president's view that the audience don't care about possible 'cheating on the budget'.' Certainly done on the cheap (check out the car chases), what is more reprehensible is the rigid adherence to the formula. The Superman-like black hero, a funky score, a little bit of Black politics and we've seen it all before.

See also: *Black Caesar*; *Black Godfather*; *Hell Up In Harlem*; *I'm Gonna Git You, Sucka*; *Original Gangstas*; *Shaft*.

Black Hand, The (La Mano Nera)

(Italy, In.Cis Films, 1973, 90 mins)

> 'A film which conveys its tediously naive hero to his long overdue end by means of a rambling plot line...'
> **(John Raisbeck, *Monthly Film Bulletin*)**

Credits
Dir/Scr: Antonio Racioppi
Prod: Carlo Infascelli
Scr: Vinicio Marinucci, Aldo Marcovecchio, Ugo Moretti, Luigi Cozzi
DOP: Riccardo Pallottini
Ed: Cleofe Conversi
Music: Carlo Rustichelli
Art Dir: Elio Balleti

Cast: Lionel Stander (Lt. Giuseppe Petrosino), Rosanna Fratello (Angela), Philippe Leroy (The Professor), Mike Placido (Antonio Turis)

An Italian immigrant becomes involved with the notorious 'Black Hand' organisation.

Shamelessly borrowing *The Godfather*'s (*qv*) most famous line (the 'offer he can't refuse' piece) just one year after that film's release, the film explores the early beginnings of the Mafia – their influences stretching to political events, as potential Governor, Republican O'Connor, is murdered to prevent the Italian community suffering higher taxes. Inside this is the story of their control of one man. Tony's seduction into the life, unwillingly substituting friendship for betrayal and perverted loyalties, as he sells worthless 'life insurance' policies, is highlighted as he realises he is as disposable as those to whom he sells. 'I have to be a murderer. I've no choice. It's the law.' Later he is told, 'You'll find in the family, you go in alive, you come out dead.' The Mafia's family structure is heavily outlined: the Black Hand, and its vows, is seen as an 'inherited disease', stressing generations. Tony's wife Angela draws this into focus: 'Our son will be the son of a gangster.' Excessively violent (a woman has her tongue cut out), it labours – but eventually gets out – the point that the Mafia are here to stay: 'the battle can't be won'.

* A 1950 Hollywood film, directed by Richard Thorpe, carried the same name, and dealt coyly with incidents clearly relating to the Mafia at the time of the film's production. Starring Gene Kelly as an Italian-American attorney out for revenge for the death of his father, it takes us back to late nineteenth-century 'Little Italy', telling the tale of Italian merchants at the mercy of the Black Hand, a group that extorts money with the threat of death.

See also: *Corleone*; *Scorta, La*; *Sicilian, The*.

Black Rain

(US, Paramount, 1989, 125 mins)

Credits
Dir: Ridley Scott
Prod: Stanley R. Jaffe, Sherry Lansing
Scr: Craig Bolotin, Warren Lewis

DOP: Jan De Bont
Ed: Tom Rolf
Music: Hans Zimmer
Prod. Des: Norris Spencer

Cast: Michael Douglas (Nick Conklin), Andy Garcia (Charlie Vincent), Ken Takakura (Masahiro Matsumoto), Kate Capshaw (Joyce Kingsley), Yasaku Matsuda (Sato)

New York vice cop escorts Japanese yakuza boss back to his own country to stand trial.

Ridley Scott's earlier film *Blade Runner* was the most-cited influence on this yakuza work, which went all out to try and prove that Japanese traditional values are useless in the modern world against the modern criminal. *Blade Runner* itself was influenced on a trip to Hong Kong on an advertising assignment, and rather like that retro vision of the future, Scott's take on Osaka is *noir* juxtaposed with hi-tech.

With the titular reference to the post-Hiroshima climate conditions setting a historical gateway, the film examines the mutual pollution of cultures, with the Japanese gangster Sato a product of America's postwar influence (effectively 'Music and Movies'). The film was accused from just about all sides as being racist. Supremacist would be more accurate, with the Japanese cop, Matsumoto, eventually emulating Conklin's colloquialisms. Japan is seen as the monolith, the vast skyscrapers and nightclubs dwarfing Conklin; as he is told, the Japanese 'make the machines... build the future'. Fear feeds the film – from a cultural and economic perspective. Conklin reasserts US dominance, but his renegade approach to police work brings him closer to the Japanese gangster, and by inference, the US closer to Japan, than is comfortable to the Western audience. Borrowing much from Sydney Pollack's *The Yakuza* (*qv*) – the quest/US vs Japanese values/codes of honour – Scott's vision tells us more about Americans than it does the Japanese.

* Chronic language problems, accelerating costs and a punishing exchange rate meant that the production, mid-shoot, had to be moved in its entirety from Osaka to New York, including shipping over Japanese vending machines and cars.

Scott also suffered from the literal-mindedness of the people. Fish-traders protested that a nightclub hostess would not have been living above the market, as detailed in the script. Permission was granted only when they informed the merchants that the character was visiting an aunt who worked at the market.

See also: *American Yakuza*; *American Yakuza II*; *Boiling Point*; *Kids Return*; *Sonatine*; *Yakuza, The*.

Bloody Mama

(US, American International Pictures, 1969, 84 mins)

Credits
Dir/Prod: Roger Corman
Scr: Robert Thom
DOP: John Alonzo
Ed: Eve Newman
Music: Don Randi

Cast: Shelley Winters (Kate 'Ma' Barker), Pat Hingle (Sam Adams Pendlebury), Don Stroud (Herman Barker), Diane Varsi (Mona Gibson), Bruce Dern (Kevin Dirkman), Robert De Niro (Lloyd Barker), Clint Kimbrough (Arthur Barker), Robert Walden (Fred Barker)

A mother and her four sons, through robbery and kidnapping, find fame and fortune in the Depression.

A reply to *Bonnie and Clyde* (qv), Roger Corman's film, based on a true story, provides a formidable critique of Penn's. The use of the less-than-glamorous Shelley Winters, along with the unflinching portrayal of sexual deviance and drug abuse, is a far cry from the Beatty/Dunaway partnership and the coy claim for Clyde's impotence (when in fact, Bonnie, Clyde and C.W. Moss were to have a menage à trois, as scriptwriters Benton and Newman had stated). Their evil is blamed on society, the wide-eyed innocence that can proclaim 'we rob banks' without turning a hair is emphasised. Corman, using newsreel footage of the Ku Klux Klan and the Wall Street Crash, places Barker as a product of the historical events of her time, when the rich fell

Bloody Mama: Lloyd (Robert De Niro) gets high, while Ma (Shelley Winters) looks on.

on the poor.

The police, busy attacking strikers at the time, may have forgotten about Ma and her boys, but Ma knows 'It's a free country, but unless you're rich you ain't free. I aim to be freer than the rest of the people.' She has the choice to plot her own destiny; she is at odds with society, not a product of it. Referring to herself as 'outside the law', by leaving her husband and sleeping with her sons she sets up a matriarchy where her authority will eventually stray beyond reason.

As *Monthly Film Bulletin*'s Philip Strick pointed out: 'the eradication of the Barkers is not, as it was with Bonnie and Clyde, the vengeful act of those unable to tolerate their beauty any longer; instead, the Barkers bring about their own ruin every step they take, a ruin charted long before they were born'. Corman's film, with its Oedipal overtones, becomes Greek tragedy. A film about the transgression of law, it is made all the more ironic by Ma's contradictory religious devotion, cookie-baking homeliness and belief in the family being 'respectable'. Corman places us, through alternating involvement with distance, in the middle ground – neither in a position to dismiss are often made to view them in pastoral settings, coloured with blues and greens, standing apart from the harm they cause. Only on occasion, such as the abrupt red fire alarm in the jewellery store, or the blood-red wall, stained with Herman's blood at the end, are we alerted to their imminent demise.

Corman, in *Sight & Sound* (Autumn 1970), stated that: 'The primary forces – fire, water the elements – symbolise certain natural powers and drives.' Significantly set around water (from the bathtub to the swamp), Ma's eventual destruction is caused as she symbolically fires on the cops from the top floor of the house, isolated as it were from the natural elements. Ma embodies nature at its most liberating, freeing the boys from the constricts of the outside world, but leaving them to face a void. While Arthur remains loyal to her until death, Lloyd seeks to escape her (he dies of an overdose), and Freddie seeks to emulate her by taking a male lover (leading to death). Only Arthur tries to re-establish the patriarchy by talking of marriage. His suicide indicates control and self-knowledge. Corman sees death as a natural process (with Lloyd's death intercut with drowning) and the only path for the Barkers.

* *Bloody Mama*, along with the Corman-produced *Big Bad Mama* (qv) series, were only a handful of films featuring the woman as the chief gangster. Bill Karn's 1960 *Ma Barker's Killer Brood* depicts the character as Corman's film, trekking from Oklahoma to Florida during the depression. So grand is her reputation, that mobsters such as Dillinger and Machine Gun Kelly come for advice. Earlier female gangster flicks included Frank Woodruff's 1941 *Lady Scarface*, in which a disfigured woman becomes the leader of a notorious gang, and Ray Enright's 1933 *Blondie Johnson*, in which Joan Blondell beats the depression by forming a gang to pull heists – only to cross swords with her lover and deputy.

See also: *Boxcar Bertha*; *Grissom Gang, The*.

Body and Soul

(US, Roberts Productions,1947, 106 mins)

Credits
Dir: Robert Rossen
Prod: Bob Roberts
Scr: Abraham Polonsky
DOP: James Wong Howe
Ed: Robert Parrish
Music: Hugo Friedhofer
Art Dir: Nathan Juran

Cast: John Garfield (Charley Davis), Lilli Palmer (Peg Born), Anne Revere (Anna Davis), Hazel Brooks (Alice), William Conrad (Quinn), Joseph Pevney (Shorty Polaski)

Professional boxer becomes the 'property' of New York East Side gangland boss and is pressured into taking a dive for financial reward.

The first venture of the Independent Enterprise Studios (formed to give film-makers greater control, leading director Robert Aldrich to state 'A marvellous place to work but the pictures were terrible!'), Rossen's film had no fewer than eight future directors working under him. Apart from Aldrich, who would go on to make *The Grissom Gang* (qv), these included Joseph Pevney, responsible for *Portrait of a Mobster* and, more importantly, Abraham Polonsky, who made *Force of Evil* (qv). Cast from the same ideology as *Force*, Polonsky – who, like Rossen, affiliated with the Communist movement in the 1930s and would face the McCarthy blacklist in the next decade – scripted the film as a statement against the evils of capitalism. The boxing ring becomes an allegorical setting for Garfield's fight for his own soul, as well as his struggle against poverty and corruption. A spiritual tussle, the fighter enters the realm of sin and temptation (with gangster Roberts' lure of money) but, untypically for *noir*, was allowed a chance for redemption. This he takes by not throwing his fight, but his statement afterwards to Roberts – 'What you gonna do? Kill me? Everybody dies!' – is a fatalistic echo of the gangster's own philosophy. Salvation, but not without reprisals, the boxer's idealism is no more intact. The film becomes a lament for the death of the dream of the honest man (symbolised by the flashback, dream-like structure). In this sequence, girlfriend Peg tells the fighter: 'Are you going to be a professional prizefighter, or are you going to run for President?', but the sordid reality, that not everything is possible, is already clear to us: 'I'm going down the drain... all these years everything down the drain.' Highly regarded as one of the most authentic boxing films ever, cinematographer James Wong Howe (a man Rossen was reportedly frightened of), shot the fights on roller skates, while inside the ring with the actors. So good is the final scene, that Martin Scorsese played the scene for Robert De Niro before they commenced work on *Raging Bull*, the pair's own take on the decline of a man's soul. As for Polonsky's script, the writer told *Film Quarterly*'s William Pechter that: 'There was a struggle during the shooting to prevent Rossen from rewriting the script and changing the ending. In fact, he shot an alternate finish in which the fighter is killed and ends up with his head in a garbage can. I think a comparison of *Body and Soul* and *The Hustler* might indicate not only the uses Rossen made of the former but where his temperament and style inevitably led him.'

* **Academy Awards:** Francis D. Lyon and Robert Parrish won for Best Editing.

See also: *Kid Galahad*.

Boiling Point (3-4x Jugatsu)

(Japan, Bandai, 1990, 96 mins)

Credits
Dir/Scr: Takeshi Kitano
Prod: Hisao Nabeshima, Masayuki Mori, Takio Yoshida
DOP: Katsumi Yanagishima
Ed: Toshio Taniguchi
Art Dir: Osamu Sasaki

Cast: Masahiko Ono (Masaki), Yuriko Ishida (Sayaka), Takahito Iguchi (Takashi), Minrou Iizuka (Kazuo), Makoto Ashikawa (Akira), Hitoshi Ozawa (Kanai)

Amateur baseball player and petrol-pump attendant crosses a yakuza member and subsequently makes a trip to Okinawa to purchase arms to defend himself.

The Japanese title (*3-4x Jugatsu*) refers to an imaginary baseball scoreline, meaning the away team scored a victory in extra time. Effectively, Masaki learns to take action, and scores his win in the last reel, as he crashes a petrol tanker into a building finally affecting others with his actions. This he learns by example from Uehara (a brief appearance from director Kitano), a deplorable misogynist, misanthrope, coward and part of the Okinawan yakuza. Only when Masaki emulates him does he fit into the baseball team (The Eagles) who, according to Japanese tradition, will pity him and let him play (badly) for just showing up. Yet the epilogue (Masaki again spending time on the toilet), suggests this as a daydream, rather like the close to Sergio Leone's *Once Upon A Time In America* (*qv*).

As Kitano's yakuza character, Murakawa, discovers in *Sonatine* (*qv*), Masaki's visit to Okinawa proves a vital part of the growth of the self. But while Murakawa rediscovered a lost innocence, relaxing at the beach like many visiting Japanese to this island, Masaki meets Uehara and the yakuza system of honourable respect. As Kitano himself has pointed out, Okinawa itself is 'a very mystical, spiritual place, protected by the gods' but also 'has the most violent and heavily armed yakuza in Japan. And the craziest. The most notorious yakuza all come from Okinawa. Mainland yakuza all long to conquer Okinawa, but there's no way that they ever will.'

See also: *American Yakuza*; *American Yakuza II*; *Black Rain*; *Kids Return*; *Sonatine*; *Yakuza, The*.

Bonnie and Clyde

(US, Warner Brothers, 1967, 111 mins)

Credits
Dir: Arthur Penn
Prod: Warren Beatty
Scr: David Newman, Robert Benton

Bonnie & Clyde: Bonnie (Faye Dunaway) fingers Clyde's (Warren Beatty) piece.

DOP: Burnett Guffey
Ed: Dede Allen
Music: Charles Strouse
Art Dir: Dean Tavoularis

Cast: Warren Beatty (Clyde Barrow), Faye Dunaway (Bonnie Parker), Gene Hackman (Buck Barrow), Michael J. Pollard (C.W.Moss), Estelle Parsons (Blanche), Denver Pyle (Frank Hamer)

The rise and demise of the world's most famous male/female bank robbing team.

The third film to approach the duo, following *Gun Crazy* and William Witney's *The Bonnie Parker Story* (*qqv*), scriptwriters Robert Benton and David Newman originally desired French New Wave hero François Truffaut to direct. Assigned Arthur Penn, his version, initially derided by critics for its violence, came to be seen as 'the crucial American film about love and death' (as David Thomson noted). Depicting not the underworld but the underside of American life, the film is black farce, with tragedy forever looming – symbolised by the black cloud that crosses the field in the final reel. Turning its back upon the urban chic of the Nouvelle Vague, the film recalls instead the myth of Edward G. Robinson's Rico and Paul Muni's Scarface, gangsters who risked their lives to live a life denied to the law-abider. Penn though changes emphasis in the genre, portraying two protagonists who operate exclusively in rural America – where innocent freedom and opportunity still existed. Bonnie and Clyde's flight is a reaction against society's sterile rules, but the pressure of living the myth is continually undermined in the personal/sexual relationships. Bonnie lies on the bed with the pistol next to her head, and later jams Clyde's cigar in her mouth – two signs that Clyde's impotence ridicules the couple's mystique. Blithely ignoring certain facts (C.W. Moss was an amalgam of two drivers, Parker left a husband to take off with Clyde, and had a lover along the way – so voracious was her sexual appetite), the film busies itself with the apparatus of myth. Penn recreates rather than reconstructs the bank robbers. Bonnie's restless romantic poem, referring to Jesse James, along with the couple's penchant for narcissistically photographing themselves (two true facts) set up the pair's belief in their own immortality. As critic Jim Cook noted, the pair 'are unconsciously arranging the legend'. They live in a twilight world between illusion and reality, escaping the thought of their first murder by going to view Mervyn Le Roy's *Gold Diggers of 1933* in a place where the public would go to indulge in fantasy. So strong is the child-like fantasy that Clyde with his 'He tried to kill me' following a near-fatal robbery is full of disbelief at the action. Theirs is a world with its own morality, as when Clyde offers the farmer a gun to destroy the 'For Sale' sign enforced by the bank on his home. But theirs is also a world like ours, full of mislived and miscalculated dreams. They are the archetypal children, who step out of line of the accepted ethic and are punished by society (in the shape of Sheriff Hamer).

* **Academy Awards:** Burnett Guffey won for Best Photography.

Estelle Parsons won for Best Supporting Actress.

See also: *Big Bad Mama*; *Big Bad Mama II*; *Bonnie Parker Story, The*; *Bloody Mama*; *Boxcar Bertha*; *Bullet For Pretty Boy, A*; *Dillinger*; *George Raft Story, The*; *Grissom Gang, The*; *Lepke*; *Lucky Luciano*; *Machine Gun Kelly*; *Rise and Fall of Legs Diamond, The*; *Young Dillinger*.

The Bonnie Parker Story

(US, American International, 1958, 79 mins)

Credits
Dir: William Witney
Prod/Scr: Stanley Shpetner
DOP: Jack A. Marta
Ed: Frank Keller
Music: Ronald Stein

Cast: Dorothy Provine (Bonnie Parker), Jack Hogan (Guy Darrow), Joe Turkel (Chuck Darrow), Richard Bakalyan (Duke Jefferson), Jim Beck (Alvin)

Fictionalised account of the famous bank-robbing couple.

A result of resuscitating the glut of lovers-on-the-run pictures from the late forties – *They Live By Night*, *Gun Crazy* (*qqv*) and *You Only Live Once* – and merging it with the biopic trend – *Machine Gun Kelly* (*qv*), *Baby Face Nelson* – this was an exploitative contribution to the genre. With the opening credits displayed next to a picture of Parker ('a real wild cat') undressing, it is evident her sexuality will be explored in the basest of ways as the route of her pathology. Based on few facts, we initially encounter Bonnie working in a bar, tarnished by the reputation of her incarcerated husband Duke Jefferson. She soon connects with Guy, ecstatically lighting his cigar after their initial robbery and potently leaving it in her mouth as she says: 'You take care of the driving, I'll take care of you.' Arthur Penn, in his version *Bonnie and Clyde* (*qv*), would recycle the image. Full of sharp, throwaway lines – 'We're gonna go out and get some kicks, some real kicks, in big city style... nobody's gonna stop me' – the film lacks the finesse

of *They Live By Night* or *Gun Crazy*, opting instead for lingering shots of Parker blazing away with a

Tommy Gun, a feature emulated by Roger Corman in the likes of *Bloody Mama* (*qv*).

See also: *Bullet For Pretty Boy, A*; *George Raft Story, The*; *Lepke*; *Lucky Luciano*; *Rise and Fall of Legs Diamond, The*; *Young Dillinger*.

Borsalino

(France, Adel/Marianne/Mars Film Productions, 1970, 126 mins)

'The result... looks rather like a Hollywood musical where someone has forgotten to insert the production numbers.'
(Monthly Film Bulletin)

Credits
Dir/Scr: Jacques Deray
Prod: Alain Delon
Scr: Jean-Claude Carriere, Claude Sautet, Jean Cau, based on the novel The Bandits of Marseille by Eugene Saccomano
DOP: Jean-Jacques Tarbes
Ed: Paul Cayatte
Music: Claude Bolling
Art Dir: Francois de Lamothe

Cast: Jean-Paul Belmondo (Capella), Alain Delon (Siffredi), Michael Bouquet (Rinaldi), Catherine Rouvel (Lola), Francoise Christophe (Mme. Escarguel), Corinne Marchand (Mme. Rinaldi)

Two rival gangsters join forces in the port of Marseille and bid for control of the town's meat and fish markets.

Borsalino & Co. (aka Blood on the Streets)

(France, Medusa, 1974, 91 mins)

'The film discouragingly ends with a flight to America and the implied threat of Borsalino Part III'
(Richard Combs, Monthly Film Bulletin)

Credits
Dir/Scr: Jacques Deray
Prod: Alain Delon
Scr: Pascal Jardin
DOP: Jean-Jacques Tarbes
Ed: Henri Lanoe
Music: Claude Bolling
Art Dir: Francois de Lamothe

Cast: Alain Delon (Roch Siffredi), Catherine Rouvel (Lola), Riccardo Cucciolla (Giovanni Volpone), Reinhard Kolldehoff (Sam), Daniel Ivernel (Commissioner Fanti), André Falcon (Commissioner Cazenave)

Seeking redress for the death of his partner, Siffredi pursues and disposes of the killers.

Given, at the time, one of the biggest ever pre-sell publicity campaigns for a French picture, the original proved a rather ineffectual pastiche. No more than a vehicle for its star personalities and their tough guy personas, the insight into French pre-war gangsters de-materialised in the rush to marry a big-budget spectacular with the corrupt City Hall/big business bandwagon. Ford and Hawks may be imbued (with the rugged sentimentality of the gangsters exchanging blows) and Jean-Pierre Melville remembered (he directed both Belmondo and Delon in his own gangster films), but Deray's work is just a shade of the pre-*Bonnie and Clyde* days. Contrasting the two personalities, Belmondo plays the nonchalant extrovert, Delon the understated opposite, their relationship mutating to co-dependency as the film takes the shape of a period buddy-buddy movie.

The sequel, picking up where the other left off with Capella's funeral, takes itself far more (too) seriously, with lines from Delon, guns-ablazing, like: 'As a kid, I thought of Marseille as Heaven. Now I'm going to make it Hell!' Lacking Belmondo's tongue-in-cheek air, at best it becomes a simplistic revenge drama. Made directly after its predecessor, but not released for four years, it's a film that seems uncomfortable with its place, both as a follow-up and a gangster flick in its own right.

* The title refers to the wide-brimmed felt hats sported by the gangsters of the period, as worn by Al Capone.

See also: *A Bout de Souffle*; *Samourai, Le*.

Bound

(US, Dino De Laurentiis, 1996, 108 mins)

'This offers the not-unappealing spectacle of gorgeous, funny, clever women making fools of hard-boiled Mafia guys.'

(Kim Newman, *Empire*)

Credits
Dir/Scr: Andy and Larry Wachowski
Prod: Andrew Lazar, Stuart Boros
DOP: Bill Pope
Ed: Zach Staenberg
Music: Don Davis
Prod. Des: Eve Cauley

Cast: Jennifer Tilly (Violet), Gina Gershon (Corky), Joe Pantoliano (Caesar), John P. Ryan (Mickey Malnato), Christopher Meloni (Johnnie Marconi), Richard C. Sarafian (Gino Marzzone)

The wife of a Mafia employee unites with her next door neighbour and double-crosses her husband and the mob.

As tightly constructed as a tourniquet, the Wachowski brothers' dazzling neo-*noir* debut ups the ante and the artifice from its forties counterparts, re-jigging the genre towards pseudo-feminist terms. Owing as much to the Coen Brothers' own debut, *Blood Simple*, as they do to the works of Hitchcock, Wilder and Siodmak, the brothers smugly manoeuvre the audience into cahoots with those who circumvent the law. In this case, femme fatale Violet and her new-found love Corky revenging themselves upon the former's husband Caesar – the motive being that men misunderstand a woman's needs, and should therefore be broken. The lesbian gimmick appears no more than an exploitive male porn fantasy (complete with hammy come-on dialogue), the 'butch' dyke Corky more like 'a witty transliteration of James Dean', as one critic noted. But, two purposes are served here. Crime is equated with sex – the more you talk about it, the wetter you get, but entering into a criminal alliance with someone you've never worked with before is no more secure than participating in a 'one night stand'. The ultimate success of the pair, allowing them to escape unharmed with the loot Caesar is baby-sitting for the mob, indicates a belief and need for trust and equality between partners, the female partnership indicating the unbalance caused by traditional destructive male-dominated relationships.

Just as loyalty was punished in forties *noir*, so was intelligence. Not so for the girls. Both cops and robbers are fooled, the only difference as Corky notes, is the mob 'have no rules and lots of money'. As if to emphasise this uncommon allegiance between both sides of the law, we are reminded that nobody calls them the Mafia anymore, just 'the business'.

Self-conscious in the extreme, the camerawork matches the lavish production design for its stylistic approach. Weaving an invisible net around the protagonists, the camera rarely stops moving, while the co-ordinated colour scheme (black, white, grey and red), right down to Tilly's fingernails, draws together the themes of sex, death and money – the staples of the genre.

Boxcar Bertha

(US, American International Pictures, 1972, 88 mins)

Credits
Dir: Martin Scorsese
Prod: Roger Corman
Scr: Joyce H. Corington, John William Corrington, based on Bertha Thompson's autobiography Sister of the Road
DOP: John M. Stephens
Ed: Buzz Feitshans
Music: Gib Guilbeau, Thad Maxwell
Prod. Des: David C. Nichols

Cast: David Carradine (Bill Shelley), John Carradine (H. Buckram Sartoris), Bernie Casey (Von Morton), Barbara Hershey (Bertha), Barry Primus (Rake Brown)

A young Arkansas woman in the Depression hooks up with a gang of train robbers.

Intended by Corman as a sequel to *Bloody Mama* (*qv*), Martin Scorsese, despite working on a budget of just $600,000 in what was only his second full-length picture, managed to weave his own concerns around the constraints of exploitation. Corman religiously adhered to the rules, championing the father of the genre: 'It's *Bonnie and Clyde* that we're doing and I think we should put a chase scene with the cars', telling Scorsese he must 'have some nudity at least every 15 pages'. As for the sound mixing (to be done in only three days), Corman argued: 'The first reel has to be good because people coming to the drive-in have to hear what's going on. Forget the rest of the film until you get to the last reel, because they just want to know how it turned out.' As it happened, for a film *Variety* described as 'routinely directed', Scorsese injected references to *The Wizard of Oz* (Hershey's hair modelled on Dorothy's), and the influential Powell/Pressburger team, naming two characters after them. The opening credits, introducing each actor with their part, harked back to the style used in the early Warner Brothers films – Union leader Big Bill Shelley, 'a notorious bolshevik', even refers to himself as 'a public enemy'. One of the most overtly political films Scorsese has handled, Shelley, not dissimilar to the child-like innocence of Bonnie and Clyde, is the idealist. His spoils go to the cause, and he vehemently denies the statement 'We're just criminals'. As if to emphasise his devotion to his fellow man – he begins to feel compromised as he becomes a gangster – the finale sees him crucified on a boxcar (a sequence later be reused, shot by shot, in *The Last Temptation of Christ*). If anything, the age-old theme of political purity and crime remaining incompatible is reiterated.

See also: *Grissom Gang, The.*

Breathless: See A Bout de Souffle.

Brighton Rock: Mirror image: Pinkie (Richard Attenborough) arrives, intent on doing some damage.

Brighton Rock (US Title: Young Scarface)

(UK, Associated British Picture Corporation, 1947, 92 mins)

'There's a certain fascination in seeing the avuncular old Dickie cast as a murdering dastard in a sharp suit.'

(Kim Newman, *Empire*)

Credits
Dir: John Boulting
Prod: Roy Boulting
Scr: Terence Rattigan, Graham Greene, based on his own novel
DOP: Harry Waxman
Ed: Peter Graham Scott
Music: Hans May

Cast: Richard Attenborough (Pinkie), Hermione Baddeley (Ida Arnold), William Hartnell (Dallow), Carol Marsh (Rose), George Carney (Phil Corkery)

The seedy side of a seaside resort is exposed as a young gang killer tries to court a waitress to set her up as his alibi.

Attenborough's chilling portrait of the 17-year-old, hat cocked menacingly askew throughout, rivals any portrait of a mobster Britain has ever produced. Somewhat apart from the trend set two years later in *It Always Rains on Sunday* and *The Blue Lamp*, Pinkie is pure psychotic, no mere chirpy spiv that would typify the British gangster – eventually to be lampooned in the Ealing comedies. A diminutive stature adds to the haunting presence evoked, the endless twisting of the cats-cradle reminds one of George Raft's habitual coin-flipping in *Scarface* (qv).

The opening credits distance the film à la *The Public Enemy/Little Caesar* (qqv) from any accusations of immorality, telling us there once was another side to Brighton, one of 'dark alleyways and gang war', that happily no longer exists – presumably because our law enforcement units have since swept away such scum and villainy.

While Pinki never drinks, smokes or consumes chocolate, he seems a precursor to Schwarzenegger's Terminator. Emotionally cold, his weapon is the razor – with one terrifying slasher sequence sending him to infamy. Yet a grim humour underlies the action: 'You're sensitive – like me' Pinkie suggests absurdly to Rose, while a-courting. He subsequently gives her his phone number, containing the figures 666. What is most ironic is the film's repetitious theme of failure; the notion that a teenager is all washed-up, a concept brought to a head in *The Last Gangster* (qv). What disappoints is the 'happy' ending; while the audience is aware of the hatred contained in the vinyl disc Pinkie has recorded for Rose, Greene's original ending is altered, and a scratch on the record prevents her discovering the true content in the epilogue.

See also: *Ladykillers, The.*

Brotherhood of the Yakuza: See The Yakuza.

Brother Orchid

(US, 1940, Warner Brothers, 91 mins)

'The other night on an obscure television channel I caught a glimpse of a man billed as Edward G. Robinson playing with Humphrey Bogart in a film called Brother Orchid. I thought they both over-acted, shouted a little too much and occasionally were very good indeed. Robinson would have played the character very differently today; I suspect Bogie would have too. It is oddly disconcerting to have a performance made permanent.'

(Edward G. Robinson, shortly before his death)

Credits
Dir: Lloyd Bacon
Exec. Prod: Hal B. Wallis
Scr: Earl Baldwin
DOP: Tony Gaudio
Ed: William Holmes

Music: Heinz Roemheld
Art Dir: Max Parker

Cast: Edward G. Robinson (John Sarto), Ann Sothern (Flo Addams), Humphrey Bogart (Jack Buck), Donald Crisp (Brother Superior), Ralph Bellamy (Clarence Fletcher), Allen Jenkins (Willie the Knife)

A racketeer, ejected from his crew after returning from a five-year absence, stumbles, wounded, upon a monastery and discovers a new meaning to life.

The last of the Robinson-Bogart pictures (until *Key Largo*, a film not regarded as part of the original cycle of Warners' gangster pictures), this would also be one of the last great gangster comedies – a tongue-in-cheek style that had rarely proved successful, but was kick-started by Michael Curtiz's James Cagney-Bette Davis vehicle *Jimmy the Gent* in 1934. In both this and *Brother Orchid*, the same rules – little gunplay, violence and certainly no death – applied. An appearance by Allen Jenkins, a specialist in gangster comedies, as the slow-witted sidekick, also seemed mandatory, and he would again reappear in Robinson's follow-up to *Brother Orchid*, *Larceny, Inc.*

Rumour had it that Robinson originally refused the role of Little John Sarto, a gangster who takes to Europe to search for 'class' only to find it through religion, and only took the role on the promise from Warners' of parts in *The Sea Wolf*, *A Despatch From Reuters* or *Dr Ehrlich's Magic Bullet*, (in all of which he featured), depending which source you believe. While this indicated a frustration at type-casting, just as Humphrey Bogart would remain equally unsatisfied with yet another supporting part opposite Edward G, as the villain of the piece, the film proved an enduring success, no doubt from the novelty value of seeing Robinson switch his top hat and tails for a monk's robes and sandals.

Full of stock characters, it is quickfire entertainment, but sharply scripted, replacing the gangster's usual desires (power, money) with 'class', a laughable pretension in itself, but the characteristic of social mobility would come to epitomise the gangster's need to reach the pinnacle of his society.

See also: *Lady Killer*; *Last Gangster, The*.

Bronx Tale, A

(US, Tribecca, 1993, 122 mins)

Credits
Dir/Prod: Robert De Niro
Prod: Jane Rosenthal, Jon Kilik
Scr: Chazz Palminteri
DOP: Reynaldo Villalobos
Ed: David Ray, Robert Q. Lovett
Music: Butch Barbella
Prod. Des: Wynn Thomas

Cast: Robert De Niro (Lorenzo), Chazz Palminteri (Sonny), Lillo Brancato (Calogero, aged 17), Taral Hicks (Jane), Joe Pesci (Carmine)

The son of a Bronx bus driver becomes involved with local mobsters after he remains silent having witnessed a shooting.

Robert De Niro's directorial debut undeniably owes its establishing sequences to Martin Scorsese's *Goodfellas* (*qv*), a film De Niro spent three weeks working on three years before. Narrated by the young Calogero, the introduction to the neighbourhood crew (the likes of Jimmy Whispers and Hankie Coffee-Cake) is a little too close for comfort. What is present, though, that *Goodfellas* lacked (some would argue to that film's credit) is the morality figure, played here by De Niro as Calogero's father – a cut-out full of obvious maxims such as 'When you do right good things happen'. He tells his young son: 'It doesn't take much strength to pull a trigger... the working man's the tough guy', adding in reference to local gangster Sonny 'People don't love him, they fear him'. This proves the turning point for the script, as the inter-racial relationship between Calogero and Jane takes over. Calogero's teenage peers, the 'little big men' dressed in their sharp suits, become caricatures; a comment is made at Sonny's funeral that 'gangsters have a thing about flowers. They think whoever sends the biggest arrangement cares the most' and the cameo of Joe Pesci, drafted in to take over the neighbourhood, also lampoons (intentionally or otherwise) the genre itself. De Niro concentrates more on developing a sense of time and space. As Producer Jon Kilik told *Screen International*: 'This area of the Bronx had a specific quality as the birthplace of doo-wop – like Liverpool in 1963 – so in the film the location is like a character.' How apt, as Robert Yates' criticism in *Sight & Sound* of the period setting being something akin to 'a guide to stock Italo-Americana' rings true for the protagonists as well. The limited characterisation stems, no doubt, from the format of the original off-Broadway production, in which actor/writer Palminteri played all 18 parts in a one-man show.

De Niro brought his traditional 'method' approach to Lorenzo (delaying production until he had passed his bus driver's test), and shot nearly twice the normal amount of footage in search of 'realism'. Shooting the film sequentially, the schedule increased from 55 to 88 days, the budget from $15 to $24 million, with De Niro injecting over $2 million of his own money into the project.

See also: *Bullets Over Broadway*

Brotherhood, The

(US, Paramount, 1969, 96 mins)

Credits:
Dir: Martin Ritt
Prod: Kirk Douglas
Scr: Lewis John Carlino
DOP: Boris Kaufman
Ed: Frank Bracht
Music: Lalo Schifrin
Art Dir: Tambi Larson

Cast: Kirk Douglas (Frank Ginetta), Alex Cord (Vince Ginetta), Irene Papas (Ida Ginetta), Luther Adler (Dominick Bertolo), Susan Strasberg (Emma Ginetta)

An old-guard Mafioso becomes a syndicate target, after killing his brother's father-in-law – the man who killed their father.

A commercial failure on release, and subsequently overlooked due to the success of the *Godfather* (qv) films, *The Brotherhood* is nonetheless notable for exploring the machinations of a Mafia family before Coppola's works. It was in fact the poor box office of Ritt's film that almost turned Paramount off adapting the Puzo novel. Just as *The Godfather* would use character actors from past gangster works, such as Richard Conte, so *The Brotherhood* would use Eduardo Ciannelli, the veteran actor from *Marked Woman* and *Dillinger* (qqv). Ritualistic deaths also pre-empted Coppola's film. A character left dead in a chair with a canary inserted in his mouth is comparable to the symbolic fish sent on behalf of Luca Brasi. Bertolo's self-strangulation, induced by Ginetta for the murder of 40 elder mob statesman (one being his father), is also echoed by Coppola with the early garrotting episode. Topics covered here would also be brushed on in *Part II*; the syndicate's desire to move into corporate business (with a potential political clash of interests) is echoed by the trouble Michael Corleone encounters with the Senator and legitimising the family business. Frank's younger and more ambitious brother Vinny claims 'There's nothing too big. Not even the Government. You can't keep operating out of a candy store.' Hyman Roth, later, will compare the syndicate the Corleone family are part of as 'bigger than US Steel'. Coppola's trilogy and *The Brotherhood* come from a recognition that gangsters were operating on a highly organised and nationwide scale. Ritt's film was a dramatisation of this process; the movement from the old-guard to the new. To keep the bloodline pure, Frank and the generations preceding him had resisted joining the syndicate ('The Family is always alive'), but as he is reminded 'There's nothing left for us but a box in the ground.'

Build My Gallows High: See Out of the Past

Bugsy

(US, Baltimore Pictures, 1991, 135 mins)

Bugsy: 'Bugsy' Siegel (Warren Beatty), caught in a pompous moment.

Credits
Dir/Prod: Barry Levinson
Prod: Warren Beatty, Mark Johnson
Scr: James Toback
DOP: Daviau Allen
Ed: Stu Linder
Music: Ennio Morricone
Prod. Des: Dennis Gassner, Leslie McDonald

Cast: Warren Beatty (Bugsy Siegel), Annette Bening (Virginia Hill), Charlie Luciano (Bill Graham), Harvey Keitel (Mickey Cohen), Ben Kingsley (Meyer Lansky), Joe Mantegna (George Raft), Elliott Gould (Harry Greenberg)

The story of the gangster who had a dream of building a gambling empire in the then little-known Nevada town, Las Vegas.

Directed by Barry Levinson, this is a 'Warren Beatty Film'. Scriptwriter James Toback worked on the script for six years, claiming 'Siegel has been in my system since I was 19', but lost out on directorial duties when Beatty brought Levinson in over his head. Not the 'campaign vehicle' that was *Dick Tracy* (qv), this, as *Sight & Sound*'s Philip Strick noted of Beatty's role as Siegel, was an amalgam of the word-savouring idealist of *Reds*, the crusader of *Dick Tracy* (qv), and the blithe bank robber of *Bonnie and Clyde* (qv). In other words, a culmination of his work to date. Just as his Clyde was a country boy who become a folk icon, so Siegel finds 'the answer to the dreams of America'. So great are his delusions of grandeur that he even hopes to assassinate Mussolini.

More a biopic than a strict gangster film (ignoring the machinations of the mobster's empire), the film is a homage to a man who wanted to build, not destroy. According to Strick, facts, such as Bugsy's violent temper, his obsession with Virginia Hill, his struggle to overcome his Brooklyn accent, and his Las Vegas dream, were 'amended, elided and enhanced to protect the audience from disaffection'. More likely to prevent this is Beatty's sympathetic portrayal of the man; almost ridiculous, he is the one who holds meetings with Meyer Lansky in a Chef's uniform, sunbathes under ultra-violet rays while travelling on a train and is shot by a sniper while watching his favourite film – his own Hollywood screen-test.

* Harvey Keitel played Siegel in the TV movie *The Virginia Hill Story* 15 years earlier.

* **Academy Awards:** Dennis Gassner won for Best Production Design.
Albert Wolsky won for Best Costume Design.

See also: *Billy Bathgate*; *Hoodlum*; *King of the Roaring Twenties: the Arnold Rothstein Story*; *Lepke*; *Lucky Luciano*; *Mobsters: the Evil Empire*; *Valachi Papers, The*.

Bugsy Malone

(UK, National Film Finance Consortium, 1976, 93 mins)

'It's a kind of Saturday matinee Godfather.'
(Philip Strick, *Sight & Sound*)

Credits
Dir/Scr: Alan Parker
Prod: Alan Marshall
DOP: Michael Seresin, Peter Biziou
Ed: Gerry Hambling
Music: Dave Garland
Prod. Des: Geoffrey Kirkland

Cast: Scott Baio (Bugsy Malone), Jodie Foster (Tallulah), Florrie Dugger (Blousey Brown), John Cassisi (Fat Sam), Martin Lev (Dandy Dan), Sheridan Earl Russell (Knuckles)

Spoof gangster musical, depicting the rivalry of two gangs in 1930s New York.

As the publicity material said: 'There's never been a movie like it'. Alan Parker, who went on to make the soulful *The Commitments* and the recent big-budget version of *Evita*, romps through cinema's gangsterland of the 1930s, using only children to play the adult roles (the eldest being just 16).

All the standards are here: from Tommy guns (called here The Splurge Gun, firing not bullets but cream) and classic cars (pedal power, of course) to sharp suits, pencil moustaches and Prohibition wars (sarsaparilla, naturally), Parker goes on to recreate a Warner Brothers feel to the film. Scenes of the prima donna actress, the dancer needing the big break and assassinations in barber shops, the Chinese laundry and speakeasy joints all help perfectly to recreate the gangster world in miniature.

References range from the (unattributable) generic, such as the prologue's alleyway killing, to the more pointed. Mob Boss Fat Sam, for example, who invokes James Cagney, calling Danny Dan 'a dirty rat'. 'You watch too many movies' replies his rival. Malone himself, a fight promoter by trade, recalls Elia Kazan's *On the Waterfront* (qv) with the oft-quoted 'I could've been a contender, Charlie' speech, while the lazy sunny afternoon that Bugsy and his girl Tallulah spend recalls the soft-focus of *Bonnie and Clyde* (qv).

See also: *Freshman, The*; *Guys and Dolls*; *I'm Gonna Git You, Sucka*; *Johnny Dangerously*; *Love Me or Leave Me*; *A Pocketful of Miracles*; *Wise Guys*.

Bullet for Pretty Boy, A

(US, American International Pictures, 1970, 89 mins)

*'Long on unremarkable action and short on
definition in acting, scripting or direction.'*
    (Richard Combs, *Monthly Film Bulletin*)

Credits
Dir/Prod: Larry Buchanan
Scr: Henry Rosenbaum
DOP: James R. Davidson
Ed: Miguel Levin
Music: Harley Hatcher

Cast: Fabian Forte (Charles 'Pretty Boy' Floyd), Jocelyn Lane (Betty), Astrid Warner (Ruby), Michael Haynes (Ned Short), Adam Roarke ('Preacher'), Robert Glenn (Hossler)

Biopic of famed gangster, eventually brought to justice by an FBI Agent.

Borrowing from more successful screen biographies of the time, *A Bullet For Pretty Boy* invokes the likes of *Bonnie and Clyde* (qv), with the appearance of Ned Short and his beret-wearing moll reminding us of Barrow and Parker. The bleached-out landscape also recalls the likes of *Bloody Mama* (qv) and *The Grissom Gang* (qv), but never escapes these influences. A quest for identity, he asserts 'I'm Charles Arthur Floyd' as he dies, an attempt to rediscover what he is, shortly after being asked to sign his infamous autograph. His life of crime – symbolised by the nickname 'Pretty Boy' that he so despises – is one of self-denial, governing all he touches. As the soundtrack sings: 'I can't run no more/But the more I run, O lore/I see it's me I'm running from.'

See also: *Bonnie Parker Story, The; Dillinger; George Raft Story, The; Lepke; Lucky Luciano; Machine Gun Kelly; Rise and Fall of Legs Diamond, The; Young Dillinger.*

Bullets or Ballots

(US, Warner Brothers, 1936, 82 mins)

Credits
Dir: William Keighley
Exec. Prod: Hal B. Wallis, Jack L. Warner
Scr: Seton I. Miller, based on the original story by Miller and Martin Mooney
DOP: Hal Mohr
Ed: Jack Killifer
Music: Heinze Roemheld
Art Dir: Carl Jules Weyl

Cast: Edward G. Robinson (Johnny Blake), Joan Blondell (Lee Morgan), Barton MacLane (Al Kruger), Humphrey Bogart (Bugs Fenner), Frank McHugh (Herman)

An undercover cop becomes a gangster's lieutenant, bringing him to blows with the boss' right-hand man.

Rather run-of-the-mill Robinson-Bogart picture, their first collaboration, with *Kid Galahad* (qv), *The Amazing Dr. Clitterhouse* and *Brother Orchid* (qv) still to come. A socially and politically conscious effort, the gangster here is not the ambitious low-life of the early Warner Brothers efforts but that of the high-ranking official. Kruger's flourishing criminal empire is funded by three anonymous bankers, and given the go-ahead by the corrupt political machine. As we learn from the statement upon violence – 'that strong-armed gangster stuff went out with Prohibition' this is attempting to examine a malaise of the present, not past. While it is evident that Kruger's numbers rackets are protected through force (a potential usurper, we are told, had acid thrown in his face), they are run by a tactic that proves far more powerful than thuggery. *Bullets or Ballots*, as the title suggests, looks at the violence of red tape. With the opening sequence (as Kruger, and his second-in-command and representative of the old-guard, Fenner watch a documentary called 'The Syndicate of Crime'), we discover 'the racketeers have the American public pretty well whipped', ruling by fear. They have control of the workforce, even the food supply – preventing wholesalers who refuse to play ball from moving their shipments. More importantly, the justice system is quite prepared to let men like Kruger off the hook. The film is a recognition that stronger laws are needed to stop racketeers (the introduction of the Grand Jury), but corruption must be wiped out behind them – the film offers a Police Department Clean-up as a start.

Bullets Over Broadway

(US, Sweetland Films, 1994, 99 mins)

Credits
Dir/Scr: Woody Allen
Prod: Robert Greenhut
Scr: Douglas McGrath
DOP. Carlo Di Palma
Ed: Susan E.Morse
Prod Des: Santo Loquasto

Cast: John Cusack (David Shayne), Chazz Palminteri (Cheech), Dianne Wiest (Helen Sinclair), Jennifer Tilly (Olive Neal), Joe Viterelli (Nick Valenti), Jim Broadbent (Warner Purcell)

Playwright compromises his work by funding the production through the mob (and later receiving literary assistance from a bodyguard), in return for casting the Boss' girlfriend.

The notion of gangster-as-writer is fairly unique, and Allen uses it to the full to meditate on the themes of art and morality, symbolically culminating in the final scene when gun shots fired in the wings are commented upon by a critic as the defining moment of the play.

Instructed to stay by gangster's moll Olive throughout, bodyguard Cheech is literally at the edge of the frame for much of the rehearsals; an ever-constant reminder of playwright Shane's compromise. Allen also bolsters the parody with the notion reminding one of past portrayals of mob involvement in the arts, shown in the likes of *The George Raft Story* (qv), with a nod to *The Cotton Club* (qv) and, with its flippancy concerning gangland, *Some Like It Hot* (qv). Allen's casting of Chazz Palminteri created (unbeknown to Allen) further resonances. Palminteri's own play *A Bronx Tale*

(qv), written while he was a struggling actor, became the source for the Robert De Niro film, which would in turn launch Palminteri's own acting career. Based on a childhood experience, Palminteri's work – like Cheech's – would reverberate with the sounds of the street, unlike Shayne's unreal 'poetic licence'.

As Allen said to Screen International's Colin Brown: 'There are a lot of actors in New York who are gangsters who are very good [actors]. This whole group of real mob guys has sprung up, you know, from the *Godfather* movies and from Scorsese's movies who now appear in films. There were several in *Bullets Over Broadway*. And oddly enough, they're graceful with dialogue and can speak and be believable.'

What transpires is a world where the characters are all creating their own moral universe. When Shayne asks Cheech if no-one had ever told him that killing is wrong, he checks himself and dryly says 'Who am I talking to?' But while Cheech has no qualms about killing, Shayne and his cast either cheat on their partners or themselves. Allen is not condoning Cheech's trade, but using him, with his stern code of 'no one squeals' ethics, to show how much closer we are to him, as art is to life, than we might think.

* **Academy Awards:** Dianne Wiest for Best Supporting Actress.

* This was not Allen's first foray into exploring the relationship between entertainment and the Mafia. *Broadway Danny Rose* told the story of a cabaret agent whose client gets mixed up with a woman whose intended has two hit-men for brothers, while her ex was a juice-man for the mob.

Bullitt

(US, Warner Brothers, 1968, 105 mins)

Credits
Dir: Peter Yates
Prod: Phil D'Antoni, Robert E. Relyea
Scr: Harry Kleiner, Alan R. Trustman, based on the novel Mute Witness by Robert Pine

DOP: William Fraker
Ed: Frank Keller
Music: Lalo Schifrin
Prod. Des: Albert Brenner

Cast: Steve McQueen (Bullitt), Don Gordon (Delgetti), Robert Duvall (Weissberg), Jacqueline Bissett (Cathy), Robert Vaughn (Chalmers)

Maverick San Francisco cop is assigned to guard a Mafia boss due to testify in front of an investigative committee.

From a script about a policeman who never solved crimes, from a novel that had already undergone four aborted adaptations, came *Bullitt* – 'one helluva film' as McQueen, who subsequently became a superstar, called it. Remembered for its visceral car chase through the hilly streets of San Francisco (taking three weeks to film 12 minutes of edited footage), it would prove to be a defining moment in US cinema. Until this point, car chases had been filmed by second-unit directors, with the star inserted at a later point using rear projection matte and a prop car. As stuntman Bud Ekins noted: 'That day was the first time anyone was using real speeds in movies. We were going well over 100mph.' An integral part of the gangster genre, the car chase has featured from the likes of *Scarface* (qv) and the Lewis Seiler-directed Humphrey Bogart effort *The Big Shot* (with the chase on ice) onwards. From *Bullitt* car action sequences would forever pale by comparison, with only William Freidkin's effort in *The French Connection* coming close. But *Bullitt* was important to the genre for another reason; the development of the maverick cop which would come to fruition in the 1970s. Stretching back to Hoover's G-Men, TV's *The Untouchables* series and film creations such as Glen Ford's Sgt. Dave Bannion in Fritz Lang's *The Big Heat* (qv), the figure upheld the law through dubious, unconventional means, often at odds with superiors and under-valued by the public he protects. Films like Freidkin's and Don Siegel's *Dirty Harry* would develop the character further, inheriting sadistic tendencies from the gangster. While *Bullitt* was liberally concerned with apprehending corrupt officials, Popeye Doyle or Harry Callaghan were exhibiting racist or fascist

behaviour, fanatically pursuing their cases. Siegel himself had already been through two gangster cycles; the remake *The Killers* (qv) and the biopic *Baby Face Nelson*. The amplification of a vigilante attitude is a clear descendent from early gangster films of the thirties, the likes of *Beast of the City* (1932) and Cecil B. DeMille's *This Day and Age* (1933). Cops, it seems, have to behave like criminals to stem the tide of criminality from filtering through to the American public at large; their only difference is a motivation by professional pride, not greed.

* Director Peter Yates went on to make *The Friends of Eddie Coyle* with Robert Mitchum as a Boston-based weapons dealer to the underworld who faces another prison term unless he informs on a gang of bank robbers. With the arrest of the leader, a contract is put on Coyle's head and it's left to his best friend (and the real informant) Dillon (Peter Boyle) to dispense with him. Based on the incomprehensible best-seller by Massachusetts assistant district attorney George V. Higgins, Yates' low-key realism preserved the seedy authenticity of a work that owed a great deal to Henry Hathaway's *Kiss of Death*.

* **Academy Award:** Frank Keller won for Best Editing.

See also: *Better Tomorrow, A; G-Men; Hard Boiled.*

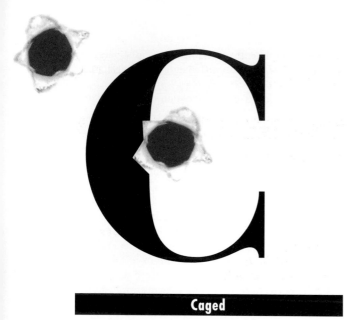

Caged

(US, Warner Brothers, 1949, 91 mins)

'It is difficult to believe in any jail quite so corrupt, or so primitively organised as this, and by piling on the horror the film reduces its own impact.'

(Monthly Film Bulletin)

Credits
Dir: John Cromwell
Prod: Jerry Wald
Scr: Virginia Kellog, Bernard C. Schoenfeld
DOP: Carl Gutherie
Ed: Own Marks
Music: Max Steiner
Art Dir: Charles H. Clarke

Cast: Eleanor Parker (Marie Allen), Agnes Moorhead (Ruth Benton), Hope Emerson (Evelyn Harper), Ellen Corby (Emma), Betty Garde (Kitty), Jan Sterling (Smoochie)

An accessory to armed robbery, a naive young woman is jailed and, after her husband's death, becomes a hardened inmate.

'In this cage, you get tough or you get killed,' fresh inmate Marie-Allen is told by Kitty, the woman paid by a syndicate to recruit new 'boosters' (shoplifters) from the inside. Marie-Allen selects the former option, and eventually cuts a deal with vice-queen Elvira Powell's own syndicate, securing her release. As she leaves, the ending is downbeat but curiously exhilarating and glamorous: 'From now on what's in it for me is what matters... You can't lick the system,' she says, adding 'For that $40 I heisted, I certainly got myself an education.' As she exits the prison door, accompanied by a sassy saxophone piece, she leaves as a chain-smoking moll, getting into a car between two hoods. A far cry from the timid kitten-like creature that entered.

A product of her environment, she is surrounded by criminal influence, much of which is attributed to men. Husbands are seen as responsible for levering the inmates into crime on the premise of love, male-dominated prison bureaucracy is present to prevent any form of rehabilitation (the denial of psychiatrists, for example, as demanded by the prison governess). And the syndicate itself – physically flanking Marie-Allen as she leaves – is an indicator that she will 'work' for a masculine organisation. The underworld reflecting society at large, it's a man's world.

* The film was remade in 1962, entitled *House of Women* and directed by Walter Doniger. Jonathan Demme's 1975 *Caged Heat* (aka *Renegade Girls*), was considered the quintessential 'women in prison' movie of the decade. Overseen by sadistic wheelchair-bound Barbara Steele, the girls undergo horrible (but legal) tortures, including lobotomy – only for the captives to rebel and cause the obligatory prison riot.

See also: *Castle on the Hudson*; *Each Dawn I Die*.

Capone

(US, 20th Century-Fox, 1975, 101 mins)

'Capone is an ill-at-ease effort to adapt old genres (and Corman's own undisputed past successes) to new exploitation angles.'

(Monthly Film Bulletin)

Credits
Dir: Steve Carver

Prod: Roger Corman
Scr: Howard Browne
DOP: Vilis Lapenieks
Ed: Richard C. Meyer
Music: Roger George
Art Dir: Ward Preston

Cast: Ben Gazzara (Al Capone), Susan Blakely (Iris Crawford), Harry Guardino (Johnny Torrio), John Cassavetes (Frankie Yale), Sylvester Stallone (Frank Nitti)

Biopic of the legendary Chicago gangster.

With the subtitle, 'the man who made the twenties roar', this is a hasty Corman production. Lacking the sardonic wit or the 'Who's-who' narration of his previous look at Capone in *The St. Valentine's Day Massacre* (qv), this is a deliberately self-conscious analysis of the Capone myth: 'Terrible things, these gangster movies. Kids come out of them and want to be someone with a gun who says "Stick 'em up!"' says Capone to the press, and eventually that is all he is reduced to. Devoid of the power and commitment in the central performance from Gazzara, which never breaks from the looming shadow of Rod Steiger's work in *Al Capone* (qv), the film instead sets about establishing simple cyclical patterns of trust and betrayal: Torrio with his underling Capone, and in turn Capone with his bodyguard Frank (an early, and impressive, part for Sylvester Stallone) who, it is claimed, turns his boss over to the Feds. Refusing to glamorise, the climactic point unusually comes not with Capone's tax evasion charge, but his terminal syphilitic condition – as *Variety* noted, only this, and not mass-murder, 'certifies badness' in America in this day and age. As the film closes, he is trying to fish in a swimming pool and the Capone image is sordid and saddening. A complex individual, he alternates between a violent and loving creature, in surroundings that do not consistently emphasise the opulence or power one would normally associate with the man. This leads us to an attempt to understand his failure; his inability to stay at the top is attributed to his ignorance of everything except how to use a gun – symbolised by his introduction of the Tommy gun to control his empire.

See also: *Gangland: the Verne Miller Story*; *George Raft Story, The*; *Lost Capone, The*; *Scarface Mob, The*; *Untouchables, The*.

Carlito's Way

(US, Universal, 1993, 145 mins)

Credits
Dir: Brian De Palma
Prod: Martin Bregman, Willi Baer, Michael S. Bregman
Scr: Leon Ichaso, David Koepp, Edwin Torres, based on his own original work
DOP: Stephen H. Burum
Ed: Bill Pankow, Kristina Boden
Music: Patrick Doyle
Prod. Des: Richard Sylbert

Cast: Al Pacino (Carlito Briganto), Sean Penn (David Kleinfeld), Penelope Ann Miller (Gail), John Leguizamo (Benny Blanco), Luis Guzman (Pachanga), Ingrid Rogers (Steffie)

Released from a 30-year sentence after only five years, a convicted heroin dealer tries to raise just enough money to buy into a legitimate business, only to find he is drawn back towards the 'life' as his crooked lawyer becomes entangled with the mob.

Complete with the De Palma signature (disposable sentimental interludes and startling set pieces), *Carlito's Way* is Al Pacino's second coming-of-age as the cinema's gangster hero, having completed the first cycle with *The Godfather Part III* (qv) three years before as the aged Michael Corleone. Pacino's Carlito is a mature advance upon his previous work with De Palma a decade before, both in terms of ability and character development. As the cocaine-head Tony Montana in *Scarface* (qv), Pacino's performance was prone to the excessive, as much a product of the eighties as Montana. As Carlito, whose past ('The J.P. Morgan of the smack business') and reputation ('Motherfucka to the masses') could be a seventies reincarnation of Montana, Pacino, using a heartfelt voiceover, gives a more lyrical and controlled turn playing the older and the wiser, achieving a pathos that he would continue to even greater effect in *Donnie Brasco*

Carlito's Way: Carlito (Al Pacino) plays voyeur.

(*qv*). Carlito, like his Brasco character Lefty Ruggiero, is 'flaked out', the 'last of the Mohicans' or 'playing Humphrey Bogart' as he labels himself. 'Ain't no more rackets. Just a bunch of cowboys ripping each other off,' he says – only young pretenders like his nemesis Blanco expect respect just because they've made a few dollars.
While Carlito is of the chivalrous old brigade, Penn's permed Kleinfeld, his best work until *Dead Man Walking*, is of the new breed. The educated and unscrupulous opposite of Carlito, he spurns the 'self-righteous code of the street' in favour of one rule only: saving himself. As Carlito points out: 'You ain't a lawyer no more, Dave. You're a gangster. You're on the other side.' An important late contribution to the genre, *Carlito's Way*, a white equivalent to the likes of *Superfly* (*qv*), depicts the vital transformation from those who held by honour and those who, fuelled by the enormous profits involved in drug dealing, did not.

Casino

(US, Universal, 1995, 177 mins)

'This is on a bigger canvas; it reflects more America, it reflects America in the seventies when anything goes. It's a world of excess, and you don't have to pay for anything, morally.'
(Martin Scorsese, *Empire*)

Credits
Dir/Scr: Martin Scorsese
Prod: Barbara DeFina
Scr: Nicholas Pilggi, based on his own work
DOP: Robert Richardson
Ed: Thelma Schoonmaker
Music: Robbie Robertson
Prod Des: Dane Ferretti

Cast: Robert De Niro (Sam 'Ace' Rothstein), Joe Pesci (Nicky Santoro), Sharon Stone (Ginger McKenna), James Woods (Lester Diamond), Kevin Pollak (Phillip Green), Frank Vincent (Frank Marino)

The true story of a gambler who manages a Las Vegas casino, with protection from a boyhood-friend-cum-gangster, but who loses it all having fallen for a beautiful hustler.

Martin Scorsese's epic self-titled 'urban Western' is an Old Testament story, and the completion of his unofficial gangster trilogy which began 23 years before with *Mean Streets* (*qv*). While he saw the tale, as he told *Vanity Fair*, as 'Vegas at the end of its heyday... almost like the end of the Wild West', it is also *Paradise Lost*, Lucifer expelled from Heaven for his pride and greed. The symbolism for both is evident. As Nicky, the desperado and gangster of the piece, violently stabs an innocent to death with a pen, cigarette fumes (or gunsmoke) drift over his face beforehand; Rothstein, the gambler in charge of the casino (his 'Paradise on Earth'), is called 'The Golden Jew' and his metaphorical descent into Hell as obvious as the Inferno-style credits created by Elaine and Saul Bass.
Based on Nicholas Pileggi's book (written while his previous Scorsese collaboration *Goodfellas* (*qv*) was in production), this true story concerns the triangle

between Frank 'Lefty' Rosenthal (renamed Sam 'Ace' Rothstein), his mercenary and substance-abusing wife Geri McGee (Ginger) and psychotic childhood pal Tony Spilotro (Nicky Santoro). In reality, the Rosenthal/Rothstein character was in charge of the Stardust, the Fremont, the Frontier and the Marina; in the final film version, it was the fictional Tangiers casino. Ultimately a lament for the frailty of the human being, Rothstein – of his relationship with Ginger (paralleled by the paranoid nature of the casino business) – spells it out with the opening sentence: 'When you love someone, you've gotta trust them... otherwise, what's the point?'

Inevitably compared to *Goodfellas* (a film that deals with the protagonist's rise, absent here), *Casino* reaches greater heights but leaves itself further to fall. Costume changes numbered 52 alone for De Niro, the rights to the panoply of poignant pop tunes totalling $2 million plus, the running time and overall budget far more than any previous Scorsese

film; all this adds up to an excess that complements the superficiality of the Vegas machine, a system now in the hands of giant corporate monoliths, as the epilogue concludes. While we're told early on that 'the bottom line is cash', Scorsese ensures that to reach an understanding of the machinations of the city and its cogs, we must negotiate the multiple narrators and visual muscle-flexing. This deliberate stubbornness, while frustrating, allows for ultimately a greater understanding of Vegas and its chain of command (skimming money past the IRS) all the way back to the mobsters in Kansas City. These men, ironically, are seen as dependant on this dwindling supply as they are on their wheelchairs and respirators; in line with the Western motif, it is the outlaw (Nicky tells Sam, 'You only exist out here because of me') who truly runs the show.

See also: *Bugsy*; *Grifters, The*; *King of the Roaring Twenties: the Arnold Rothstein Story*.

Casino: Nicky Santoro (Joe Pesci) takes a little advice from Sam 'Ace' Rothstein (Robert De Niro).

Castle on the Hudson

(US, Warner Brothers, 1940, 77 mins)

Credits
Dir: Anatole Litvak
Prod: Sam Bischoff
Scr: Seton I. Miller, Brown Holmes, Courtney Terrett, based on the book by Lewis E. Lawes
DOP: Arthur Edeson
Ed: Tom Richards
Music: Leo F. Forbstein
Art Dir: John Hughes

Cast: John Garfield (Tommy Gordon), Ann Sheridan (Kay), Pat O'Brien (Warden Long), Burgess Meredith (Steven Rockford), Jerome Cowan (Ed Crowley)

A gangster convicted for 30 years in Sing-Sing prison is temporarily released by his warden (who believes in rehabilitation rather than incarceration) so he can see his injured girlfriend, only to avenge himself against his crooked lawyer.

A virtual remake of the 1933 Michael Curtiz film *20,000 Years in Sing-Sing* (itself spawned from trend-setting social-conscience prison dramas such as George Hill's *The Big House* and Mervin Le Roy's *I am a Fugitive from a Chain Gang*), this film modified the original to include footage of Gordon's racketeer activities. The prison sub-genre itself allowed the criminal ethic to boil in an environment, where men – as the Warden notes in *The Big House* – have nothing to do 'but brood and plot'. A desire to escape the cramped conditions, leading to the obligatory prison break, was a recognition that gangsters become so for social as well as economic reasons.

Just as Paramount had found Alan Ladd to head the second generation of gangster pictures, so Warner Brothers chose the pugnacious John Garfield, who took the role Spencer Tracy had in the original. Two others would follow for Garfield with the studio: *East of the River* and *Out of the Fog*, the latter (again directed by Litvak) the only Warners contribution to the genre to be based on a stage play, Irwin Shaw's *The Gentle People*.

* Special effects were produced by Byron Haskin, a task he also performed for other gangster dramas including *The Roaring Twenties*, *Brother Orchid* and *High Sierra* (qqv). By 1947, he would direct his own take on the genre, *I Walk Alone* (See: *Out of the Past* for further discussion). In 1956 he directed *The Boss* – a film, based on the Pendergast regime of Kansas City, which emphasised the political dimensions of the genre (See *Kansas City*).

See also: *Caged*; *Each Dawn I Die*.

Charley Varrick

(US, Universal, 1973, 111 mins)

Credits
Dir/Prod: Don Siegel
Prod: Jennings Lang
Scr: Dean Riesner, Howard Rodman, based on the novel by John Reese
DOP: Michael C. Butler
Ed: Frank Morris
Music: Lalo Schifrin
Prod. Des: Fernando Carrere

Cast: Joe Don Baker (Molly), Walter Matthau (Charley Varrick), Felicia Farr (Sybil Fort), Norman Fell (Mr Garfinkle), Sheree North (Jewell Everett), Jacqueline Scott (Nadine Varrick), Andy Robinson (Harman Sullivan)

Intelligent bank robber becomes involved with the mob when he unwittingly steals $750,000 of Mafia money in a raid.

A tightly constructed Don Siegel production, made during the period when Walter Matthau took time out from his comic roles to remind the public there was more to him than *The Odd Couple* – see: *The Taking of Pelham 123* (qv). With Joe Don Baker as a racist, misogynist Mafia functionary pursuing Matthau and the mob money (being laundered via a corrupt President of the Western Fidelity Bank), some disconcerting points are uncovered about the wholly unseen Mafia's system of operations. As Matthau points out, when they realise just who the money belongs to, the police will give up looking sooner or later: 'The difference is, the Mafia kills you... they don't stop looking for you until you're dead.' (Or as the plot brings to bear, with Matthau switching dental records with his soon-to-die partner Harman, until they *think* you're dead.) More explicitly, as President Maynard Boyle (John Vernon) informs his colleague, when they catch you 'they'll strip you naked and go work on you with a pair of pliers and a blow torch' (a line lifted directly by Ouentin Tarantino in *Pulp Fiction* (qv) for gang boss Marsellus Wallace). Another point of interest stems from the comment 'The Cosa Nostra's everywhere'; this is shown by Baker's leads gleaned from Tom's Gun Shop and the respect shown to him in the brothel (where he claims, at least knowingly, that he 'never sleeps with whores'). Siegel is careful to underplay this – allowing for the Mafia's presence to be felt but their influence, and vast network of connections, to resonate through the film.

See also: *Outfit, The*; *Point Blank*; *Prime Cut*.

China Girl

(US, Vestron Pictures, 1987, 90 mins)

'It's a story about love in a racist society. The neighbourhood is changing; more Italians are leaving and more Chinese are moving in, and you're bound to have a volatile situation... our films do contain some element of violence but they all show that violence is wrong. Violence is never the answer.'

(Nicholas St. John, City Limits)

Credits
Dir: Abel Ferrara
Prod: Steven Reuther
Scr: Nicholas St. John
DOP: Bojan Bazelli
Ed: Anthony Redman
Music: Joe Delia
Prod. Des: Dan Leigh

Cast: James Russo (Alberto 'Alby' Monte), Richard Panebianco (Tony Monte), David Caruso (Johnny Mercury), Sari Chang (Tyan-Hwa), Russell Wong (Yung-Gan), Joey Chin (Tsu-Shin)

An Italian-American boy falls for a Chinese girl, sparking a gang war between the couple's families.

Reputedly Abel Ferrara's favourite from his own body of work, this modern-day *Romeo and Juliet* borrows more from *West Side Story* than Shakespeare's play (though the director claimed all he took from the musical 'was the chainlink fence'). In fact, character names (Tony), settings (the fire escape), plot (inter-racial gang killings) and dialogue (the 'How do you say 'I Love You' in Chinese/Italian sequence) ensure the film is close to its source. While the central love story, between Tony and Tyan-Hwa, is as traditional as they come, the notion of organised crime as peacekeeper – the Mafia godfathers sharing formal meals with the Triad uncles – is an unusual one. The Chinese invasion of Little Italy ('In five years, you'll have to go to Brooklyn to eat pizza') is put aside, as 'business' interests take precedence. Negative racial feeling engendered by juvenile delinquents in both camps lead the older generations to pull together, 'the communality of Capitalist crime', as one critic noted. As they confirm: 'We must never allow ourselves to be divided by war' (or, importantly, interfered with by the police). The older, essentially business-oriented crime lord is a stabilising force in the ethnic community (hence the Chinese term *sunxi*, a gentleman of the people), while the younger, more territory-oriented street gangs are volatile and destabilizing because they have abandoned the traditional criminal ethical codes. The message, encouraging racial harmony within the boundaries of a community subjected to a criminal system of control, is positive.

See also: *Funeral, The*; *King of New York, The*.

City on Fire

(Hong Kong, Cinema City, 1987, 98 mins)

Credits
Dir: Ringo Lam
Scr: Tommy Sham
from a story by Ringo Lam
DOP: Andrew Lam

Ed: Sone Ming Lam
Music: Teddy Robin
Art Dir: Luk Tze Fung

Cast: Chow-Yun Fat (Ko Chow), Sun Yeuh (Inspector Lau), Lee Sau Yin (Ah Foo)

After his predecessor is killed ex-undercover cop goes back on the force to penetrate a gang of professional thieves by setting up an arms deal.

This film became infamous some years after its release, due to the furore surrounding the plot points 'borrowed' from director Lam's work by Quentin Tarantino for his debut *Reservoir Dogs* (qv).
Using a 'jewel heist gone wrong' scenario, the downfall occurs through the rat in the group, whose final identity is revealed to Fu, the one who had trusted him throughout. Three-way Mexican stand-offs, dark glasses and slow-mo shots of the boys walking the streets (to the words 'Let's go to work'), along with a discussion of how to extract safe combinations from the shop manager, are all echoed in Tarantino's work.
Unlike Tarantino, Lam – adopting a style less frenetic than John Woo – attempts to define human emotion within his characters, detailing Ko Chow's abortive relationship with his girlfriend and Fu's hopes for his son's normality, having graduated from a family of thieves.
The gangster's world here is one of phoney camaraderie, addressing each other as 'Brother', while simultaneously adopting an attitude of cold-blooded indifference, to each other. They view their own lives as disposable (on cops: 'It's fortunes of war. We kill them, they kill us'), very much second fiddle to the price of success.
Betrayal is very evident: Chow, in a recurring nightmare, remembers having old friend Shing arrested; he later will repeat the process with gang-member but kindred spirit Fu. The CID, distrusting Chow, betray him as they do with Chow's old-timer uncle, bringing the ruthless Inspector Lau onto the case over his head. The themes of friendship and the law are much in evidence, with Ko Chow's potentially redemptive relationship with Fu all the more powerful after Chow's treatment of Shing. This highlights the far-reaching power of the law over those that enforce it, even the loose cannons such as Ko Chow.

City Streets

(US, Paramount, 1931, 82 mins)

Credits
Dir: Rouben Mamoulian
Prod: E. Lloyd Sheldon
Scr: Oliver H.P. Garrett, Max Marcin,
based on the story by Dashiell Hammett
DOP: Lee Garmes
Ed: William Shea
Music: Sidney B. Cutner

Cast: Gary Cooper (The Kid), Sylvia Sidney (Nan Cooley), Paul Lukas (Big Fellow Maskal), William 'Stage' Boyd (McCoy), Guy Kibbee (Pop Cooley)

Carnival sharpshooter falls for the step-daughter of a bootlegger, and eventually joins the gang and gets a taste for the high life.

A melodramatic, even operatic, film, making up for what it lacked in realism with technical artistry. As Eugene Rosow noted, it was the first 'talkie' film to use the sound flashback, when Sylvia Sidney lies in jail remembering her conversation with her Gary Cooper, who has just told her during a visit that he has joined the gang: 'Her fear and worry about his safety are expressed in repeated fragments of the conversation, which becomes increasingly loud and jarring as the girl becomes more frightened.' Remarkably lit and shot, the film was photographed innovatively by Lee Garmes: from a close-up of Sidney's eyeball as she takes aim at a shooting gallery to the final burst of backlit birds, the visuals set the tone. This rather set apart the film from its less-lofty peers, but the image of the car (a symbol of what can be termed as the myth of the gangster's success) brought it into line with other works of the era. Gleefully showing his new vehicle off to his girl, he later drives her off into the sunset, using his transport to evade his old gang who are trying to take him for a ride. But even this is atypical – ending in the open country, the enclosed urban shootout is denied.

Clockers

(US, 40 Acres/Mule Filmworks, 1995, 128 mins)

'I just hope that people will see some of the insights they might not see on the news at 6 and 11. For the young black males, I hope they wake up and see we gotta stop killing ourselves.'
(Spike Lee, US Premiere)

Credits
Dir/Prod/Scr: Spike Lee
Prod: Martin Scorsese, Jon Kilic
Scr: Richard Price, based on his own novel
DOP: Malik Hassan Sayeed
Ed: Sam Pollard
Music: Terence Blanchard
Prod. Des: Andrew McAlpine

Cast: Harvey Keitel (Rocco Klein), John Turturro (Larry Mazilli), Delroy Lindo (Rodney), Mekhi Phifer (Strike), Isaiah Washington (Victor), Keith David (Andre the Giant)

A 16-year-old Brooklyn drug-dealer (or 24-hour 'Clocker') based in the Projects becomes a favourite of local crack kingpin and is subsequently pursued by a veteran homicide detective in connection with the murder of another dealer.

No doubt had Martin Scorsese not passed on directing Richard Price's 600-page novel, we would have had a very different work, concentrating perhaps on the novel's original subject, the identity crisis of white, middle-aged homicide cop, Klein. As it is, Spike Lee runs against the grain, the startling credit sequence (police file photographs of bloody, and more importantly real, corpses murdered in drug-related incidents), brutally setting the tone. His use of real crack addicts as extras completes the haunting evocation of reality. As Strike says: 'This ain't no TV movie violence bullshit. This stuff out here is real. Real bullets hurt and real guns kills you dead.' This is not a 'ghetto-centric' hood film, in the mould of *Boyz N the Hood* or *Menace II Society* (*qv*). Despite sharing concerns, it deliberately lacks their visceral punch and avoids the gangsta rap score, preferring Seal and Des'ree. A far cry from his own political *Do the Right Thing*.

Hope (which Lee claimed comes from tracing his family tree, a need to be aware of roots and history) is offered in the final reel, as dealer Strike escapes the city on a train. Some have seen this as self-conscious grasping but the recurrence of the single-mother struggling against the pushers throughout shows the optimism is not last ditch. While praising the film, *Sight & Sound*'s Amy Taubin called it 'the 'hood movie to end all 'hood movies'. Far subtler than that, Lee depicts the Projects, without recourse to melodrama, as a constant siege of violence: not just guns, but gangsta video games, slasher movies and MTV – visuals that excite impulses and incite action.

The character of Rodney, the crack dealer, is taken from the stock files of the gangster. The benevolent type, he even cuts the kids' hair still, running a convenience store to cover his operations. As Lee told *US Premiere*'s Anna Deavere Smith: 'This guy is selling drugs, but at the same time he makes sure that all those little kids in his store do their homework, obey their mother and go to church. But once they get old enough, he's going to try to recruit them... Just look at Nicky Barnes, who was one of the biggest drug dealers in Harlem. He was considered a hero because he would buy people turkeys on Thanksgiving. And people would look at that and look past all the devastation and death he was inflicting.' Strike models himself in the same way, lecturing the young Tyrone to ensure he doesn't play hookey, but the figure of Erroll, AIDS victim and Rodney's own mentor, is a reminder that the gangster (just as with 1930s bootleggers) can never succumb to his own product.

See also: *New Jack City; Superfly.*

Cookie

(US, Lorimer Film Entertainment, 1989, 93 mins)

Credits
Dir: Susan Seidelman
Prod: Laurence Mark
Scr: Alice Arlen, Nora Ephron
DOP: Oliver Stapleton
Ed: Andrew Mondshein

Music: Thomas Newman
Prod. Des: Michael Haller

Cast: Peter Falk (Dominick 'Dino' Capisco), Diane Wiest (Lenore), Emily Lloyd (Carmella 'Cookie' Voltecki), Michael V. Gazzo (Carmine Tarantino), Brenda Vaccaro (Bunny)

Ex-con and Mafia kingpin struggles to keep his feisty daughter in line.

Complete with all the trademarks of Susan Seidelman's earlier hit, *Desperately Seeking Susan* (screwball female fantasy), *Cookie* dissects the Mafia film to create either a piece of post-feminist satire or a Runyon-esque slice of whimsy, depending on your point of view. The latter, mainly inspired by the performance of Peter Falk, who began his career in the Runyon vein with Frank Capra's *A Pocketful of Miracles* (qv), is perpetuated by the bland soundtrack, which includes Kylie Minogue's *I should be so Lucky*. The film targets the suburban veneer that disguises the macho world of the gangster, a topic also seen in *My Blue Heaven* (qv). The patriarchal family, where women are relegated to running part-time businesses (such as Bunny's pet-grooming service) also comes under fire. Cookie herself, dressed like Madonna's character from *Desperately Seeking Susan*, is not the role model for the romantic dreams and conventional family life to which her mother aspires. Playing the working woman, she ascends through the ranks within the genre. An assertion of female independence, she becomes a chauffeur for her father; she then moves to gangster's moll, reading a potboiler called *Mafia Princess*, and finally, with Dino asking Cookie if she'll be going straight, to the natural inheritor of her father's own crooked values – a role normally taken by the son.

Set pieces (the ending is a funeral and a wedding), nicknames (Mikie 'Pork Chop' Rozello), themes (loyalty, paranoia) all point towards the gangster film, as does the use and abuse of fashion – in this case, Americana tack, seen also in Jonathan Demme's *Married to the Mob* (qv). These being merely trimmings, the film is best seen as a Mafia fairy tale.

Cook, The Thief, His Wife and Her Lover, The

(UK, Allarts Enterprises/Erato Films, 1989, 124 mins)

Credits
Dir/Scr: Peter Greenaway
Prod: Kees Kasander
DOP: Sacha Vierny
Ed: John Wilson
Music: Michael Nyman
Prod. Des: Ben Van Os, Jan Roelfs

Cast: Michael Gambon (Albert Spica), Helen Mirren (Georgina Spica), Richard Bohringer (Richard Borst), Alan Howard (Michael), Tim Roth (Mitchel)

Crude and cruel restaurateur-cum-gangster receives a most appropriate come-uppance having slain his brow-beaten wife's lover.

Not a gangster film, more a Jacobean revenge drama (Greenaway cited *Tis Pity She's a Whore* for his assaults on taboo sexuality), or as the director himself called it 'a violent and erotic love story set in the kitchen and dining room of a smart restaurant'. The monstrous Albert Spica, a bigoted gangster of the basest impulses, is the villain of the piece, as he holds court each night at his favourite table in his own restaurant. Greenaway's work, never more so than in the creation of Spica, revels in its own artificiality. In a film that bears little resemblance to its genre, ironically in Spica's ludicrous and inflated presence, we are given the most foul addition to the British cinematic criminal, making exclusion from this book impossible. As if to reinforce the point, a highly staged scene reminds of the Cagney/Clarke grapefruit scene in *The Public Enemy* (qv) when Spica jabs a fork into a girl's cheek.

It is a film about consumption, power, desire and vulnerability. Georgina's nightly public humiliation at the dining table indicates she has had her identity consumed, the bruises a submission to Spica's gross personality. He forces debtor Roy to eat dog shit; Pup, the kitchen boy and umbilical cord between the lovers and sympathetic cook, to consume his own navel, and Michael to swallow pages of the books he catalogues. In the world of

The Cook, The Thief, His Wife & Her Lover: Left -Right: Lover (Alan Howard), Cook (Richard Bohringer), Wife (Helen Mirren) and Thief (Michael Gambon) share dinner, while sidekick Mitchell (Tim Roth) plays with his food.

the La Hollandais restaurant, anything – including corpses – may be cooked and consumed. As Spica says: 'It all comes out as shit in the end.' At gunpoint, Spica is forced to eat the penis of the cooked Michael – to 'penetrate himself at the orifice which symbolises his power: his dictatorial and consuming mouth', as Joy McEntee phrased it. His abuse of other men highlights not only the weakness of the flesh (as do so many other aspects of the film), but his own potential for violation. Greenaway invites a political reading, the split in the crowd following Spica's cannibalistic exercise representing the new order. Spica's old regime is framed by the reproduction of Frans Hals' *Banquet of the Officers of the St. George Civic Guard Company* which sits behind his table. The French Revolution is invoked (a book on the topic is used to stuff Michael), and Spica can be seen not only as the overthrown French aristocracy, but also the bourgeois revolution (the humiliated Roy as *roi?*), that consumed itself. As each set takes us through a period of history (just as the changing hues of characters' costumes represent the fickleness of their natures), Greenaway is obliquely exploring the abuses of power: between nations, fellow countrymen and partners. The gangster, with his desire for control, becomes a symbol for this.

Corleone

(US, Capital Films, 1978, 120 mins)

Credits
Dir/Scr: Pasquale Squitieri
Prod: Mario Cecchi Gori
DOP: Eugenio Bentivoglio
Ed: Mauro Bonanni
Music: Ennio Morricone
Art Dir: Umberto Turco

Cast: Giuliano Gemma (Vito Gargano), Claudia Cardinale (Rosa

Accordino), Francisco Rabal (Don Giusto), Stefano Satta Flores (Natale Calia), Michele Placido (Michele Labruzzo)

The rise of a Sicilian gangster, who becomes the sole power behind the Mafia only to give himself up for trial.

Already having explored the Mafia in Sicily between 1900 and 1930, in *I am the Law* (*Il Prefelto Di Ferro*), Pasquale Squitieri this time focused upon post-1952 Mafia-justice system/State interdependence, with Sicily a symbol for this increasingly worldwide phenomenon. Concurrent with the rise of Vito, from beggar to Mafia king, is his increasing disregard for his union manifesto promise to 'emancipate our fair land'. Compared to Charlemagne, he later adds 'Palermo's mine now'. The corruptible nature of power goes hand-in-hand with the idea that the revolution and freedom are pipe-dreams. The gangster is no more benevolent than the politician.

Described by *Variety* as 'an action director who goes a step beyond bloodletting to analyze social and political motivations behind it', Squitieri's plodding and unbalanced work even tries to emulate the Leone Western. With its Morricone soundtrack, the screen freezes as a victim dies and gun shots ring out – but any merit in merging the two genres is lost.

See also: *Black Hand, The*; *Scorta, La*; *Sicilian, The*.

Cotton Club, The

(US, Zoetrope, 1984, 128 mins)

> *'Coppola has become the poet of crime... [the] film is not only a compendium of underworld history as we know it from the movies, but a refinement of his own work in the genre.'*
> **(John Kobal, *Films and Filming*)**

Credits
Dir/Scr: Francis Ford Coppola
Prod: Robert Evans
Scr: William Kennedy
DOP: Stephen Goldblatt
Ed: Robert Q. Lovett, Barry Malkin

Music: John Barry
Prod. Des: Gregory Bolton, David Chapman, Richard Sylbert

Cast: Richard Gere (Dixie Dwyer), Gregory Hines (Delbert 'Sandman' Williams), Diane Lane (Vera Cicero), Lonette McKee (Lila Rose Oliver), Bob Hoskins (Owney Madden)

Set around Harlem's Cotton Club, a Jazz cornet player saves the life of gangster Dutch Schultz and is taken under his wing.

Begun as a dream of *The Godfather* (*qv*) producer Robert Evans, he paid $350,000 for the rights to the work, sensationally raising $8 million with just a poster and a pitch ('*The Godfather* with music'). As Evans later told critic Barry Norman: 'The picture I had in mind is on the cutting room floor.' Amid a spiralling budget (peaking around $47 million), a disgruntled cast and crew, and 30 to 40 script rewrites, accusations of Mob financing and murder surrounded the project. Evans' company was funded by big-time drug traffickers Laynie Jacobs and Roy Radin, the latter mysteriously turning up dead in a quarry.

Grossing only half the budget back in the US, the film received criticism from all sides. Accused of being 'empty as it is emphatic', it was seen as 'panoramic, not profound' – Coppola achieving no insights into the underworld or racism in showbusiness – with the structure as teasing and divergent as a series of jazz beats. In his defence, Coppola is not revisiting *Godfather* territory. He is examining the relationship between the musical and the gangster genre – the idea of showbiz and gangsterdom as spectacles – symbolised by the cross-cut scene of rapid tap and machine gun fire. He invokes the Cotton Club era, a place undergoing a cultural renaissance in a time when blacks performed but were not permitted as customers, but plays down the relationship between the gangster film and social/historical events. Gangsters and jazz musicians, in fact, led an affable co-existence, Fats Waller reportedly delighted at being kidnapped for Al Capone's three-day birthday party celebrations. Yet Diane Lane's nightclub owner was based on club queen and gangster's moll Texas Guinan, who used to greet her customers with the phrase 'Hello suckers!', paraphrased by Lane. Cornet player Dwyer also gets a screen test via Cotton Club owner Owney Madden, following the pattern of George Raft's own story. Coppola, with bloodshed reduced to a drop on a girl's cheek, is drawing his story from gangster fable. He inverses tradition, reviving the grand old Hollywood musical, but imbuing it with social significance. Here, the numbers are no show-stoppers – woven instead into the fabric of the film. The 'musical' is present to highlight the inter-racial relationship between Delbert Williams and Lila Rose. Such dexterity itself comments on how inextricably linked high society, the Mob, show-business and politics are.

See also: *Billy Bathgate*; *Harlem Nights*; *Hoodlum*.

Criss Cross

(US, Universal, 1948, 98 min)

Credits
Dir: Robert Siodmak
Prod: Michel Kraike
Scr: Daniel Fuchs, based on the novel by Don Tracy
DOP: Franz Planer
Ed: Ted Kent
Music: Miklos Rozsa
Art Dir: Bernard Herzbrun, Boris Leven

Cast: Burt Lancaster (Steve Thompson), Dan Duryea (Slim Dundee), Richard Long (Slade Thompson), Yvonne de Carlo (Anna), Stephen McNally (Ramirez)

Returning to LA, a divorced man finds himself involved with his ex-wife, and her second husband, a gangster with whom he participates on a heist, but then tries to abscond with the loot.

A fatalistic love story, Robert Siodmak's dark-drenched *noir* draws its thrust from the heist movie sub-genre. Combining a complex narrative structure, a realism born of location shooting and Siodmak's expressive stylisations (note his acutely angled interiors) the film resembles Siodmak's earlier *The Killers* (qv) by depicting a disastrous love and a man prone to winning gesture. Racked with a lonely, helpless mood, the film is subjectively viewed through Steve's eyes; notice the shot of his brother and future sister-in-law kissing in the living room, distanced from where Steve sits. His entrapment continues as he later lies in hospital after the raid, waiting for Slim's vengeance to be executed. Nihilistic in tone, it's a film that, as *Film Comment's* David Thomson pointed out, shows 'fools try crime to prove they're grown up'. One of the finest exchanges comes between Steve and the femme fatale ex-wife, Anna. 'Love? Love? You have to watch out for yourself... you just don't know what kind of world it is,' she admonishes. 'I'll know better next time,' is his murmur. A creature of insincerity, immaturity and grasping ambition, she is cast in the mould of Ava Gardner in Siodmak's *The Killers*. True to the *noir* formula, the film treats its characters as losers caught in a force beyond their control. What draws Steve back to Anna? A chance sighting, as a Union Station cigarette clerk bends down to restock his shelves, revealing her in the distance. Although the racketeer Slim would appear the winner, shooting the ex-husband and wife in the final reel, he, like his adversary, only realises Anna's limitations when it becomes too late. He too loses.

The supporting players add also to the atmosphere of hopelessness. A fascinating array of failure: Alan Napier's alcoholic Finchley, who plans the caper for a month's credit at the liquor store; the humiliated head waiter; Steve's mother, who knows her son is a no-hoper; even the Chinaman who can't place his bet in time.

* An unbilled Tony Curtis, in his first screen role, can be seen dancing the rumba with Anna in the early club scene.

See also: *Asphalt Jungle, The*; *Face*; *Heat*; *Killing, The*; *Reservoir Dogs*; *Taking of Pelham 123, The*; *Usual Suspects, The*.

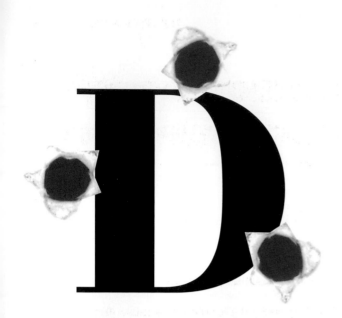

Dang Bireley's and the Young Gangsters
(2499 Antapan Krong Muang)

(Thailand, Tai Entertainment, 1997, 110 mins)

Credits
Dir: Nonzee Nimibutr
Prod: Visute Poolvoralaks
Scr: Wisid Sartsanatieng,
based on a true story by Suriyan Saktaisong
Ed: Sunit Ussavinikul
Music: Orange Music
Prod. Des: Ek Eiamchurn

Cast: Jesdaporn Pholdee, Noppachai Muttaweevong, Attaporn Teemakorn, Suppakorn Kitsuwan, Chatchai Ngamsun

Set in the early 1960s, this is the true story of one of Thailand's most notorious gangsters.

Cut to the sound of Elvis Presley, Nimibutr's film is the highest grossing in Thai history, taking over 75 million baht at the domestic box office. Nicknamed after his own favourite soda pop, Dang – who idolises, and eventually dies like, James Dean – becomes, through a series of killings (his first at only 13), a feared force in Pra-Nakorn (now Bangkok). Stylistically borrowing from John Woo (well-choreographed gunfights, slow-motion squibs) and Martin Scorsese (extensive use of freeze-frames and stills), the story is told in flashback by Dang's

former gang member, Piak – now an old man leafing through sepia-tinted photographs and vintage memories. As much his story as Dang's, the film depicts how both boys have little chance to survive within society. As Piak reflects: 'To find a job is harder than finding a gun.' Corrupt politicians, martial law (driving the gangs in 1961 to the countryside), a crumbling economy all contribute – but the film makes the important distinction that these teen hoodlums (moving from school to gang warfare) are partially to blame. While Dang may have a prostitute for a mother, her insistence on having him ordained as a Buddhist monk (to clear both their sins away) is his chance to escape the life. Although in the final scene he travels to take his vows, the fact that 'more hoodlums than monks' were present indicates where his loyalties really lie. Piak himself, well-educated and urged by his peers to complete his schooling and find a job, drops out to commit to the gang full-time. Complementing this, characterisation is by no means black and white: 'Even though we were fierce gangsters, sometimes we were scared like teenagers,' says Piak. Although the film insists that a boy-child must soon exert his masculinity (another social pressure faced by the characters), it takes a side-step to look at those who occasionally let the mask slip, revealing vulnerability. It concludes by depicting the gangster as part-sociological phenomenon, part-desire-driven individual, both a warrior and boy. In many ways, a symbol for the uncertain political climate that heralded the era.

Dead End

(US, Samuel Goldwyn, 1937, 93 mins)

Credits
Dir: William Wyler
Prod: Samuel Goldwyn
Scr: Lillian Hellman, based on the play by Sidney Kingsley
DOP: Gregg Toland
Ed: Daniel Mandell
Music: Alfred Newman
Art Dir: Richard Day

Cast: Humphrey Bogart (Joe 'Baby Face' Martin), Joel McCrea (Dave Connell), Sylvia Sydney (Drina Gordon), Wendy Barrie (Kay Burton), Claire Trevor (Francey)

A gangster returns to his birthplace, the slums of New York's East River.

The Broadway sensation of 1936, Sidney Kingsley's play about a group of people living in a New York slum celebrated the same success on screen. Re-using the six actors (Billy Halop, Leo Gorcey, Huntz Hall, Bobby Jordan, Gabriel Dell and Bernard Punsley) who played the streetwise Dead End kids (see below) on stage, the film benefited greatly from Gregg Toland's photography, prefiguring his work with Orson Welles in *Citizen Kane* and *The Magnificent Ambersons*. Toland, together with director Wyler, created a series of haunting images around the warren-like slum set, juxtaposed against the opulent Manhattan skyscrapers. We – like the gangster figure played by Bogart – are 'watchin' life in the slums', with his character the destructive role model for the kids, advising them to use bottles and knives illegally in a pre-determined street fight with a rival gang. More idealistic than the Warner Brothers films of the time, the upstanding architect played by Joel McCrea, who shuns the dishonest route taken by Bogart to escape the slums he hopes one day to tear down, represents a desire for social change. The triumph of his relationship with Drina over that of his lust for the rich Kay indicates integrity; a quality needed to resist a life of crime and implement his dream. That the camera rises above the tenement buildings in the closing shots tells us this will happen, and so the film becomes more complex than simply denouncing all poverty-stricken people as criminals. Good and evil exist around the kids and they must choose their own paths.

* The kids were subsequently signed to long contracts by Warner Brothers, and made appearances collectively in various B grade gangster flicks, firstly under the mantle that made their fame (in the likes of *Angels with Dirty Faces* (qv) and *Junior G-Men*), and later as the East Side Kids and then the Bowery Boys, starring in films like *Mob Town* among others.

Deadly is the Female: see Gun Crazy.

Desperate Hours, The

(US, Paramount, 1955, 112 mins)

Credits
Dir/Prod: William Wyler
Scr: Joseph Hayes, based on his own novel and play
DOP: Lee Garmes
Ed: Robert Swink
Music: Gail Kubik
Art Dir: Hal Pereira, J. MacMillan Johnson

Cast: Humphrey Bogart (Glenn Griffin), Frederic March (Dan Hilliard), Arthur Kennedy (Jesse Bard), Martha Scott (Eleanor Hilliard), Dewey Martin (Hal Griffin), Gig Young (Chuck)

Desperate Hours

(US, Dino De Laurentiis, 1990, 105 mins)

Credits
Dir/Prod: Michael Cimino
Prod: Dino De Laurentiis
Scr: Lawrence Konner, Mark Rosenthal
DOP: Douglas Milsome
Ed: Peter Hunt
Music: David Mansfield
Prod. Des: Mel Dellar, Victoria Paul

Cast: Mickey Rourke (Michael Bosworth), Anthony Hopkins (Tim Cornell), Kelly Lynch (Nancy Breyers), Mimi Rogers (Nora Cornell), Lindsay Crouse (Brenda Chandler)

A group of escaped convicts hold a suburban family hostage.

Based on a real incident, the original Broadway play in 1955 featured a young Paul Newman in the role of criminal Glenn Griffin, immediately before he made his motion picture debut in *The Silver Chalice*. But, with the actor at the peak of his career (this his penultimate film, just two years before his death), Humphrey Bogart would return to the genre that had brought him popularity and play the part on screen. Bearing a resemblance to *The Petrified Forest* (*qv*), the film that got him noticed 19 years before, Hayes' play was optioned by Bogart with the intention of performing alongside his good friend Spencer Tracy. This was not to be, with neither actor willing to consent to second billing, and the actor instead reunited with director William Wyler – who filmed him in *Dead End* (*qv*). Bogart's performance was, like Cagney's in *Angels with Dirty Faces* (*qv*), definitive. As *Variety* (*qv*) noted, he was 'in the type of role that cues comics to caricature take-offs. Here he's at his best, a tough gunman capable of murder, snarling delight with the way his captives must abide by his orders, and wise in the ways of self-preservation strategy.'

On one level, it's a study of man's innate ability to kill, with the mild-mannered middle-class Hilliard going some way to understanding the mindset of the desperate criminal. Bogart represents a rejection not only of suburban 'smart-eyed, respectable suckers' but also of the upwardly mobile gangster. He despises 'shiny-shoed wiseguys with white handkerchiefs'; the absence of musical score distancing the film further from the Warner efforts of the thirties, and veering it towards the documentary-style gangster films begun in the mid-fifties.

Cimino's remake, while miscasting the father-figure (Hilliard/Cornell) role with Anthony Hopkins, proved an efficient enough thriller. The director was most influenced by Wyler's use of long, uninterrupted takes; his finest sequence (cut in the US version) a four-minute, one-shot scene between lawyer Lynch (obsessed with the Rourke character) and the FBI agent (Lindsay Crouse), attempting to turn her against the criminal.

As with *Heaven's Gate* and *The Deer Hunter* respectively, Cimino's love for the American West and his obsession with self-destruction were revisited. As the simple hoodlum Albert (David Morse) is surrounded by snipers in the canyon, he whistles *The Red River Valley* and raises a pistol to his head, moments before he is shot down. As the director explained to *Sight & Sound*'s John Pym, the ritual of dying drew him closer to Wyler's version: 'The original *Desperate Hours*, the movie, is painful to watch because Bogart was so ill then, he knew he was dying. It was shot in the simplest way possible, but when the camera came in on this great actor's eyes, you can see they are focused on something far beyond the movie. It was difficult to watch because I went through that experience with John Cazale. John was dying the whole time we were shooting *The Deer Hunter*.'

* Cimino, again with Mickey Rourke (and co-scripted by Oliver Stone), made an earlier exploration of mob culture in *Year of the Dragon* – as a police captain attempts to crack down on crime lords who rule New York's Chinatown.

Dick Tracy

(US, Touchstone Pictures, 1990, 105 mins)

> 'All dressed up with nowhere to go, Warren Beatty's comic striptease is huge globs of extravagant style with absolutely no substance or story whatsoever.' **(Starburst)**

Credits
Dir/Prod: Warren Beatty
Scr: Jim Cash, Jack Epps Jr., Lorenzo Semple, Bo Goldman
DOP: Vittorio Storaro
Ed: Richard Marks
Music: Danny Elfman, Stephen Sondheim
Prod. Des: Richard Sylbert, Harold Micheson

Cast: Warren Beatty (Dick Tracy), Madonna (Breathless Mahoney), Glenne Headly (Tess Trueheart), Al Pacino (Big Boy Caprice), Dustin Hoffman (Mumbles), Paul Sorvino (Lips Manlis)

Live action rendering of the cartoon detective who attempts to rid the city of various deformed gangsters.

While Peter Biskind in *US Premiere* described the film as 'a breathtaking marriage of nostalgia and violence, a coldly expressionistic world that owes much to G.W. Pabst and Bertolt Brecht, but is also shot with Dickensian and Chaplinesque sentiment', the more pertinent comment of the time came from Disney's CEO Jeff Katzenberg. Faxing producer Don Simpson, who was behind rival summer blockbuster *Days of Thunder*, he said 'Wait till you see how big my Dick is.' As Beatty told co-writer Bo

Goldman: 'I don't want to see any psychology or behaviour... this is entertainment.' A production in development for 16 years, names such as Martin Scorsese, John Landis, Walter Hill and Roman Polanski had all been attached at one point. But from the very beginning Beatty was in favour to play the lead and it has always been his project; rejecting Hill, for example, when he preferred the movie to be a slice of realism rather than loud and exaggerated.

Eventually the top grossing film of 1990, taking over $103 million, it was a production (at a total cost of $23 million for Walt Disney) that included one lawsuit, one script arbitration and one just off-camera affair, between Beatty and co-star Madonna. Of course, the real star was the set. With filming in Chicago an expensive nightmare, art director Sylbert set about creating 'an artificial generic world shot against an artificial sky in bold, primary comic-book colours'. Only the seven hues used by Tracy's creator Chester Gould are featured to create an under-detailed 2-D landscape, where products are labelled by their term – the newspaper called The Daily Paper, for example. The scant plot inflates the gangster's ambitions to match the lurid colour scheme and gross physical deformities suffered by fellow mobsters. Al Pacino's Big Boy, a Napoleonic figure with a vision of organising a syndicate of all the unnamed city's hoodlums, believes 'the future is me'. In a film where size is everything, that's about as prophetic as one gets.

* Previous filmed versions of Gould's Dick Tracy have included four 15-chapter movie serials in the thirties and forties and four forties feature films, as well as a TV series in the 1950s and children's cartoon show, beginning in 1961.

* **Academy Awards:** Rick Simpson and Richard Sylbert won for Best Art Direction.
Stephen Sondheim won for Best Song ('Sooner or Later').
John Caglione Jr won for Best Makeup.

Diexue Shuang Xiang: See The Killer.

Dillinger

(US, Monogram Pictures, 1945, 70 mins)

Credits
Dir: Max Nosseck
Prod: Frank and Maurice King
Scr: Leon Charles, Philip Yordan
DOP: Jackson J. Rose
Ed: Otho Lovering, Edward Mann
Music: Dimitri Tiomkin

Cast: Lawrence Tierney (Dillinger), Anne Jefferies (Helen), Edmund Lowe (Specs), Eduardo Ciannelli (Murph), Marc Lawrence (Doc), Elisha Cook Jr. (Kirk)

Dillinger: 'I rob banks!': John Dillinger (Warren Oates) at work.

Dillinger

(US, American Inernational Pictures, 1973, 107 mins)

Credits
Dir/Scr: John Milius
Prod: Buzz Feitshans
DOP: Jules Brenner
Ed: Fred. R. Feitshans

Music: Barry DeVorzon
Art Dir: Trevor Williams

Cast: Warren Oates (John Dillinger), Ben Johnson (Melvin Purvis), Michelle Phillips (Billie Frechette), Cloris Leachman (The Lady in Red), Harry Dean Stanton (Homer Van Meter), Steve Kanaly ('Pretty Boy' Floyd), Richard Dreyfuss ('Baby Face' Nelson)

Biopic of the notorious bank robber

Director of the 1973 version, John Milius, wrote in the preface to the script of his film *The Life and Times of Judge Roy Bean*: 'If this story is not the way it was, then it's the way it should have been and furthermore the author does not give a plug damn.' Milius, a resident expert on legendary Americans, is loose with the facts of the death of Nelson and Floyd, to make a neat end to the gang, but is more concerned with the way the public view robbers, but not cops, as charismatic. Dillinger, from his opening 'I rob banks for a living. What do you do?' is secure in his reputation; a self-publicist, he is ever concerned with image: 'What would your public think?' asks a female companion when he considers living his life 'like a Pharaoh'. FBI Bureau Chief Melvin Purvis, despite being the first to be labelled a G-Man, must exceed Dillinger's myth. Equally concerned with press coverage he receives, one by one he works his way up to Dillinger, capturing Wilber Underhill and Machine Gun Kelly and bypassing their status – 'He had a name he didn't deserve' observes Purvis of Kelly. Re-hashing the blood-letting of *Bonnie and Clyde* (*qv*), along with its romantic glow, is a far cry from Max Nosseck's 1945 Monogram version, an unglamorous, factual account of the man's rise through the ranks of his gang – with an increasing reliance on murder (witness the waiter he returns to kill, having suffered an insult from him years before).
Critics at the time commented upon that fact that the screenwriters 'simply record the passing events in newsreel fashion, instead of creating a screenplay in which the killer's character is brought before the cameras against the background of the action' (*New York Herald Tribune*). Little psychological analysis is presented, and as Alton Cook in the *New York World Telegram* pointed out,

gangsters' 'dreams rode on bullets, not flights of fancy' – rather limiting the action. While both versions connect at certain points (Dillinger's assassination while watching *Manhattan Melodrama* (*qv*), carrying a fake gun to escape from prison), it is Milius's film that reaches for a higher place in history for the man.

* A rather lifeless ABC telefilm, directed by Rupert Wainwright, and also entitled *Dillinger*, was produced in 1990. Starring Mark Harmon as the man (and with a reappearance from Lawrence Tierney), the film echoes Milius's version, focusing on the media hype that surrounded his Public Enemy myth. A laughing stock for not holding Dillinger, Purvis is told by Hoover 'In this country, the press rules. It moulds people's opinions.' Its only true authenticity is the filming itself, taking place in Wisconsin, a state frequented by the real gangster.

See also: *Bonnie Parker Story, The*; *Bullet For Pretty Boy, A*; *George Raft Story, The*; *Lepke*; *Lucky Luciano*; *Machine Gun Kelly*; *Rise and Fall of Legs Diamond, The*; *Young Dillinger*.

Donnie Brasco

(US, Mandalay, 1997, 127 mins)

> 'The problem with the gangster genre is that like any genre it becomes self-sustaining. And then the only thing that's left to do is mannerism, or some kind of crazy quilt of the genre like Tarantino. But it gets further and further away from the life.'
>
> **(Paul Attanasio, *Sight & Sound*)**

Credits
Dir: Mike Newell
Prod: Barry Levinson, Mark Johnson, Louis DiGiaimo, Gail Mutrux
Scr: Paul Attanasio, based on the book Donnie Brasco: My Undercover Life in the Mafia by Joseph D. Pistone and Richard Woodley
DOP: Peter Sova
Ed: Jon Gregory
Music: Patrick Doyle

Donnie Brasco: Donnie (Johnny Depp), Lefty (Al Pacino) and Sonny (Michel Madsen), Mafia foot-soldiers with bad dress sense.

Prod. Des: Donald Graham Burt

Cast: Al Pacino (Lefty Ruggiero), Johnny Depp (Joe Pistone/Donnie Brasco), Michael Madsen (Sonny Black), Bruno Kirby (Nicky), James Russo (Paulie), Anne Heche (Maggie Pistone)

Undercover FBI agent infiltrates New York crew, using a veteran (and overlooked) Mafia foot soldier to reach the top at the expense of his home life.

Based on the true story of FBI Agent Joe Pistone, who infiltrated the Bonanno crime family between 1975 and 1981 leading to over 100 mob convictions (and a $500,000 contract on his head), Paul Attanasio's script had remained on ice since the 1990 release of Martin Scorsese's *Goodfellas* (qv), when Stephen Frears was originally slated to direct. At the time Scorsese was one of the few to see the differences: 'Mine's about the life,

yours is about relationships,' he told Frears. Truly, the film is more, as director Newell phrased it *'Death of a Salesman* than *The Godfather'*. It's about the guys who stand in the cold on the street corner waiting to pay their respects to the big shots – the spokes on the wheel, as Lefty would term it. Ultimately it is about the price of betrayal: Pistone/Brasco using Lefty as a stepping stone parallels Lefty's own hit on old friend Nicky: 'You go in alive, you come out dead and it's your best friend that does it.' Newell, through a connection named Rocco 'The Butcher' Mussachia – also an advisor on *The Freshman* (qv) – learnt the way the Mafia communicate. As he told *Sight & Sound*'s Geoffrey MacNab: 'They can't express themselves abstractly at all... One day a guy from another crew in Queens said to the capo of the gang that I was with, 'Hey, I don't see Tommy no more!' The leader looked him dead in the eye and said, 'Eh' –

and there was a little click of a pause and the guy looked at the leader and said, 'Eh. So Tommy's gone... There were volumes spoken in a few syllables.' Such cadences (including the meaning of the phrase 'Forget about it'), along with street aphorisms, make it to the screen. Lefty, obsessed with the 'rules', takes Brasco under his wing, telling him 'a wiseguy never pays for a drink', and is 'always right. Even when he's wrong'. A film about the tragedy of the working man, while Lefty comes to realise that, after 30 years, he commands no respect, the Depp character becomes drawn into playing the game: 'I'm not becoming like them. I am them', he tells his wife.

See also: *Carlito's Way*.

Driver, The

(US, 20th Century Fox, 1978, 91 mins)

'As beautifully crafted as a booby-trapped Fabergé egg, The Driver is the ultimate urban thriller.'
(**Philip French**, *Radio Times*)

Credits
Dir/Scr: Walter Hill
Prod: Lawrence Gordon
DOP: Philip H. Lathrop
Ed: Tina Hirsch, Robert K. Lambert
Music: Michael Small
Prod Des: Harry Horner

Cast: Ryan O'Neal (The Driver), Bruce Dern (The Detective), Isabelle Adjani (The Player), Ronee Blakley (The Connection), Matt Clark (Red Plainclothesman), Felice Orlandi (Gold Plainclothesman)

A game of cat and mouse between an obsessed cop and the best getaway driver in the business.

Following a long apprenticeship as screenwriter for John Huston and Sam Peckinpah, Walter Hill's sparse, elliptical second film is a B movie par excellence. Originally sent by Hill to a 90-year-old Raoul Walsh for his input, it's a work which drew inspiration from Jean-Pierre Melville's *Le Samourai* (*qv*) – itself influenced by Frank Tuttle's *This Gun*

for Hire (*qv*) – with Ryan O'Neal's impassive stoic clearly modelled on the Delon/Ladd characters. Extolling the gangster as the hero, Hill sees the modern cityscape as frontier territory, a deserted arena to play out the existential drama. 'Some of the criminal types these days are real cowboys. Think they can just drive around and do whatever they want to do whenever they want to do it', The Driver is told. It's a theme that is played on – The Driver's only indulgence is a tape recorder that blares out Country and Western, prompting The Detective to note 'Cowboy music. Always tells a story. Drunks, whores, broken hearts...' The Driver himself is referred to as a cowboy (a slang term for freelancer in his trade), but it helps emphasise not only his status as the outlaw, but the Detective's role as the corrupt Sheriff (who, in order to catch his man, blackmails two criminals to hire O'Neal for a set-up bank robbery). It is The Driver who emerges with his integrity intact; in spirit a throwback to the highly amoral films of Cagney and Robinson. Arguably allegorical, with the 2-D characters known only by their tag names (The Player, The Connection) and only ever seen in connection with their profession, the film can be read in the manner of David Cronenberg's version of J.G. Ballard's *Crash*, whereby we are only able to function as human beings through the machine.

See also: *Fallen Angels*; *Killer, The*; *Leon*; *Samourai, Le*; *Little Odessa*; *Prizzi's Honor*; *This Gun For Hire*.

Duoluo Tianshi: See Fallen Angels.

SOLIHULL S.F.C.
LIBRARY

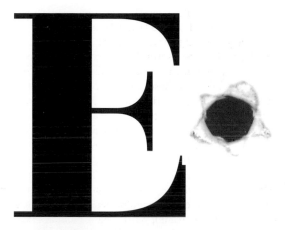

A highly underrated Cagney vehicle, this offers one of his most explosive performances as the framed reporter sent to prison. A veritable cauldron of disparate elements (the gangster, prison and newspaper drama stirred together), the film - unlike, say, *The Big House* - uses the setting not to explore the iniquities of the prison system but to drive the narrative. Raft plays the gangster, admittedly without the charisma displayed as Rinaldo in *Scarface: the Shame of a Nation* (qv), but the performance is to be savoured if only for the reason that it was the sole time that both he and Cagney appeared together on screen. Newcomer Jane Bryan completed the principal players, replacing Cagney favourite Ann Sheridan - who starred alongside the man in *Angels with Dirty Faces* (qv) - at the last minute.

It was also the last time Cagney would appear in a gangster picture, before *White Heat* (qv) saw a blazing return to the genre that made his name a decade later. With *Each Dawn I Die* due to have been his official retirement from such crime films, both he and Raft turned an average Warner Brothers pot-boiler into something memorable. Raft's Stacey - who 'doesn't think there's anyone, man or woman, that money couldn't buy' is initially sketched as the classic thirties gangster, serving a 199-year life sentence. 'A slum kid who never had a chance', he 'chose the easy way', and 'never did one decent thing in all his life'. Yet his turnaround represents post-Hays Code sensibilities. A rare generic effort where friendship lasts to the bitter end, Stacey is as good as his word, returning to prison after his escape when he discovers the man behind Cagney's set-up. Not 'used to straight guys', his efforts to free Cagney may be seen as self-serving, hoping to vicariously live through Ross' existence on the outside once he's free. Nevertheless, his death - unlike most of his peers - is honourable, a trait that became increasingly prominent in works like *All Through the Night* and *The Roaring Twenties* (qqv).

See also: *Caged*; *Castle on the Hudson*.

Each Dawn I Die

Original US Title: Killer Meets Killer)

(US, Warner Brother, 1939, 92 mins)

'It's a grim story... until a final tear gas battle proves that Cagney has been the victim of a frame-up and that Raft has that perverse streak of honesty that distinguishes all the leading American gangster heroes.'

(Alan Page, *Sight & Sound*)

Credits
Dir: William Keighley
Prod: David Lewis
Scr: Norman Reilly Raine, Warren Duff
based on the original novel by Jerome Odlum
DOP: Arthur Edeson
Ed: Thomas Richards
Music: Max Steiner
Art Dir: Max Parker

Cast: James Cagney (Frank W. Ross), George Raft (Hood Stacey), Jane Bryan (Joyce Conover), George Bancroft (Warden John Armstrong), Maxie Rosenbloom (Fargo Red)

A reporter, framed for murder, befriends a gangster in prison in the hope that it will aid his escape.

Each Dawn I Die: Frank Ross (Jimmy Cagney) and Hood Stacey (George Raft) go stir crazy.

Enforcer, The

(US, United States Pictures, 1950, 87 mins)

'Purports to show realistically the workings of a criminal ring such as was revealed by the Kefauver hearings... The picture of the crime ring lacks the sobriety and realism of, for instance, The Asphalt Jungle, and does not carry its conviction.'

(Monthly Film Bulletin)

Credits
Dir: Raoul Walsh
Prod: Milton Sperling
Scr: Martin Rackin
DOP: Robert Burks
Ed: Fred Allen
Music: David Buttolph
Art Dir: Charles H. Clarke

Cast: Humphrey Bogart (Martin Ferguson), Zero Mostel ('Big Babe' Lazich), Ted De Corsia (Joseph Rico), Everett Sloane (Albert Mendoza), Roy Roberts (Captn. Frank Nelson)

Assistant DA digs deep to prosecute the leader of Murder Inc, a syndicate with assassins for hire.

A curious film for several reasons, *The Enforcer* was directed by Raoul Walsh (though oddly credited as Bretaigne Windust), his first but one film after the glorious *White Heat* (*qv*). The appearance of Humphrey Bogart, following his work in John Huston's *Key Largo* (*qv*) three years earlier, marked another appearance in a gangster picture despite his departure in the 1940s towards more serious fare. Again on the right side of the law, Bogart had come full circle: his kudos now enough to ensure he would no longer play the two-bit snarling support. Based loosely on the exploits of DA Burton Turkus (but changing characters' names to protect the innocent), it follows a crusading Bogart as he uncovers a special assassination squad, meticulously piecing together evidence from dozens of strands. Everett Sloane, who had been brought to Hollywood by Orson Welles to star in *Citizen Kane*, played small-time thug and organiser of the syndicate Albert Mendoza with a malevolent offhand approach, suitable both to the lurid tone imbued by Walsh and the reputation of Mendoza's real-life counterpart, Louis 'Lepke' Buchalter - who went to the electric chair in 1944. Like *The Valachi Papers* (*qv*) would, the film was one of the first to latch onto the terror and nationwide scope of such organisations that retained power through murder and intimidation. A far-cry from traditional gangsters, who generally stuck to killing their own, this new and dangerous breed would kill indiscriminately - at the right price.

* A remake of sorts appeared in 1960, directed by Stuart Rosenberg, but this time bravely titling itself *Murder Inc.* after the very organisation on which it was based. Gleaning Peter Falk an Academy Award nomination as killer Abe Reles who squeals on the mob to gain immunity, the film (from Turkus' book, based on Reles' testimony 20 years previously) does dare to use the real identities of those involved, though reveals little about the operations of the

syndicate. Instead, Louis 'Lepke' Buchalter (David J. Stewart) and his murder-for-hire operation are set against a fictional story of a nightclub singer and dancer. Off-beat casting - TV comic Henry Morgan as Turkus and 'human joke machine' Morey Amsterdam as a gunned-down cabaret entertainer - make for an uneasy ride.

See also: *Lepke*.

Escort, The: See La Scorta.

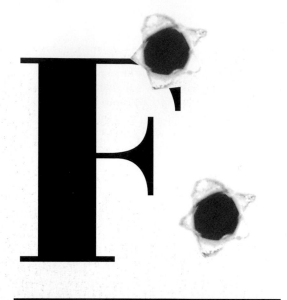

F

Face

(UK, BBC/Distant Horizon, 1997, 105 mins)

Credits
Dir: Antonia Bird
Prod: David M. Thompson, Elinor Day
Scr: Ronan Bennett
DOP: Fred Tammes
Ed: St John O'Rorke
Music Sup: Andy Roberts
Art Dir: Eddy Andres

Cast: Robert Carlyle (Ray), Ray Winstone (Dave), Phil Davis (Julian), Damon Albarn (Jason), Lena Headley (Connie), Steve Sweeney (Weasel)

A gang of 'faces' pull off a dangerous heist, only for one to betray the others.

Placing The Clash's 'London Calling' on the soundtrack may have been an oblique cry, heralding the return of the UK gangster movie, but Antonia Bird's heist drama sets its own agenda, one character wryly spurning crime films for never showing the criminals in a true light. An unusual outing for a female director to take, Bird's influence was Stateside: 'I'm always looking at American genre movies', she told *Sight & Sound*'s Bob McCabe. Drawing more from Michael Mann's *Heat* (qv) than its more obvious forefathers, namely *The Long Good*

Friday and *Get Carter* (*qqv*), the movie hones in on the reasons that drive a man to such desperate measures, the emotion of violence. Carlyle's Ray, once a committed Trades Union activist (with posters in his house for Ken Loach's *Land and Freedom* and *Hidden Agenda* indicating his political persuasion), now is 'just chasing money like everybody else'. His revolutionary idealism gone, the security depot raid represents a misconceived attempt at clashing with authority. As it is later pointed out, 'You and your sort are always on your own – that's why the law's against you. There are no public servants. There is no public service. All there is, is money.'

Winstone's Dave, it transpires, is the devoted father; the financial difficulty he has in maintaining his suburban lifestyle, and sending his children to private school, represents a class struggle as he symbolically betrays his roots. Ultimately, the film blames the political climate as much as human frailty for the robbery and its backlash. Working on both a national and universal level, alienation (be it political or social) is the real menace to society.

See also: *Asphalt Jungle, The; Criss-Cross; Killing, The; Reservoir Dogs, Taking of Pelham 123, The; Usual Suspects, The.*

Fallen Angels (Duoluo Tianshi)

(Hong Kong, Jet Tone, 1995, 95 mins)

'To me, each film is only a postcard, not a book.'
(Wong Kar-Wai, US Premiere)

Credits
Dir/Scr: Wong Kar-Wai
Prod: Jeff Lau
DOP: Christopher Doyle
Ed: William Chang, Wong Ming-Lam
Music: Frankie Chan
Prod. Des: William Chang

Cast: Leon Lai (Wong Chi-Ming), Michele Reis (The Killer's Agent), Takeshi Kaneshiro (He Zhiwu), Karen Mong (Baby), Charlie Young (Charlie Young)

Fallen Angels: The Killer (Leon Lai) stops off for some Light refreshment.

Two Hong Kong stories: a contract killer, who takes commissions from an agent in love with him, decides to quit the life, and a mute ex-con, who hijacks shops and videotapes his father.

Described by one critic as a 'riff on the Hong Kong gangster film, albeit with a somewhat more interesting plot line', the hitman is yet another outlet for Kar-Wai's concerns: the problems of loneliness, insecurity and the inability to commit. As if it needs emphasis, his coded instructions to carry out hits are disguised as messages to meet friends. While we a told 'even a killer has friends in junior high school', as our man bumps into one, their meeting is cold and vapid. Just as the murders themselves are motiveless and without emotion, so the gangster's life reflects this.

The plot was due to be the third strand to Kar-Wai's previous (surprise) hit, *Chungking Express* (the story of two lovelorn cops) and fragments/in-jokes from that film can be seen here (tinned pineapple, the Agent's predilection for entering her unrequited love's apartment). Abruptly switching between this neo-*noir* drama and the farcical exploits of the nocturnal Zhiwu, the multiple narrators and stringent use of monochrome increases the isolation each feels from the other, lost in the frenetic blur of the Hong Kong cityscape.

* *As Tears Go By* (*Wangjiao Kamen*), Kar-Wai's 1988 debut, was a generic attempt at *Mean Streets* (*qv*), originally intended as the first part of a trilogy by Patrick Tam. Set in Triad-ridden Mongkok, an enigmatic hitman is drawn into fire by his protégé, time and again. Introducing a key theme to Kar-Wai's work, the hitman's demise is based around a romantic decision. Kar-Wai, unable to decipher his very much 'alive' work, commented to *Sight & Sound*'s Tony Rayns: 'I'm still always trying to understand the character played by Andy Lau... He's a gangster, and I don't know what he thinks or what motivates him.'

See also: *Driver, The*; *Killer, The*; *Leon*; *Samourai, Le*; *Little Odessa*; *Prizzi's Honor*; *This Gun For Hire*.

Force of Evil

(US, Enterprise Productions, 1948, 78 mins)

'I was committed to a representational film. It was a method I would have tried again and again until solved. After all, we had that big Hollywood machine which the success of Body and Soul had delivered into our hands and we didn't mind seeing what we could do with all that horsepower. But the blacklist took the machine away from us. While we had possession, like those bicycle fanatics at Kitty Hawk, we couldn't wait to waken in the morning, knowing that each day would surprise us. We had the right feelings. Only our plane never flew.'

(Abraham Polonsky, *Film Quarterly*)

Credits
Dir/Scr: Abraham Polonsky
Prod: Bob Roberts
Scr: Ira Wolfert, based on his novel Tucker's People
DOP: George Barnes
Ed: Art Seid
Music: Rudolph Polk
Art Dir: Richard Day

Cast: John Garfield (Joe Morse), Thomas Gomez (Leo Morse), Beatrice Pearson (Doris Lowry), Marie Windsor (Edna Tucker), Howland Chamberlain (Freddy Bauer)

Unscrupulous attorney, in the pocket of a New York crime boss, attempts to look out for his honest brother, persecuted by the syndicate.

One of the few films of the era to explore fully the relationship between business and crime, and to detail the day-to-day operations of the numbers racket, the film was Abraham Polonsky's last for 21 years – until the 1969 effort *Tell Them Willie Boy is Here*. Perhaps the most original expose of organised crime ever made, it took the expressionism of film *noir* and the essentials of the gangster drama and redefined what audiences had come to expect from such staples into an almost avante-garde, multi-layered examination of the corruption of society. Yet the film suffered. While John Garfield would die four years on from the film's release, the trauma of facing the House of Un-American Activities Committee said to have caused his heart attack, Polonsky – self-described as a 'Democrat, Anarchist, Radical, Confused' – would be doomed to writing for TV under various pseudonyms, the McCarthy-era blacklist having scarred him for life. Not even *Force of Evil*'s redemptive ending, included to secure approval, could save him.

The film in some ways is a masterpiece. Polonsky experimented with a poetic dialogue akin to blank verse, 'the babble of the unconscious' as he called it. A great poignancy was introduced into the urban thriller, hitherto unseen in the genre, in particular the final scene as mobster lawyer Joe Morse descends to the river to discover the body of his brother, as if he was entering the ninth circle of Dante's *Inferno* (he calls it 'like going to the bottom of the world'). Visually, the film's hallucinatory quality haunts, echoing, even taunting, Garfield's tortured brilliance (Polonsky himself envisaged 'visual image, actor, word' as 'equals'). Thematically, Polonsky echoes his previous work as writer, Robert Rossen's *Body and Soul* (*qv*). The protagonist (boxer or lawyer) becomes corrupted by evil, only to revolt against this having first caused a loved one irreparable damage. Central to *Force of Evil* is Joe's relationship with his brother, the Freudian love story that leads to a moral awakening in the lawyer as he utters his last words 'I decided to help', referring, of course, to informing upon his boss, Ben Tucker. Ironically, it was such an activity that would afflict Polonsky for the rest of his life.

See also: *Big Combo, The*; *Big Heat, The*; *Frightened City*; *Street With No Name, The*; *Underworld USA*; *Valachi Papers, The*.

Freshman, The

(US, Tristar Pictures, 1990, 103 mins)

Credits
Dir/Scr: Andrew Bergman
Prod: Michael Lobell
DOP: William Fraker
Ed: Barry Malkin
Music: Harlan Goodman
Prod. Des: Ken Adam, Daniel Davis, Alicia Keywan

Cast: Marlon Brando (Carmine Sabatini), Matthew Broderick (Clark Kellogg), Bruno Kirby (Victor Ray), Penelope Ann Miller (Tina Sabatini), Paul Benedict (Arthur Fleeber)

NYU film student takes on a part-time delivery job for a seemingly familiar screen Don, who indulges in importing endangered species to be eaten.

Marlon Brando's parody (his suggestion, at a cost of $3.3 million plus 11 per cent gross) of his character Don Corleone from *The Godfather* (qv) makes for a likeable, if one-dimensional, comedy. Adopting the voice, clothes, familiar gestures and family values in his portrayal of Carmine Sabatini, the likeness causes one character to remark 'they saw him and based the film on him'.
As director Bergman told *US Premiere*'s Fred Schruers, 'In the thirties, guys did that all the time; their job was to play a certain kind of gangster, then they would just out-and-out parody it in another picture. Edward G. Robinson did *Little Caesar* and then he did *The Little Giant*, which is a sort of take off of that movie.'
Emulating a scene from *The Godfather Part II* (qv), when Robert De Niro (the younger version of Don Corleone) strolls through his local marketplace, Broderick's wet-behind-the-ears film-student Clark Kellog observes Brando do the same – as if he is reclaiming the role from the actor who would go on to surpass him. But, as he would infamously tell a reporter from the *Toronto Globe and Mail* on the set of what was his first film in ten years, 'It's going to be a flop... an extremely unpleasant experience. I wish I hadn't finished with a stinker.'
Rather more awkwardly, the film attempts to parody *The Godfather Part II*'s themes. Kellog tutor expounds the theory that 'All corruption is equal. There's no separation between politics and gangsterism', after Michael Corleone refuses to bow to the Senator's fiscal demands. This is borne out through the plot's superfluous use of corrupt government agents, defrauding Clark of the money gleaned from an endangered species racket.

See also: *Bugsy Malone*; *I'm Gonna Git You, Sucka*; *Johnny Dangerously*; *Wise Guys*.

Frightened City

(UK, Zodiac Productions, 1961, 98 min)

Credits
Dir/Prod: John Lemont
Prod/Scr: Leigh Vance
DOP: Desmond Dickinson
Ed: Bernard Gribble
Music: Norrie Paramor
Art Dir: Maurice Carter

Cast: Herbert Lom (Waldo Zhernikov), John Gregson (Sayers), Sean Connery (Paddy Damion), Alfred Marks (Harry Foulcher), Yvonne Romain (Anya)

Six London protection rings join forces to extort money from the city.

Notable for the early appearance of Sean Connery (*Variety* commented upon the distinct impression made by this 'virile young man who combines toughness, charm and Irish (?) blarney'), the film is somewhat ahead of time in comparison to its UK peers, thankfully spurning the chirpy East End rogues of earlier efforts. Drenching the gritty milieu with a laconic sense of humour, the film follows the American gangster pictures of the late fifties and early sixties that dealt with nationwide syndicates spreading across the country, such as *The Valachi Papers* (qv). Restricting it to London may seem parochial, but it matches mastermind Lom's own profession – that of an accountant. A trend, incidently, that would continue in a diverse range of gangster sub-genres, from *Black Caesar* (qv) to *The Brotherhood* and *The Godfather* (qqv), indicating the rise of the middle-man in a profession becoming more business-oriented. This is reflected in Lom's plans to halt the progress of the building of an office block, in order to gain from the penalties the builders would incur. The success would lead to an assault on chains of stores and cinemas – a rather unusual method of extortion. Innovation continued with John Gregson's portrayal of Detective Inspector Sayers, a precursor to Clint Eastwood's rogue cop Harry Callaghan, as he breaks into a solicitor's office to retrieve some jewels (as opposed to finding a magistrate to procure a warrant).

Part psychological-profile ('The criminal mind is the dark side of the moon'), part attack on the justice system (Sayers believes if the law is left stagnant 'the hoodlums and mobsters will be dominating this country before we know what's hit us'), its low-budget nature belies the contribution it made to both British and US films.

See also: *Big Combo, The*; *Big Heat, The*; *Force of Evil*; *Street With No Name, The*; *Underworld USA*.

Funeral, The

(US, October Films/MDP/C&P, 1996, 98 mins)

Credits
Dir: Abel Ferarra
Prod: Mary Kane
Scr: Nicholas St. John
DOP: Ken Kelsch
Ed: Bill Pankow, Mayin Lo
Music: Joe Delia
Prod. Des: Charles M. Lagola

Cast: Christopher Walken (Ray Tempio), Chris Penn (Chez Tempio), Vincent Gallo (Johnny Tempio), Benicio Del Toro (Gaspare Spoglia), Annabella Sciorra (Jeanette), Isabella Rossellini (Clara Tempio)

Two 1930s mob brothers mourn the death of their younger sibling, and grieve in different ways; the elder searching out the killer for revenge.

In the opening scene, the soon-to-be-killed 22-year-old Communist Johnny Tempio sits alone in a theatre watching Archie Mayo's *The Petrified Forest* (qv). While he may aspire to be Bogart's grizzled

Duke Manti, his brother Ray would more than likely identify with Leslie Howard's existential Squire. But then, as Johnny himself says, accused of reading too many books, 'That's the American tragedy. We need something to distract us – the radio or the movies.' The suggestion that the gangster is a symbol of the cultural and spiritual desolation of Mankind is present. While the hijack of a truck-full of radios shows impending technological change (implied, for the worse), the Priest laments for the Tempio family's 'Practical atheism' – they must pray for themselves.

Ferrara works within the boundaries of tradition, his Gaspare a slick amalgam of Cagney, Robinson and Muni, but also goes beyond the Warner Brothers era, creating strong female characters that provide oblique commentary on mob life but also remain responsible for binding the 'Family'.

Nicholas St. John's script, as far removed from his previous Ferrara mob collaborations *China Girl* and *King of New York* (qqv) as you could get, paints a much broader canvas than these former efforts, uniting underworld preoccupations with death, religion, politics and commerce. Ray believes people of his ilk should be running the Ford Motor Company: 'We're just a bunch of street punks, nobody's watching us. What is it – greed, pride, stupidity – that takes over us?' He concludes that the 'flaw in the criminal character' is a sense of the untrustworthy. All that can be managed, though, is a switch from terrorizing Union strike-scabs to hooking up with the employer of such breakaways, compromising Johnny's ideals in the process.

Death, meanwhile, is mythologised and internalised: gangsters never go to each other's funeral, it is suggested, as the wounds of the victims would begin to bleed, recalling Christ-like religious imagery. Ray, a devout Catholic, is assured he will 'Roast in hell', and as he searches for the truth, wrestling with his conscience – 'the way God sees it' – he knows his eternal damnation is secure.

See also: *Sonatine*.

office success, opening to rave reviews claiming it was his best film since *The Public Enemy* (qv), the heavy marketing campaign focused on Cagney's unusual turnaround, from mobster to Federal policeman. The real key to success was retaining Cagney's two-fisted, boisterous approach; the Government Men, having grown up in the same areas as the hoods, are seen as the only force capable of stopping their erstwhile neighbours. Cagney's character only avoided crime as a benevolent older gangster paid for his schooling to 'make something of himself'. This refashioning grew in part as a response to propaganda for a strong federal government, emphasising the gangster further as a scapegoat for the country's troubles rather than any political or religious target. The G-Man may be on the side of the law, but with an ominous spirit of fascism imbued (the Men rather like a police army) he is permitted to arm himself – 'to shoot to kill with the least possible waste of bullets'. More importantly, the 'hero' lives to the end, gaining respectability. While the gangster was made even more of an outcast, the crusading (and now unconventional) law-enforcer was allowed, dangerously, to fight fire with fire. Will Hays himself in his annual President's Report lauded the film and

G-Men

(US, Warner Brothers, 1935, 84 mins)

Credits
Dir: William Keighley
Prod: Louis Edelman
Scr: Seaton I. Miller, based on the original novel Public Enemy No.1 by Gregory Rogers
DOP: Sol Polito
Ed: Jack Killifer
Music: Leo F. Forbstein
Art Dir: John Hughes

Cast: James Cagney (James 'Brick' Davis), Margaret Lindsay (Kay McCord), Ann Dvorak (Jean Morgan), Robert Armstrong (Jeffrey McCord), Barton Maclaine (Brad Collins)

A lawyer, whose education was financed by a gangster, becomes a G-Man after his cop pal is killed in a gangland shooting.

Following Hays Code stipulations, Warner Brothers brilliantly poured 'old wine in new bottles' (as *Monthly Film Bulletin* called it), reinventing the gangster by placing James Cagney firmly on the side of the law. The original gangster melodrama intended to glorify the police not the gunman, *G-Men* was fashioned from a story entitled *Public Enemy Number 1*, shot in just six weeks but on a (then) lavish budget of $450,000. A huge box-

G-Men: Jimmy Cagney turns Government Man as 'Brick' Davis.

its belief in authority for its 'healthy and helpful emphasis on law enforcement' – urged on by the publicity-hungry J. Edgar Hoover, chief of the FBI. As a result, Warner Brothers released *Special Agents* in the same year, also directed by Keighley. This saw a number of Washington D.C. G-Men decide to use the income tax laws to entrap gangsters who were running a number of racketeering operations from a nightclub. Such ruthless methods laid seeds for the maverick cop seen in *The Big Heat* and *The Big Combo* (qqv), to be then perverted in *Dirty Harry* and *The French Connection*.

* Reissued in 1949 to coincide with the FBI's 25th anniversary, a newly shot prologue was added to the re-released prints. David Brian appears as a bureau chief addressing a classroom full of rookies, telling them that they (and the audience) are about to see the 'grand-daddy' of all FBI pictures. 'The hoodlum', of course, is 'the same today as he was then. He is still a public enemy.' Other G-Men related films include Fred Brannon's *G-Men Never Forget* and *The Bonnie Parker Story* (qv) director William Witney's *G-Men vs The Black Dragon*.

See also: *Bullitt*.

Gangland: the Verne Miller Story

(US, Three Aces Productions, 1987, 95 mins)

'Dialogue ridden with genre clichés and direction that substitutes episodic hopscotching for pacing and suspense.'

(Variety, Sep. 1987)

Credits
Dir/Scr: Rod Hewitt
Prod: Ann Brooke Ashley
DOP: Mikhail Suslov
Ed: John O'Connor, Paul Dixon
Music: Thomas Chase, Steve Rucker

Cast: Thomas G. Waites (Al Capone), Scott Glenn (Verne Miller), Barbara Stock (Vi Miles), Lucinda Jenney (Bobby), Sonny Carl Davis (Frank 'Baldy' Nash), Andrew Robinson (Pretty Boy)

A one-time South Dakota Sheriff becomes embroiled with Al Capone, eventually to mastermind 'The Kansas City Massacre'.

Hewitt's film suffers in part from low production values (the budget was reported at $2.5 million) but also from a failure to recognise the dramatic possibilities in watching Miller's change from law-maker to breaker. Coyly narrated by Miller's female companion Bobby, we begin with the man committing a bank robbery (killing his fellow robbers in the process for murdering a child witness) and then to Chicago, where Miller tells Capone 'I don't want to work for you. I want to work with you'; an equality that eventually manifests itself a little too much as both contract incurable syphilis.

Some unique, if historically questionable, episodes are interwoven with the standard fact-churning (Hoover and the FBI, Prohibition, etc). Capone's use of Chicago's sewer system, and a suggestion of his sexual inadequacy, along with Miller's seduction of an incorruptible Judge's daughter and his attack on Moran's men by disguising himself as a shop dummy all hold interest. Though Waites tackles the role of Capone with gusto, the plot's decision to follow the Kansas Massacre, an event that eventually spurred Congress into empowering the FBI to use guns and arrest across State lines, typifies the small-scale nature of the film, and the man it celebrates.

See also: *Al Capone*; *Capone*; *George Raft Story, The*; *Lost Capone, The*; *St. Valentine's Day Massacre, The*; *Scarface Mob, The*; *Untouchables, The*.

Gang That Couldn't Shoot Straight, The

(US, MGM, 1971, 96 mins)

'...not so much a film but a sloppy assemblage of out-takes of the movie-that-almost-was.'
(Peter Buckley, Films & Filming)

Credits
Dir: James Goldstone
Prod: Irwin Winkler, Robert Chartoff

Scr: Waldo Salt, based on the orginal novel by Jimmy Breslin
DOP: Owen Roizman
Ed: Edward A. Biery
Music: David Grusin
Art Dir: Robert Gundlach

Cast: Jerry Orbach (Salvatore 'Kid Sally' Palumbo), Leigh Taylor-Young (Angela), Jo Van Fleet (Big Momma), Robert De Niro (Mario), Lionel Stander (Baccala).

A South Brooklyn gang declare war on one of New York's five big Mafia bosses, making several bungled assassination attempts.

Paltry comedy, notable only for an early turn by De Niro as an Italian cyclist who becomes embroiled in this embarrassing spectacle. Director James Goldstone said to John Cutts in *Films & Filming*, the film was 'A funny look at corruption. If it isn't, I'm in serious trouble.' The use of Lionel Stander, whose early career included *The Last Gangster* (qv), and the reference to *Kiss of Death* (qv), with an aspiring gangster emulating the infamous snigger of Richard Widmark's hood Tommy Udo, add little to the film's fabric. With both book and movie parodying the life of Crazy Joe Gallo, neither were well received in the underworld. As Peter 'Pete the Greek' Diapoulas, Gallo's bodyguard, explained in his book *The Sixth Family*: 'The writer our crew would have loved giving a beating to was Jimmy Breslin.'

General, The

(UK/Ireland, Merlin Films/J&M Entertainment, 1998, 123mins)

'This was the great challenge: to make a film about a man who was fundamentally a bad person and to try to see the world as he saw it.'
(John Boorman, *Sight and Sound*)

Credits
Dir/Scr/Prod. : John Boorman, based on the book by Paul Williams)
DOP.: Seamus Deasy
Ed: Ron Davis

Music: Richie Buckley
Prod Des: Derek Wallace

Cast: Brendan Gleeson (Martin Cahill), Adrian Dunbar (Noel Curley), Sean McGinley (Gary), Maria Doyle Kennedy (Frances), Angeline Ball (Tina), Jon Voight (Inspector Ned Kenny)

Biopic of the notorious Irish crimelord, Martin Cahill.

As Boorman told *Sight & Sound*'s Phillip Kemp, the true life figure of Irish gangster Martin Cahill appealed to him in a mythic dimension, harking back to figures from previous films *Zardoz* and *Excalibur*. 'He also relates to those Irish Mafioso bosses in Chicago, it's very much the same character,' he later added. A lyrical film, shot in black and white, to show 'a more contiguous world, more connected to dreams and the unconscious', *The General* is a work of tragic beauty. Winning Boorman Best Director in Cannes, it's apolitical - despite his assassination (which encircles the narrative) by the IRA. Cahill, born and brought up on the Hollyfield estate in Dublin, viewed the terrorist organisation as just another aspect of the authority he despised. As Boorman noted: 'for Cahill, it was a case of saying, 'Well, I don't accept any of the laws of this society - the laws of God or man.'' His V-sign to the Police, led by his nemesis Jon Voight, reaches a hysterical peak as he keeps his cool, discovering his flock of pigeons, killed by the law. To the IRA, he simply spits 'They're amateurs!' More than just a criminal (his crimes we see, such as the art theft, seem petty and hilarious), Cahill is a complexly drawn character. While his minor activities may seem more at home in an Ealing comedy, the harshly-adhered to codes of loyalty recall works like *The Godfather* (qv). The archetypal Celtic chieftain, the adoration from the public elevates him, in the tradition of the gangster movie, to the status of myth. Referred to as 'Robin Hood' by Voight, Cahill further adds to this image by giving money from his spoils to neighbours: 'It's my way of paying taxes', he notes. Ironically, while Cahill is pursued on an income tax charge, in the manner of Al Capone's demise, his reaction is simple: blow the tax inspector's car up. His image is all-important. Upon hugging his right-hand man

Curley, he breaks quickly from the lock: 'We're not fuckin' Italians,' he notes. He's a gangster, but more in the spirit of Cagney than Capone. Violent (he crucifies, in a reference to *The Long Good Friday* and *The Krays (qqv)*, the hand of a suspected traitor in his gang to the snooker table), Cahill is also loving and caring. Living in a bizarre ménage à trois with his wife and sister-in-law (Kennedy and Ball respectively), he raises children by both but lives in harmony. Not drinking, smoking or 'cheating' on his wife(s), Cahill is a family man. With his oiled side parting and comfortable sweaters in many ways he is the very antithesis of the sharp-suited womanisers seen in the likes of *Goodfellas (qv)*. Yet, with his descent into paranoia, as his gang breaks up and his neighbours view him as a traitor for selling his hoard of art to the UVF, he in some ways follows the tradition of the gangster once more. Later suspecting his sister-in-law of informing to the police, sympathy from the audience's perspective begins to wane. Swelled by ambition, his reality is brought around him. 'What do you stand for? Thieving and killing and scaring people to death,' he is told. His answer: 'Nobody believes in nothing anymore, except me.' A dying breed, Cahill is the last of the 'gentleman gangsters'. While set some years before, Stuart Townsend's thug in *Resurrection Man (qv)* is of the new schism, likely to eclipse those of the old school. Cahill may be hero and villain, but Boorman is careful not to demonise him, using him instead as a telescope towards his adopted country of Ireland. As Boorman noted: 'It is the story of an iconoclast. Cahill invented his own world, his own rules and lived by them. What Cahill did in taking on the police, state and church was to illuminate the changing society here in Ireland. The church has lost its influence, there is corruption in politics, and people are changing tremendously. With old values disappearing people are very uncertain about what they believe in whereas Cahill was coming from a philosophy which he lived out.'

George Raft Story, The (UK title: Spin of a Coin)

(US, Allied Artists Picture Corporation, 1961, 106 mins)

Credits
Dir: Joseph M.Newman
Prod: Ben Schwalb
Scr: Crane Wilbur
DOP: Carl Gutherie
Ed: George White
Music: Jeff Alexander
Art Dir: David Milton

Cast: Ray Danton (George Raft), Jayne Mansfield (Lisa), Julie London (Sheila), Barrie Chase (June), Brad Dexter (Benny Siegel), Barbara Nichols (Texas Guinam)

Biopic of the 1920s small-time gangster-cum-hoofer, turned Hollywood star.

Tepid work, following the likes of *The Al Jolson Story*, with little to recommend it, except the scenes depicting Raft filming Howard Hawks' *Scarface (qv)* and his subsequent meeting with Al Capone. Like a series of variety acts, featuring overlong dance and comedy-double-act numbers, the film unites crime and the stage as Raft is wrongly arrested by the LAPD as he enters Tinseltown. On letting him go, the Police Chief cautions: 'Just keep on being an actor, Mr Raft. This department's going to be your fiercest critic.' Money is seen as the root of all evil. Sick of being poor, Raft knows 'Without money you're nothin'. With it, you're goin' places.' But, as it proves, devotion to the lifestyle, once he makes it, becomes all the more tragic when the parts dry up and Raft turns into a suicidal loner. As much about the shark-infested waters of Hollywood (with the pressures of the public's image of Raft influencing his roles), as about New York gangsters, his comeback supporting role in Billy Wilder's *Some Like It Hot (qv)* epitomises the film: 'It's the story of my life,' he ruefully comments.
Through shooting *Scarface* (for which Raft becomes the ideal choice as unofficial technical advisor), insight is gained into the boundaries that divide art and life. Improvising upon the script in his famous death scene, he tells the director how a real gangster would act – 'I've seen 'em die. They don't

die no different from anyone else. And they don't seem to like it.' After gaining rave reviews, he is called to see Capone and becomes 'one of the boys', even gaining his own Al-appointed bodyguard. Neville Brand's (a role he played in Phil Karlson's *The Scarface Mob*) Capone is disgruntled that his 'character' was bumped off; and in a sharp reminder of the era's censorship Raft reveals this was due to the Hays Office Production Code, insisting that criminals were not presented sympathetically.

See also: *Al Capone; Bonnie and Clyde; Bonnie Parker Story, The; Bullet for Pretty Boy, A; Capone; Dillinger; Gangland: the Verne Miller Story; King of the Roaring Twenties: the Arnold Rothstein Story; Lepke; Lost Capone, The; Lucky Luciano; Rise and Fall of Legs Diamond, The; St. Valentine's Day Massacre, The; Scarface Mob, The; Untouchables, The; Young Dillinger.*

Get Carter

(UK, MGM, 1971, 112 mins)

'I think in its own way, it was ahead of its time. I remember [producer] Michael Klinger going to America with the film and Don Siegel seeing it and being completely stunned, because nothing quite like it had come out of Britain before.'
(Mike Hodges, *Film Review*)

Credits
Dir/Scr: Mike Hodges, based on the novel Jack's Return Home by Ted Lewis
Prod: Michael Klinger
DOP: Wolfgang Suschitzky
Ed: John Trumper
Music: Ted Lewis
Prod. Des: Assheton Gorton

Cast: Michael Caine (Jack Carter), Britt Ekland (Anna Fletcher), John Osborne (Cyril Kinnear), Ian Hendry (Eric Paice), Bryan Mosely (Cliff Brumby), Geraldine Moffatt (Glenda), Dorothy White (Margaret)

A hitman travels to Newcastle to avenge the death of his brother.

Exerting massive influence on subsequent British gangster films from *The Long Good Friday* to *Face* (qqv), Mike Hodges' *Get Carter*, along with Michael Tucher's lesser-known *Villain* (qv), would come to epitomise the cold-blooded bleakness of our own gangster films. As Hodges told *Film Review*'s Howard Maxwell: 'Up until then, gangsters had been portrayed as kind of jolly characters in British films. But there was a meanness to them as well as a softer side, and I really wanted to bring this out. I wanted to give the film that sense of hardness you saw with the Krays and the Richardsons when their cases finally went to court.' While containing a gruesome double-knifing, the threat of brutality that pervades the film is far worse. This, of course, did not prevent inevitable criticism and censorship; the BBC, on a television airing, hacked the film so much that the scene where Carter forces a woman to overdose was cut after she is told to strip, making the incident look like rape.

Caine's Carter, an 'East End Alfie gone bad', as one publication called him, is the authentic post-permissive hero, an avenging angel who systematically and sadistically sets about pursuing the leaders of a blue movie empire (that features Doreen, his niece, or possibly daughter, as is hinted). On the train shuttling him from the impersonal London to the seedy alleyways, pubs and lodging houses of Newcastle, Carter reads Raymond Chandler's *Farewell, My Lovely*. While inviting the interpretation that he is a latter-day Bogart-Marlowe incarnation, the film's Tyneside setting with its slum streets and Carter's encounter with them, lead one to witness an evolution of a class-conscience in his character. He may order a pint of bitter in a thin glass, but as he tells local bigwig Brumby, 'the Doreens of the world' (unlike Brumby's daughter) are the ones that will never get away with it. The cynical sneer is replaced by a protective feeling for the victims of those who, like pornographers, willingly exploit them.

* The film was remade in the following year as *Hit Man* (directed by George Armitage), riding on the wave of the popular Blaxploitation films. Starring Bernie Casey as Tyrone Tackett (the Carter figure), the film follows events from Hodges' work to the letter, with Tyrone searching for his brother Cornell's killer and uncovering a pornography ring. As with most white-produced black films, there is no attempt at

raising the viewer's consciousness; black pimps, prostitutes and porno stars just represent another side to Blaxploitation (this time, specifically female). In keeping with the longevity of the black hero crucial to the genre, Tyrone survives an assassination attempt (even utilising *Get Carter*'s beach setting used for Caine's demise) in the final reel.

Get Shorty

(US, Jersey Films, 1995, 105 mins)

Credits
Dir: Barry Sonnenfeld
Prod: Danny DeVito, Michael Shamberg, Stacey Sher
Scr: Scott Frank, based on the novel by Elmore Leonard
DOP: Mark Plummer
Ed: Jim Miller
Music: John Lurie
Prod. Des: Peter Larkin

Cast: Martin Weir (Danny DeVito), John Travolta (Chili Palmer), Gene Hackman (Harry Zimm), Rene Russo (Karen Flores), Dennis Farina (Ray 'Bones' Barboni), Delroy Lindo (Bo Catlett)

Miami loan shark turns Hollywood producer, using a real-life gangster swindle as the basis for his plot.

At its time of release, the most successful of all attempts to convert an Elmore Leonard novel, Barry Sonnenfeld's slick realisation is part Tinseltown satire, part crime story – letting us know that the Hollywood film business is no more respectable than Miami's underworld. *Pulp Fiction* (*qv*) meets Robert Altman's *The Player*, as one critic suggested, it is inspired by Tarantino's world of dismissive death, undesirables' casual banter and an obsession with movies, in particular *Rio Bravo* (as seen in *True Romance* and *Natural Born Killers*). The Leonard-Tarantino connection itself goes deeper; the film-maker once stating that while writing *True Romance* he was 'trying to write an Elmore Leonard novel as a movie' (achieved rather literally with *Jackie Brown*, his 1997 adaptation of *Rum Punch*). Such incestuous influences cannot help but feed into each other – both writer and director are turned on by juxtaposing comedy with

violence, murder with the mundane.

Get Shorty (co-starring De Vito, who executive-produced *Pulp Fiction*) is the bastard offspring. Loan shark and racketeer Chili, who wears a leather coat 'like the one Pacino wore in *Serpico*', plans to save an ailing cinema, in order to 'show some old Cagney movies'. De Vito's character, Hollywood star Martin Weir, made his name in *The Cyclone* as a mob man; so convincing was his turn that Chili says he was convinced Weir was 'a made man'. Weir himself wonders if Chili's script proposal is funded by wise-guy money. Even actor Dennis Farina (as the film's one true mobster Ray 'Bones' Barboni), after leaving his profession as a Chicago cop, starred in previous gangster works – *Romeo is Bleeding* and *Men of Respect* (*qqv*) in particular. In a film that revels in self-referential dialogue (Travolta alluding to his own *Look Who's Talking* series by deriding males acting with babies), these are movie gangsters in more ways than one. A definable new phase for the gangster film, the gangster has moved from tragic hero to cartoon cut-out.

* The real Chilli Palmer, a reformed gangster and muse for Leonard, can be glimpsed in the opening exchanges between Travolta and Ray 'Bones' Barboni.

See also: *Kiss of Death*; *Things To Do In Denver When You're Dead*.

Getting Gotti

(US, Kushner-Locke, 1994, 120 mins)

Credits
Dir: Roger Young
Prod: John M. Eckert
Scr: James S. Henerson
DOP: Ron Stannett
Ed: Benjamin A. Weissman, Terry Blythe
Music: Patrick Williams
Prod. Des: William Beeton

Cast: Lorraine Bracco (Diane Giacalone), Anthony Denison (John Gotti), Jeremy Ratchford (Harvey Sanders), Ellen Burstyn (Diane's mother), Jason Blicker (Diane's mother)

A lawyer dedicates herself to tracking down John Gotti.

Made-for-TV it may be, but *Getting Gotti* offers an unusual attempt to dispel the myth of mob life. As pugnacious Assistant DA Diane Giacalone (played by Ray Liotta's 'wife' from *Goodfellas* [qv], Lorraine Bracco) notes: 'They're not romantic. They're a bunch of money-grabbing little thugs who are too dumb to make a buck without hitting someone over the head.' While she cites Italy's positive contributions to the world – Puccini and Verdi, for example – she is ashamed that these mobsters originate from the same country. As Mike Newell's *Donnie Brasco* (qv) would later do, the film spends its time showing the unglamorous side of crew life, the mobsters all hanging outside the club door in the cold, waiting for Gambino crew chief Gotti. Sweeping away all thought of 'Al Pacino looking soulful' in *The Godfather* (qv), the film opts for the anti-climactic ending as Cotti successfully circumvents the law and avoids imprisonment. The case, and the film, are about justice and corruption: 'the system versus the street', where the law could only be won if the jury had been bought. Appropriately enough, the epilogue informs us that, while Gotti was finally convicted in 1992, the crusading Giacalone moved to the Political Corruption Unit of the US Attorney's office.

* Another worthy biopic, Robert Harmon's *Gotti* was released in 1995. Made for HBO, the 'Dapper Don' is portrayed with authority by Armand Assante, with heavyweight support from Anthony Quinn.

Glass Key, The

(US, Paramount, 1935, 77 mins)

Credits
Dir: Frank Tuttle
Prod: E. Lloyd Sheldon
Scr: Kubec Glasmon, Harry Ruskin, Kathryn Scola, based on the novel by Dashiell Hammett
DOP: Henry Sharp
Ed: Hugh Bennett

Cast: George Raft (Ed Beaumont), Edward Arnold (Paul Madvig), Claire Dodd (Janet Henry), Rosalind Keith (Opal Madvig), Ray Milland (Taylor Henry)

Glass Key, The

(US, Paramount, 1942, 85 mins)

Credits
Dir: Stuart Heisler
Prod: Fred Kohlmar
Scr: Jonathan Latimer
DOP: Theodor Sparkuhl
Ed: Archie Marshek
Music: Victor Young
Art Dir: Haldane Douglas, Hans Dreier

Cast: Alan Ladd (Ed Beaumont), Brian Donlevy (Paul Madvig), Bonita Granville (Opal Madvig), Veronica Lake (Janet Henry), Moroni Olsen (Ralph Henry)

Crooked political boss, a prime suspect in the murder of his young sister's boyfriend, backs a candidate for mayor, only to be on the end of a smear campaign from an ambitious racketeer.

Frank Tuttle's original came at a lull in the first cycle of the genre. In 1932, 35 films using a gangster character or plotline were released; by 1935, only 12, including Tuttle's film, were seen, partly through the Hays Code denting creative licence for the genre. Minimising the novel's relationship between Janet Henry and Ed Beaumont, the fiancée and friend respectively of accused boss Madvig, George Raft's character was also made more intelligible: the novel suggesting room for other inexplicable ambitions. His motives for repeatedly taking beatings from Jeff (William Bendix), henchman for gangster Shad O'Rory (Robert Gleckler), can now be seen as a simple loyalty to Madvig. While Tuttle carefully captures Hammett's mood, with airless interiors and low-key photography, the underlying pessimism is lacking. The bleak ending in the source, with the Beaumont/Madvig friendship severed but the corrupt political system still in place, is replaced by Madvig, his name cleared, now backing an honest candidate.

The Heisler version similarly was unable (or unwilling) to realise Hammett's dark vision fully for the movie-going public. Scripted by Jonathan Latimer (himself a detective fiction writer in the Hammett vein), the text was here rendered in a more faithful manner. The Henry/Beaumont relationship is restored, with Latimer emphasising her arrogance, contemptuousness and duplicity.

But, as Saul N. Scher termed it, the film with its muted, neutral style, was 'interim *noir*', arriving in a year when patriotic trips like *Yankee Doodle Dandy* were popular, and before cynical mid-1940s dramas like *Double Indemnity* were readily accepted by audiences. Madvig's buffoonish portrayal by Donlevy (inviting comparison with his character in Preston Sturges' *The Great McGinty*) rather renders the 'Politics is simple. All you need is a little muscle' strain impotent. With campaign slogans like 'A vote for Henry is a vote for honesty' the irony fails to bite; the humour offers relief for the audience from hard facts.

* This was Alan Ladd's second vehicle for Paramount, who capitalised on the recent rushes of Ladd's debut *This Gun For Hire* (qv) and Warner Brothers success with Hammett's *The Maltese Falcon* by ushering the star into a remake of the 1935 film. Ironically, with *This Gun For Hire* still unreleased, the screen chemistry between Ladd and Veronica Lake had gone largely unnoticed. Patricia Morison had been cast opposite Ladd for Heisler's film, and it was only a quirk of fate (Morison being deemed too tall) that reunited the pair.

Gloria

(US, Columbia Pictures, 1980, 121 mins)

Credits
Dir/Scr: John Cassavetes
Prod: Sam Shaw
DOP: Fred Schuler
Ed: George C.Villasenor, Jack McSweeney
Music: Bill Conti
Prod. Des: Rene D'Auriac, Fred Schuler

Cast: Gena Rowlands (Gloria Swenson), John Adames (Phil Dawn), Julie Carmen (Jeri Dawn), Lupe Guarnica (Margarita Vagas), Buck Henry (Jack Dawn), Val Avery (Sill)

One-time gangster's moll and showgirl goes on the run from the Mob, taking with her some incriminating evidence and the child belonging to her deceased Mafia-connected neighbour.

At the double-urging of wife Rowlands and an MGM executive (who was looking for a part for their child-star of the time Ricky Schroder), Cassavetes wrote the script as something he would sell, not direct himself. MGM lost Schroder to Disney, and the project fell into Columbia's hands – who agreed Rowlands could star, providing Cassavetes would direct. While it is the kind of film Cassavetes would normally act in for another to fund his own work (he admitted the script was 'no great shakes'), *Gloria*, unlike *The Killing of a Chinese Bookie* (qv) which deconstructed the genre, keeps conventions in line with his own personal concerns, allowing the characters to stray upon occasion into the gangster film.

Here, Cassavetes is allowed inside a cinematic myth, within a tightly constructed discipline, to work through the clichés, exaggerating them to become truth: hitmen turning up late for their work, the outsider-hero a woman, the 'man' of the piece a child (bequeathed to him by his father) – all help Cassavetes in his struggle to 'beat the system' (as little Phil notes is possible). Gloria's final 'confrontation' scene with former lover and mob boss Tanzini, where she hopes to trade Jack Dawn's account book for her and Phil's life, is typical of this, as Cassavetes directs against tension. Having been made to wait around as if for a job interview, she receives a slap on the wrist ('You can't go around shooting our people') and then is able to simply walk out. This disarray reflects Cassavetes' take on how movie gangsters just aren't like real gangsters (something *Bookie*, with its physically impaired types, showed more explicitly).

Cassavetes also reverses the process, ironically using conventions to comment: the idea of a mother's unconscious need for a son (and vice versa), is raised by, and because of, an organisation traditionally based around the family structure. 'I know you all approve of mothers', says Gloria to Tanzini's boys in her plea for her life (recalling the

Oedipal fixation). 'Every woman is a mother', they reply; Gloria's own latent maternal affection, brought to a head in the most striking image of the film as she stands astride on a street corner and fires at a carload of hoods, for once straddling both the 'real' and the 'illusional' of the two worlds of Cassavetes films.

* A remake, directed by Sidney Lumet and featuring Sharon Stone, was released in 1998.

Godfather, The

(US, Paramount, 1972, 171 mins)

'I always wanted to use the Mafia as a metaphor for America... Both the Mafia and America have roots in Europe.'

(Francis Ford Coppola, *Sight & Sound*)

Credits
Dir/Scr: Francis Ford Coppola
Prod: Albert S. Ruddy
Scr: Mario Puzo, based on his own novel
DOP: Gordon Willis
Ed: Marc Laub, William Reynolds, Murray Solomon, Peter Zinner
Music: Nino Rota
Prod. Des: Dean Tavoularis

Cast: Marlon Brando (Vito Corleone), James Caan (Sonny Corleone), John Cazale (Fredo Corleone), Al Pacino (Michael Corleone), Robert Duvall (Tom Hagen), Diane Keaton (Kay Adams), Sterling Hayden (Captain McClusky)

The tale of a crime family, headed by the 'Godfather' of the Manhattan Mafia, set in Post-World War II New York.

Godfather Part II, The

(US, Paramount, 1974, 200 mins)

Credits
Dir/Prod/Scr: Francis Ford Coppola
Scr: Mario Puzo
DOP: Gordon Willis

Ed: Barry Malkin, Richard Marks, Peter Zinner
Music: Carmine Coppola, Nino Rota
Prod. Des: Angelo P. Graham, Dean Tavoularis

Cast: Al Pacino (Michael Corleone), Robert De Niro (Vito Corleone), Robert Duvall (Tom Hagen), Diane Keaton (Kay), John Cazale (Fredo), Lee Strasberg (Hyman Roth)

The saga continues, intertwining Michael's reign as head of the family with the early life of his father.

Godfather Part III, The

(US, Paramount, 1990, 140 mins)

Credits
Dir/Prod/Scr: Francis Ford Coppola
Scr: Mario Puzo
DOP: Gordon Willis
Ed: Barry Malkin
Music: Carmine Coppola
Prod. Des: Alex Tavoularis

Cast: Al Pacino (Michael Corleone), Diane Keaton (Kay), Bridget Fonda (Grace Hamilton), Sofia Coppola (Mary Corleone), Andy Garcia (Vincent Mancini)

The ageing Michael attempts to pull away from organised crime, only to find himself drawn back in.

The Godfather, Francis Ford Coppola's intimate epic, moved the gangster from the urban renegade of the thirties to congenial patriarch-cum-corporate businessman. No other work has single-handedly redefined the gangster's image in the eye of the public so drastically. Based on the best-selling novel by Mario Puzo (as was *Part II*), it would go on to gross $150 million worldwide by the end of the year. It was called the *Gone With the Wind* of gangster movies, and Coppola was only brought on board by producer Robert Evans because he was Italian, cheap (his previous film *The Rain People* had flopped) and directors like Arthur Penn, Peter Yates and Costa-Gavras had declined. Clashing with the studio, from his casting choices of the then has-been Brando and newcomer Pacino to the shooting schedule (he wanted 80 days, they gave him 53), the production experienced controversy from the start. *Chinatown* scribe Robert Towne was brought in on an uncredited rewrite, the Italian-American league petitioned every elected official in national government not to allow the film to defame their race. And yet the movie, with its characterisations, codes, language and lines, impinged upon popular consciousness. Brando's Don Vito, with his hoarse mumblings and saggy cheeks, became the archetypal gangster, the memories of explosive pint-pots like Cagney and Robinson dispensed with instantly.

Set in the decade following the end of World War II, Gordon Willis' buttery photography and Nino Rota's nostalgic score beautifully recreate the 1940s. Acknowledging its debt to previous gangster films, an elaborate montage of newspaper headlines (partly designed by George Lucas) is included, while cameos for Richard Conte and Sterling Hayden are found, with Coppola mentor and *St. Valentine's Day Massacre* (*qv*) director Roger Corman appearing in *Part II*. The film, and its successor, see the Corleone family as a paradigm for American capitalism – survival of the fittest, the ruthless annihilation of critics and an accumulation of power and wealth. Numerous crimes are committed in the name of the

The Godfather: Luca Brasi (Lenny Montana) receives an offer he can't really refuse.

Family, an indivisible loyal commitment to the concept of the male-dominated familial structure. Personal feeling infiltrates everything; business is family business. The family becomes a microcosm for the world at large; the Don's private system of justice, with its quasi-confessional feel, reflects both the temporal and spiritual aspects to life. Ultimately, he is the man that must protect his kin from the hostile world. For a generation of film-goers *The Godfather* was the ultimate expression of the souring and hypocrisy of the American way of life.

The Godfather Part II. As Coppola told *Time*: 'Right under the surface is a loose metaphor for America. Like Michael, we all have blood on our hands.' The only sequel ever to win Best Picture, Coppola saw it more as a continuation, a process of evil reverberating over generations, just as this film in each scene would recall a shot or moment of dialogue from the original ('the first film ought to haunt the second like a spectre' said the director). Structurally wrapping itself around *The Godfather, Part II*, now with the courage to use the words 'Mafia' and 'Cosa Nostra', expands its canvas, examining the rise and fall of the family as a metaphor for modern American history. Michael's decline into paranoia recalls McCarthyism; Roth's Miami airport assassination a reconstruction of Jack Ruby's murder of Lee Harvey Oswald; the Senate hearings smack of Watergate; the Cuban episode a comment on the American support of Third World dictators – a place, as Roth notes, beyond the reach of Kefauver, who had exposed a network of crime syndicates back in 1950. During Michael's period as don, a terrible sense of the world falling apart is felt; while the government collapses in Havana before rebels, the in-laws don't understand Italian. With the symbolic inclusion of the Statue of Liberty in the young Vito's story, the film is a yearning for past ideals, vanished in the wake of drugs, ruthless capitalism and violence. On a more personal level, the sombre lighting of Michael contrasts with the warm, amber lighting of his father. Vito's murderers solicit approval, Michael's (now carried out by others) do not. Vito's 'humanity' is rejected by the new generation, with Michael caught in between Old World values and the postwar American Dream. The saga traces a decline from the Robin

The Godfather Part II: Michael Corleone (Al Pacino) becomes the Don.

Hood-altruism of Vito to the greed and self-interest of his son, his fall Luciferian in stature. Michael loses his faith in the concept of family, even blood (as he orders the death of brother Fredo). Kay's 'miscarriage', Fredo's spouse's alcoholism, Connie's neglect of her children all lead to Michael's increasing sense of loss and alienation: with the final three-way execution of his enemies, he sits alone, his life void of meaning.

Coppola has repeatedly compared himself to Michael. In the way that Michael brought class to the Corleone family, so Coppola would reduce the vulgar elements from the original in this film. Just as his elder brother August was the expected success of the family, so Francis 'stepped over' him, as Michael did to Fredo. He enhanced the comparison: 'I'm a powerful man in charge of an entire production, and my wife... you see, there are personal things that emerge in this film.' Throughout the trilogy, he had used his family as extras, his father even co-composed the score. Uniting the two plots through the theme of generations, the film effortlessly glides between the two time periods (five episodes each, devoted to Vito and Michael), using the image of the child as a thread between cuts. As much then a family portrait as an indictment of the gangster as a symbol for Corporate America, August summarised the project: 'Every aspect of the story is tied into our own family in some way... The irony is that you begin to respond to this Mafia story as a celebration.'

The Godfather Part III. Coppola, after a 16-year gap, was in it for the money. Receiving $5 million plus 15 per cent of the gross, the cash generated was to fund an independent project entitled *Megalopolis*, an epic tracing the parallels between ancient Rome at the time of Cicero and the Catiline conspiracy (63 BC) and the Ed Koch era in New York City. With *The Godfather Part III* going through some 30 script revisions (Coppola requesting six months to write the first draft, getting only six weeks), he told *US Premiere*'s Cyndi Stivers that much of the plot left him cold: 'I really am not interested in gangsters... I always sort of resented that it took up so much of my life and that, you know, it's about shooting people.' Freely admitting at the time that he set the film partly in Italy to stay out of the studio's clutches, this new-found freedom didn't help the final project. Winona Ryder suffered a nervous breakdown one day before she was due to begin filming as Mary; the inexperienced Sofia Coppola took over, and it showed – Pacino and Shire having words with her father over his nepotism. Robert Duvall's Tom Hagen was also written out of the script, Duvall having demanded a $3.5 million fee (with Pacino already getting $5 million).

The film itself echoes its predecessors in structure, opening with yet another gathering – this though to award Michael the highest accolade in the Catholic Church, the order of St. Sebastian. Now set in 1979, Michael is in the state of mind where he wants to resolve what kind of man he was (still haunted by ordering his brother's death, he is in perpetual penance), asking at Don Tommasino's (Vittorio Duse) coffin: 'You were so loved... why was I so feared?' Pregnant with religious imagery, the film attempts to draw comparisons with the Vatican and the Corleone family, just as it did with corporate business. Attempting to invest $500 million in a European Real Estate company in which the Church has a 25 per cent stake, Michael would wipe out much of the $769 million deficit faced by the Church. As a priest tells him, 'The power to absolve debt is greater than the power to absolve sin.' This inclusion would simultaneously wash away his family's dubious history. Moving away from the intimate nature of Parts I and II, the family, like the film, has become fractured and dispersed; Michael's increasing lack of control an echo of Coppola's grip; the concluding opera an unpleasant reminder of the film's hysterics.

* Broadcast by NBC between 12 and 15 November 1977, 'Mario Puzo's *The Godfather* : the complete Novel for Television' was presented. Re-edited in chronological order, with an extra hour's footage included, the programme ran at 7hrs 15mins. With *Part II*'s design originally conceived specifically for this purpose, the telecast now adhered more to Puzo's novel, ending not with the telling close-up of Michael, but of Kay in worship.

Additional scenes include Brando's Don Vito listening to Hagen's report about his unsuccessful negotiations with Woltz in Hollywood; Vito also disposes of two men in Sicily who had been involved in the murder of his father; Michael, as Don, is also shown speaking to a wealthy suitor of Sonny's daughter, Francesca, urging him not to be ashamed of his fortune.

* **Academy Awards:** *The Godfather* – Best Picture
Marlon Brando won for Best Actor
Francis Ford Coppola & Mario Puzo won for Best Adapted Screenplay

Part II Best Picture
Robert De Niro won for Best Supporting Actor
Francis Ford Coppola won for Best Director
Nino Rota & Carmine Coppola won for Best Score
George R. Nelson and Dean Tavoularis won for Best Art Direction
Francis Ford Coppola & Mario Puzo won for Best Adapted Screenplay

See also: *Brotherhood, The; Freshman, The*

Godfather of Harlem, The: See Black Caesar.

Godson, The: See Le Samourai.

SOLIHULL S.F.C.
LIBRARY

Goodfellas

(US, Warner Brothers, 1990, 145 mins)

'I know... there were film-makers and critics who felt I was morally irresponsible to make a film like Goodfellas. Well, I'll make more of them if I can.'
(Martin Scorsese, *Sight & Sound*)

Credits
Dir/Scr: Martin Scorsese
Prod: Irwin Winkler
Scr: Nicholas Pileggi
DOP: Michael Ballhaus
Ed: Thelma Schoonmaker
Prod. Dir: Maher Ahmad, Bruce S. Pustin, Kristi Zea

Cast: Robert De Niro (Jimmy Conway), Ray Liotta (Henry Hill), Joe Pesci (Tommy DeVito), Lorraine Bracco (Karen Hill), Paul Sorvino (Paul Cicero), Frank Vincent (Billy Batts)

Three decades of life in the Mafia.

The synopsis says it all. Based on Nicholas Pileggi's non-fiction account of Mafia foot-soldier-turned FBI informant Henry Hill, Scorsese initiates us in 'the life', as no other gangster picture ever has. Hill's opening voice-over candidly states: 'As far back as I can remember, I always wanted to be a gangster.' By the end of the picture, so do we.

Merging the spirit of docudrama detail with techniques of the Nouvelle Vague, in particular Truffaut's use of stills in *Jules et Jim*, Scorsese creates a dialectic between the objective and subjective – a love/hate relationship epitomising the amoral, non-judgmental stance of the film, typified in the scene where psychotic hood Tommy, midway through regaling his crew with an anecdote, turns on Hill for calling him 'Funny'. Laughter and violence have never been so dangerously intertwined. As onlookers we are appalled – not at Tommy – but at our own seduction, as this juxtaposition, so typical of Scorsese's technique, truly turns us on. Described by Scorsese as 'not a Hollywood movie [but] an in-spite-of-Hollywood movie', it takes the traditions of the American gangster film apart; the end credits song, Sid

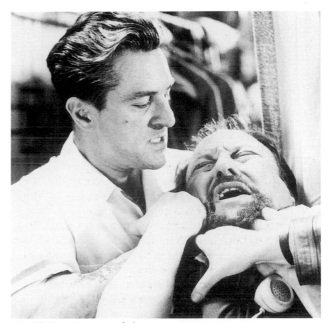

Goodfellas: 'Give me my fuckin' money!' Jimmy Conway (Robert De Niro) strangles Morris Kessler (Charles Low) with a telephone wire.

Vicious's idiosyncratic version of *My Way*, is as much as sign of defiance as the brief beyond-the-grave appearance of Tommy firing a gun to camera. Hill's daydream has come and gone (ending the film on a Witness Protection Programme, living in suburbia 'like a schnook'); there is no moral growth, only a yearning for the high life once again. An extreme example of self-conscious realism, Scorsese's exuberant filmic vocabulary (freeze-frames, fluid steadicam and swooping tracking shots) comment upon the life as much as the poignantly assembled soundtrack. Both express a simplicity to the hierarchical and structural order of the film and its motley crew. Tony Bennett croons *Rags to Riches*, while minutes later we watch in horror as the camera freezes upon Henry receiving a beating from his father. Intense, defining moments from a world with its own primitive sense of law and order – 'You get outta line, you got whacked.' Charting 30 years in the life of Hill, which included organising the record-breaking $6 million Lufthansa heist, the film plays like a history of

The Grifters: Mother love: Roy Dillon (John Cusack) and Lily Dillon (Angelica Huston) get too close for comfort.

postwar American consumer culture, as one critic noted. From the romanticism and naiveté of the fifties (echoed by the young Henry's childlike wish to be a wiseguy), through to the disillusionment felt in the post-Nixon era (shown by Hill's physical deterioration via cocaine abuse), Hill becomes a mirror held up to American society, its rise and fall, its innocence corrupted.

* **Academy Award**: Joe Pesci won for Best Supporting Actor.

See also: *Bronx Tale, A*; *Casino*.

Grifters, The

(US, Miramax, 1990, 114 mins)

Credits
Dir: Stephen Frears
Prod: Martin Scorsese, Barbara de Fina, Robert A. Harris, James Painten, Peggy Rajski
Scr: Donald E. Westlake, based on the novel by Jim Thomson
DOP: Oliver Stapleton
Ed: Mick Audsley
Music: Elmer Bernstein

Art Dir: Leslie McDonald
Cast: John Cusack (Roy Dillon), Annette Bening (Myra Langtry), Anjelica Huston (Lilly Dillon), Pat Hingle (Bobo Justus), Henry Jones (Desk Clerk), J.T. Walsh (Cole)

The story of three con artists (a mother, son and his girlfriend), the first of whom works for the mob.

Scripted by Donald E. Westlake, who wrote – under the pseudonym Richard Stark – the novel that inspired John Boorman's *Point Blank* (*qv*), this is a film not so concerned with the scam, but – as *Film Comment*'s Maitland McDonagh puts it – 'it's a film about passing. Not passing for white, but passing for bourgeois, passing for rich, passing for respectable, passing for family, passing for friends.' Ensuring that racetrack odds are lowered to protect bookies against long-shot winners, Lilly (suffocating mother to short-con operator Roy) spends her time at the tracks strategically placing bets, while skimming mob money on the side for her own nest egg. Bobo Justus, her mob-connected boss present on the fringes of the film, reminds them of the prizes and penalties of moving into the big time. When the betting goes awry, he has no qualms about punching Lilly in the stomach, burning her hand with a cigar or threatening to hit her with a potentially haemorrhaging orange wrapped in a towel. But, in line with the love-hate triangle that exists at the eye of the film, effects a strangely paternal relationship with her. 'Motherhood!' he exclaims. 'It's a side of you I never knew.' Justus is the oracle, fit for Greek tragedy. The opening three-way split-screen curtain call, demonstrating our three protagonists' belief in the total command of their performances, belies the rest of the film. Unable to resist conning each other but more importantly themselves, so the mechanics take over. As they attempt to escape the life and/or dominate each other, for reasons of revenge, seduction and revulsion, they are helplessly swept to their fates. Lily is the only survivor – but, with Justus alerted by Myra to her scam, will forever live in fear. Roy and Myra (played by Benning who was cast because of her likeness to Gloria Grahame's Debbie, the recipient in *The Big Heat* (*qv*) of a scalding pot of coffee from Lee Marvin) suffer death; the result of selfishness and greed respectively.

Grissom Gang, The

(US, ABC Pictures, 1971, 128 mins)

Credits
Dir/Prod: Robert Aldrich
Scr: Leon Griffiths, based on the novel No Orchids For Miss Blandish by James Hadley Chase
DOP: Joseph Biroc
Ed: Michael Luciano
Music: Gerald Fried
Art Dir: James D. Vance

Cast: Kim Darby (Barbara Blandish), Scott Wilson (Slim Grissom), Tony Musante (Eddie Hagan), Irene Dailey (Ma Grissom), Robert Lansing (Dave Fenner)

Family of 1920s kidnappers ransom a wealthy debutante.

A re-make of the tawdry 1948 British thriller *No Orchids For Miss Blandish*, itself spawned from the salacious James Hadley Chase novel, Aldrich – who made *Kiss Me Deadly* – directs what is an attempt to appeal to box-office whim, following Corman's *Bloody Mama* and Penn's *Bonnie and Clyde* (*qqv*). At best an off-beat love story between kidnapped beauty Barbara and slow-witted beast Slim, Aldrich peppers the film with quirky, yet strangely fitting, clements. The final shoot-out at the Grissom nightclub, with its careering police cars, is reminiscent of the Keystone cops; the nouveau riche 'luxury' room decorated for Blandish by Slim is a camp riot of art-deco styles, right down to the gold-leaf embossed fixtures. Irene Dailey's Ma is, at once, ruthless and homely, baking cookies then stating 'After we get the dough, we kill the girl.' These plot elements point towards the central theme, that of the family and its breakdown. While the Grissoms ostensibly appear a solid unit, the boys' sexual deviances and Ma's penchant for violence ensure that the Grissoms are a perverse reflection of the American way of life. Meanwhile, Blandish's father – a millionaire and prominent Missouri socialite – while representing the respectable well-to-dos, is shown to have even less capacity for love than the Grissoms. On her return, her father is horrified at her surroundings: 'I was only trying to stay alive,' she protests. 'Was it worth it?' he coldly replies.

See also: *Big Bad Mama*; *Big Bad Mama II*; *Boxcar Bertha*.

Gun Crazy
(Original US Title: Deadly is the Female)

(US, United Artists, 1949, 87 mins)

Credits
Dir: Joseph H. Lewis
Prod: Frank King, Maurice King
Scr: MacKinlay Kantor, Millard Kaufman
DOP: Russell Harlan
Ed: Harry Gerstad
Music: Victor Young
Art Dir: Gordon Wiles

Cast: Peggy Cummins (Annie Laurie Starr), John Dall (Bart Tare), Berry Kroeger (Packet), Morris Carnovsky (Judge Willoughby), Anabel Shaw (Ruby Tare)

A World War II veteran and a carnival sharp-shooter embark on a crime spree.

Widely regarded as a minor classic, Lewis's B picture, with its couple-on-the-run dressed in trenchcoats and dark glasses, was a probable influence on *A Bout de Souffle*, Jean-Luc Godard's own take on this most austere of sub-genres (Nicholas Ray and Fritz Lang also contributing with *They Live By Night* (*qv*) and *You Only Live Once*). Lewis's film is best described as a Freudian tragedy in which the lovers – a principally good but cowardly male, and a dominant, even demonic, female – head towards self-destruction, neither strong enough to halt the other. Rife with sexual tension (the shooting contest becomes a firework display of sexual desire), Lewis encouraged this, directing their first encounter by telling the actors: 'Remember, you're a female dog on heat, he's a male dog, and you're just all around him.' Along with the rather phallic obsession with the gun (Bart repeatedly cleans his), the film revels in role reversal, dressing its female lead in trousers and even getting the characters to swap clothes at one point. Not gangsters as such, more desperadoes, Annie still demonstrates the take-what-you-desire ethos ('I don't want to be afraid of life') that drives all mob men to seek fortune. Her character gleefully threatens to overthrow the cultural and sexual certainties afforded to women in middle American life.

With Lewis distinctly improving the original shooting script with scene improvisation, several scenes enhanced the film's reputation considerably. The Hampton Savings and Loan Company robbery allows the camera to accompany the couple as they nervously drive towards the bank, wondering if they are to find a parking place. While the hold-up is performed by Bart, Annie flirts with a policeman, only to clobber him as Bart emerges allowing for their getaway. All is filmed in only one take, in an actual location using members of the public as unsuspecting extras – both Cummins and Dall had no idea when driving into town if they really would be able to park. By contrast, the second robbery (of the Meat-Packing factory) is fragmented, panicky in style – both indicating through rhythmical variations the tensions between the self-effacing Bart and the predatory Annie. The final scene in the swamp is another inspired set-piece. A third key moment in their relationship, after firstly Annie persuades him that crime is the only option, and Bart to his disgust later realises 'we're killers', the scene takes on a dreamlike quality – enforcing Bart's feeling 'that nothing is real anymore... the rest is a nightmare'. He and Annie are excluded from the rest of the world – just as she, travelling circus trick shot, and he, as an ex-reform school inmate, were always destined to be outsiders.

Guys and Dolls

(US, Samuel Goldwyn, 1955, 150 mins)

Credits
Dir/Scr: Joseph L. Mankiewicz, based on the original play by Jo Swerling and Abe Burrows from a story by Damon Runyon
Prod: Samuel Goldwyn
DOP: Harry Stradling
Ed: Daniel Mandell

Music/Songs: Frank Loesser, Jay Blackton
Prod. Des: Oliver Smith
Cast: Marlon Brando (Sky Masterton), Jean Simmons (Sarah Brown), Frank Sinatra (Nathan Detroit), Vivian Blaine (Adelaide), Robert Keith (Lt. Brannigan)

A New York hustler, who maintains a 'floating crap game', seeks a location and cash for his latest, and highest stake, scam – raising money by betting that a fellow gambler cannot romance a Salvation Army member.

Beginning life as two short stories from Damon Runyon, the most prominent of which was *The Idyll of Miss Sarah Brown*, it became a two-act libretto by Abe Burrows and Jo Swerling – then set to music by Frank Loesser and directed by George Kaufman – and rose to become one of Broadway's hottest shows. In what was Samuel Goldwyn's penultimate film (his swansong *Porgy and Bess* would prove disastrous), all the lavish components one came to expect from the producer were present, in particular the girls and the large, extravagant sets (including Oliver Smith's stylised version of Times Square). Casting non-musical screen stars in major roles proved a successful experiment, with Brando pulling off the numbers admirably, in his role as the high-stakes compulsive gambler Sky Masterton sent to woo stuffy Jean Simmons. While the artificial feel to the studio sets (check out Havana) rubs rather against the naturalistic turns of Brando and Sinatra (whose part was expanded, with Loesser contributing another number *Adelaide*), and the double-wedding finale smacks of gross sentimentality, our racketeers achieve at least some verisimilitude to their Warner brothers.

* Goldwyn considered in 1992 remaking the film, having already planned – in the 1970s – an all-black version, to be directed by Bob *All That Jazz* Fosse.

See also: *Bugsy Malone*; *Love Me or Leave Me*; *Pocketful of Miracles, A.*

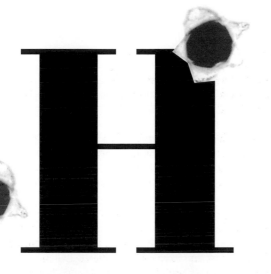

Hard Boiled (Lat Sau San Tam)

(Hong Kong, Milestone Pictures, 1992, 126 mins)

Credits
Dir/Ed: John Woo
Prod: Linda Kuk, Terence Chang
Scr: Barry Wong
DOP: Wong Wing-Heng
Ed: Kit Wai Kai, David Wu
Music: Michael Gibbs
Art Dir: James Leung, Joel Chong

Cast: Chow Yun-Fat (Inspector 'Tequila' Yuen), Tong Leung (Tony), Teresa Mo (Teresa), Philip Chan (Superintendent Chan), Anthony Wong (Johnny Wong)

Hong Kong arms smugglers, hiding a huge ammo dump under a hospital, are pursued from the outside by a maverick cop, while an undercover man masquerades as an assassin from within.

John Woo's Eastern swan-song, before wasting his evident talent in Hollywood on the likes of *Broken Arrow*, is technically the culmination of the pyrotechnical, frenetic style that had become his trademark. While *Screen International*'s Leonard Klady called it 'more fun than being in a toy store', echoing much of the deserved praise heaped upon the film for its expertly choreographed shootouts, Woo received criticism for his failure to develop the characters' relationships as he did in *The Killer* (qv), instead contriving a plot to set up the next big action set-piece. *Sight & Sound*'s Tom Tunney went so far as to draw the comparison between the anonymous, disposable villains of Woo's work with the showgirls of a Busby Berkeley musical, leaving him not in the territory of Peckinpah but of the synthetic and safe 'action' category.

Woo does try to create, in the character of the undercover Tony, the contradictions of gangster and cop, leading him to admit '[I was] so busy being a gangster, I don't know which me is real'. Every time he kills, he makes a paper crane to celebrate the fact. Questions of identity are raised: Chow Yun-Fat's 'Tequila' says of his partner/rival: 'He's not really a criminal, but not really a cop.' Tony, later, enforces this himself: 'To you I'm a thief, to my mother a son, to the Triads a hero.' Yet this internal division of the self leads nowhere, lost as it is in the explosive finale.

What Woo does achieve is a nod towards the economics of gang war. 'Most things will go in and out of fashion – except war,' comments Boss Wong wryly, adding later that rival Hoi's low prices are destroying his market. The pressures of supply and demand ensure capitalists and gangsters become inseparable.

Far better than his attempt at humanising his characters, Woo draws distinctions between the Triad bosses Johnny Wong and Uncle Hoi, who demonstrate opposing attitudes to their work. Wong is of the new school – 'In this world, the man who holds the gun wins', whereas Hoi is old fashioned: 'I know that respect and face are final.' With the triumph of the younger generation, Woo recognises his place within the genre. His is a very modern gangster film, where moral values are indistinct, and respect is a redundant word.

* An appalling sequel, *Hard Boiled 2: The Last Blood*, directed by Wong Ching, followed, bearing little resemblance to its predecessor. Tracing the Japanese army, out to assassinate religious leader the Daka (sic) Lama on the 25th National Day of Singapore, its one highlight has a character selling memorabilia of the stars, including the watch of Chow Yun-Fat!

See also: Better Tomorrow, A.

Harder They Come, The

(Jamaica, International Films, 1972, 110 mins)

'[It's] a deeply subversive film because it attacks the whole basis of the commercial society... the next revolution has to be a cultural revolution, for people.'

(Perry Henzell, *Cinema Rising*)

Credits
Dir/Prod/Scr: Perry Henzell
Scr: Trevor D. Rhone
DOP: Frank St. Juste, Peter Jessop, David MacDonald
Ed: John Victor Smith, Reicland Anderson, Richard White
Music: Jimmy Cliff, Desmond Dekker
Art Dir: Sally Henzell

Cast: Jimmy Cliff (Ivan), Carl Bradshaw (Jose), Basil Keane (Preacher), Janet Bartley (Elsa), Bobby Charlton (Recording Company Manager)

Country boy comes to the big city and gets involved in violence, dope peddling and racketeering.

The first Jamaican feature film ever made, the opening night in Kingston, Jamaica, saw over 6,000 people swarm up from West Kingston to the capital's largest theatre, The Carib, break in and occupy it – with only eight of the original 200 VIPs invited managing to get in. Even star Jimmy Cliff was stranded a quarter of a mile away. Such was the excitement created over the first film entirely produced, acted and directed by Jamaicans. Conceived by BBC-trained director Perry Henzell as the first part of a trilogy (the third to be based on his own novel *Power Game*), the film was released in its home country uncut – underlining its uncompromising nature. With subtitles added to translate the Jamaican dialogue, the film sings its post-Colonial national pride; we either accept the Jamaican experience or not.

The film is partially based on the life of Raz Daniel Hartman (aka Raigan), who terrorized Kingston circa 1960. A member of the secret Rasta organisation, he was imprisoned, brutalised and became a national hero subsequent to his death at the hands of the police. The plot mechanics were also suggested by the life of Jimmy Cliff himself (who was, like Ivan,

exploited having cut his first disc). Singer-pusher Ivan is part folk-hero, part media-manipulator, singing 'You Can Get It If You Really Want' as he evades the capitalist record producer hoping to cash in on his success. His penchant for sending photographs to the newspaper of himself dressed in a cowboy outfit suggests a love of image and notoriety, modelling himself on the Man With No Name. Both he and the song become symbols of resistance. Ivan himself is a Robin Hood, an incarnation of this early gangster. He becomes an American-Jamaican hybrid, straddling church music and reggae, the Shanty towns and luxury villas, the 'missionary' religion and the native Rastafarian sect. At once a critique of Colonial rule and an advocation of the American dream, the film alternates between anger and humour. As Henzell told *Cinema Rising*'s Martin Hayman: 'It's a film in which the fantasy of the celluloid and the reality of everyday life constantly overlap.'

* Henzell, while shooting in the slums, had to make contact with local gang The Spanglers, in order to get their go-ahead to film. The Jamaican government also interfered during filming on several occasions because it recognised the picture's outright insurrectionist tone.

Hard Men

(UK/France, Dacia Films/Venture Movies, 1996, 85 mins)

'It might also serve as a good indication of what film students are up to currently.'

(David Tse, *Sight & Sound*)

Credits
Dir./Prod./Scr: J.K. Amalou
Prod: Georges Benayoun
DOP: Nick Sawyer
Ed: Victoria Boydell
Music Sup: Nicola Fletcher
Prod. Des: Simon Elliott

Cast: Vincent Regan (Tone), Ross Boatman (Bear), Lee Ross (Speed), 'Mad' Frankie Fraser (Pops Den), Ken Campbell (Mr Ross), Mirella D'Angelo (Chantal)
Two gangland collectors are instructed to kill off their

friend and third member of the group, after he decides to quit the life for the ex-girlfriend and baby who have just reappeared on the scene.

Branded as sub-Tarantino material, *Hard Men* was unable to resist the lure of pop culture banter, lurid café and bathroom sequences, dismemberment and intertextual reference points, namely *Get Carter, Mean Streets* and Tarantino's own *Pulp Fiction* (*qqv*). Add the use of 'Mad' Frankie Fraser, a former member of London's notorious Richardson gang (echoing the stunt Tarantino pulled with the use of Eddie Bunker as *Reservoir Dogs*' [*qv*] Mr Blue), and the Hollywood calling-card is complete.

In saying that, this uneven 24-hour crawl around Soho's seemingly lawless landscape is full of zest, steered by fledgling Amalou somewhere between pastiche and fable. Bear's weight problem and Tone's lust for suburbia, singing his baby to sleep over a mobile phone, disarms the hard man image. A unique touch, and an ironic jibe towards the traditional mould that has shaped the British celluloid gangster.

Harlem Nights

(US, Paramount, 1989, 116 mins)

> '*Harlem Nights* remains a cumbersome monument to one man's swelling ego, and rapidly dwindling comic charm. With black directors blithely recycling such brain-dead stereotypes, who needs mainstream Hollywood ignorance? To paraphrase *Public Enemy*, it takes a nation of Spike Lees to redress the balance.'
>
> **(Jonathan Romney, City Limits)**

Credits
Dir./Scr. Eddie Murphy
Prod: Robert D. Wachs
DOP: Woody Omens
Ed: George Bowers
Music: David Allen Jones
Prod. Dir: Larry Paul

Cast: Eddie Murphy (Quick), Richard Pryor (Sugar Ray), Redd Foxx (Bernie Wilson), Danny Aiello (Phil Cantone), Michael Lerner

(Bugsy Calhoune)

A black 1930s nightclub owner stands up to a white mobster intent on muscling in on his territory.

A real shot in the foot for Eddie Murphy, this foul-mouthed and inarticulate 'comedy' does little for its director-star, or a catatonic Richard Pryor. Murphy plays Quick ('Quick, like in quick to whip someone's ass' – see what I mean?), rather PC it would seem, telling his cohorts to 'get out of the jungle' when they discuss the Creole nationality of Dominique. Further racial issues are grossly over-simplified; a white runner for Bugsy (our boys' chief rival) comments to Sunshine (Lela Rochon): 'Normally, I wouldn't consider a black girl.' While this touches on *The Cotton Club* (*qv*) territory (the notorious club where blacks could perform but not watch), such lines are never pursued, or if so, only flippantly in embarrassingly prolonged skitlets.

Evocative production design and Herbie Hancock music aside, the film bears little resemblance to what we know of 1930s Harlem. An uncalled for moral sense, drawing the line between big-time operators and club-owners, is also tentatively drawn. As Pryor says to Murphy: 'We're not gangsters, we're club owners.' As Murphy has recently acquired a gun and expresses a desire to use it, this seems a mite incorrect. Or maybe that's irony.

See also: *Hoodlum.*

Heat

(US, Forward Pass Productions, 1995, 172 mins)

Credits
Dir./Prod./Scr: Michael Mann
Prod: Art Linson
DOP: Dante Spinotti
Ed: Dov Hoenig, Pasquale Buba, William Goldenberg, Tom Rolf
Music: Elliot Goldenthal
Prod. Des: Neil Spisak

Cast: Robert De Niro (Neil McCauley), Al Pacino (Vincent Hanna), Val Kilmer (Chris Shiherlis), Jon Voight (Nate), Tom Sizemore

Heat: Neil McCauley (Robert De Niro) and Chris Shiherlis (Val Kilmer) turn on the heat.

(Michael Cheritto), Ashley Judd (Charlene), Amy Brenneman (Eady)

An obsessive cop hunts the leader of a gang of professional thieves.

'I do what I do best: I take scores. You do what you do best: you try to stop guys like me.'
At the centre of Michael Mann's sprawling crime/heist epic, the cop/criminal struggle is refined to its bare essentials. Both homicide cop Hanna ('All I am is what I'm going after') and his nemesis McCauley, a single-minded loner, admit in the infamous (and curiously intimate) coffee-shop scene, they can do no other job, nor would they want to. McCauley sneers at regular life – 'barbecues and ball games' – extolling the credo 'Allow nothing to be in your life that you can't walk out on in 30 seconds flat if you spot the heat around the corner.' But his desire to be with young graphic designer Eady, and Hanna's dysfunctional marriage, flesh out the latter's comment: 'You and I are like a couple of regular fellas.' They share, as Mann noted, 'commonality', symbolised by the scene at the refinery, where Hanna tries to guess what McCauley has been looking at, by standing in his exact spot, only to realise it was him. Both minds are grafted from the same stock. Mann suggests this manhunt is a modern-day equivalent to his Mohicans and Hurons from *The Last of the Mohicans* (partly through casting Wes Studi in both works). Shot in the urban jungle of LA, a 'dead tech post-modern' version of John Huston's own heist effort *The Asphalt Jungle* (qv), Mann recognises his men, criminal and cop, as predatory hunters,

with the heist (or prevention of it) as the prize.

* The film was a virtual remake of Mann's earlier, less successful film, *LA Takedown*.

See also: *Criss-Cross*; *Face*; *Killing, The*; *Reservoir Dogs*; *Taking of Pelham 123, The*; *Usual Suspects, The*.

Hell Up In Harlem: See Black Caesar.

High Sierra

(US, Warner Brothers, 1941, 100 mins)

Credits
Dir./Prod./Scr: Raoul Walsh
Exec. Prod. Hal B.Wallis
Scr: John Huston, W.R. Burnett, based on Burnett's own novel
DOP: Tony Gaudio
Ed: Jack Killifer

Music: Adolph Deutsch
Art Dir: Ted Smith

Cast: Humphrey Bogart (Roy Earle), Ida Lupino (Marie Garson), Arthur Kennedy (Red), Alan Curtis (Babe), Joan Leslie (Velma), Henry Hull (Doc Banton)

In the Sierra Mountains, Nevada, an ageing gangster — while planning a daring raid on a Californian resort — befriends a family, and financially assists their daughter's operation, only to suffer unrequited love.

Raoul Walsh, whose early work had included the Charles Butterworth gangster parody *Baby Face Harrington*, went onto make a trio of classic contributions to the genre. After *The Roaring Twenties* and before *White Heat* (qqv) came *High Sierra*, the vehicle that finally cemented Humphrey Bogart's reputation as a major league player. Both James Cagney and Edward G. Robinson had passed on the part of 'Mad Dog' Roy Earle, as did George Raft, reportedly because he would not consent to play another character who died on screen, but

High Sierra: Earle (Humphrey Bogart) spreads the word.

Bogart, at his most surly, provided the right balance of defiance and strength.

In some respects, *High Sierra* is a lament for the Cagney/Robinson/Raft era – 'All the A1 guys are gone: dead or in Alcatraz. Sometimes I feel I don't know what it's about any more.' Bogart, since his emergence from an eight-year prison stretch has to contend with young 'soda drinkers', and as a result remains loyal to Big Mack, the racketeer setting up the El Tropico resort job. Yet Earle is not a city-slick underworld man of the thirties. Drawn with complexity, he is as cruel as he is compassionate, as ready to show affection to a dog as to strike a deal with his girl to 'pop' [kill] her if he wants. He is a desperado, a modern-day outlaw in the mould of Clyde Barrow or John Dillinger, using crime as a means of survival. As the Doctor reminds Bogart, quoting Dillinger's comment about people such as himself, he is 'Just rushing towards death'.

This is lived out through the central theme of incarceration. After his release, Bogart is taunted by nightmares, mumbling in his sleep about 'crashing out' [escaping]. Marie, Earle's second-choice partner, having suffered rejection from Velma, compares this to her own life, forever 'escaping' from scenarios with which she finds it difficult to cope. Characters are on the run from life, prompting Marie to ask 'What does it mean when a man crashes out?' and concluding that, as Earle is shot by local lawmen in the mountains, 'It means he's free.' The radio news report's running commentary in the finale stresses that the landscape, which includes one of the highest peaks in the USA, becomes Earle's judge, jury, executioner and even prison – but through death he finds a spiritual freedom, escaping from his physical self and the desires/needs that drove him to crime.

* The film was faithfully remade in 1955 by Stuart Heisler, entitled *I Died A Thousand Times*. Jack Palance took the Humphrey Bogart role, with Shelley Winters assuming the part vacated by Ida Lupino. Produced on a lush budget, incorporating colour photography, the film is noteworthy mainly for an early appearance by Lee Marvin and a cameo by Lon Chaney, who played 'Big Mack', the dying gangster who engineers Earle's release from prison.

See also: *Bonnie and Clyde*; *Dillinger*.

Hit, The

(UK, Zenith/Central Productions, 1984, 98 mins)

Credits
Dir: Stephen Frears
Prod: Jeremy Thomas
Scr: Peter Prince
DOP: Mike Molloy
Ed: Mick Audsley
Music: Eric Clapton, Paco de Lucia
Prod. Des: Andrew Sanders

Cast: John Hurt (Braddock), Tim Roth (Myron), Terence Stamp (Willie Parker), Bill Hunter (Harry), Laura Del Sol (Maggie), Lennie Peters (Mr Corrigan)

Two hitmen track down a stool-pigeon, now living a self-imposed exile in Spain ten years after his betrayal.

Produced by Jeremy Thomas, Nicolas Roeg's producer for *Bad Timing* and *Eureka*, it has been suggested by *Sight & Sound*'s Richard Combs that *The Hit* 'could be ascribed to a producer following an (absent) director whom he in turn may have influenced'. Certainly, links to Roeg's own surreal gangster flick *Performance* (*qv*) exist – namely the fractured shots of Braddock moments before executing Parker, recalling the earlier film's structural dismemberment. The Hurt/Stamp doppelgänger theme, brought on by Myron's comparison, also reflects the Jagger/Fox symbiosis. More obviously, Stamp – with his metaphysical preparations for the afterlife – recalls Leslie Howard's philosophic Alan Squier in *The Petrified Forest* (*qv*), as he attempts to unnerve his captors by calmly accepting his fate. While the apocalyptic nature of the dialogue suggests something more than what it actually is – a conventional road movie – the film casts an eye over the changing nature of British life. From the wishful mysticism and breezy violence of the sixties, the abrupt cut to the selfish, cynical eighties indicates obliteration. The chorus of 'We'll Meet Again', sung at Parker in his courtroom appearance, harks for a nostalgia further afield but this is wishful thinking. Times have changed.

Symbolised by an early hyperactive performance by Tim Roth as the novice bullyboy sidekick, who carries a sand-filled kosh and wears razor-blades in his lapels, he is the archetypal lager lout on holiday. The opposite to Hurt's introspective hit man or Stamp's cultivated traveller, he represents a change from the loveable wideboy two decades before to the impulsive sociopath of the time; a view in itself a comment of the transient nature of 'the times'.

Hoodlum

(US, Universal, 1997, 142 mins)

Credits
Dir: Bill Duke
Prod: Frank Mancuso Jr
Scr: Chris Brancato
DOP: Frank Tidy
Ed: Harry Keramidas
Music: Elmer Bernstein
Prod. Des: Charles Bennett

Cast: Larry Fishburne (Ellsworth 'Bumpy' Johnson), Tim Roth (Dutch Schultz), Andy Garcia (Lucky Luciano), Vanessa Williams (Francine Hughes), Cicely Tyson (Madame Queen), Richard Bradford (Captain Foley)

The relationship between the Harlem community and gangster Dutch Schultz, who aimed to operate the city's only illegal lottery.

Disappointing and woefully inaccurate spin on the Luciano/Schultz story from the director who used actor Fishburne to much better advantage in his dark drugs cartel tale *Deep Cover*. Duke ensures the film is rooted in routine Warner Brothers stylistics, the montage sequence (complete with calendar dates, newspaper clippings and various murders) the most obvious. Later influences upon the film must include *The Godfather Part III* (qv), with an ambush sequence cut to an operatic performance. References to the Depression, The Cotton Club and the numbers racket contextualise the film, as ex-con 'Bumpy' re-emerges in his neighbourhood to fight off control from Schultz. While the plot hurriedly slides 'Bumpy' further along the downward morality spiral ('I'm a coloured man and the white folks haven't left me nothing but the underworld'), Frank Tidy's repeated use of slow-motion photography ensures we see the designer violence (including a shot of a man's severed testicles) in full glory.

Of most interest is Roth's portrayal of Schultz as an unhinged control freak, complete with Cheshire cat smile. But towards the final quarter the quarrel between Schultz and 'Bumpy' (managing Harlem bigwig Madame Queen's affairs while she resides in jail) simply alternates scenes of violent retribution between the two, until finishing with a downbeat double cross and assassination for Schultz.

See also: *Billy Bathgate*; *The Cotton Club*; *Harlem Nights*.

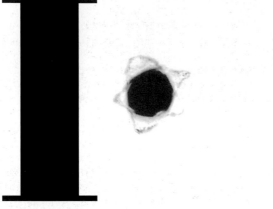

I

I'm Gonna Git You, Sucka

(US, Ivory Way/Raymond Katz Productions, 1988, 89 mins)

'I think Mississippi Burning is exploitation. That's true exploitation when you take someone's history, meddle with it and change all the facts. Totally different to gangster movies which were really just bad films.'
(Keenan Ivory Wayans, *City Limits*)

Credits:
Dir./Scr: Keenan Ivory Wayans
Prod: Peter McCarthy, Carol Craig
DOP: Tom Richmond
Ed: Michael R. Miller
Music: David Michael Frank
Prod. Des: Catherine Hardwicke

Cast: Keenan Ivory Wayans (Jack Spade), Bernie Casey (John Slade), Antonio Fargas (Flyguy), Steve James (Kung Fu Joe), Isaac Hayes (Hammer), Jim Brown (Slammer)

Blaxploitation spoof in which the hero avenges the death of his brother, who died from wearing too many gold chains.

Despite the cycle having long since given up the ghost, the film was the first to mock the Blaxploitation culture with such merciless abandon. Wayans, who went on to formulate the innovative US sketch show *In Living Color* but then best known for co-writing Eddie Murphy's *Raw* and Robert Townsend's satire *Hollywood Shuffle*, cast a number of performers from the era. Unlike *Original Gangstas* (qv), which did the same but took itself far too seriously, Wayans' players get to reverse the type-casting. Isaac Hayes, composer of the 'Theme from Shaft', and star of various Blaxploitation efforts (*Truck Turner*, *Three Good Guys*) finally, for example, gets to play the good guy; Bernie Casey, who featured in *Cleopatra Jones* and *Black Gunn* (qv), Jim Brown, also *Gunn and Slaughter*, and Antonio Fargas, seen in *Shaft* (qv) all get to contribute to spoof the base elements of their own work. This constitutes incoherent jive talk, corrupt and oppressive white law-enforcers, and a perpetual funk soundtrack.

Taking its blueprint from the Zucker Brothers' *Airplane!* series, Wayans was able to mix quickfire gags with current themes, namely a poignant note that black films must progress from this hero-worship cult that surrounds pimps and pushers. With the film contemporary to Spike Lee's early films, and preceding works like *New Jack City* (qv) it apparently worked.

* The film itself underwent severe problems in pre-production. Apart from having to take a serious suggestion that Charles Bronson should appear as the lead, Wayans also was told by one company to write a white half-brother in for lead character Jack Spade, to be played by a white actor who was to pretend to be black!

See also: *Black Caesar*; *Black Godfather*; *Bugsy Malone*; *Freshman, The*; *Hell Up In Harlem*; *Johnny Dangerously*; *Wise Guys*.

Invisible Stripes

(US, Warner Brothers, 1939, 82 mins)

Credits
Dir: Lloyd Bacon
Prod: Louis Edelman
Scr: Warren Duff,
based on the book by Warden Lewis E. Wawes

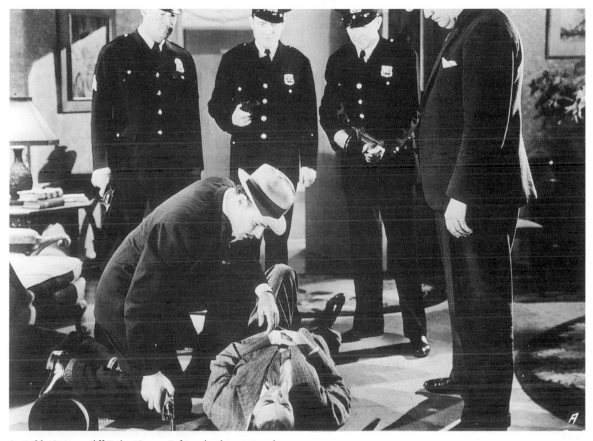

Invisible Stripes: Cliff Taylor (George Raft) makes his exit in style.

DOP: Ernest Haller
Ed: James Gibbon
Music: Heinz Roemheld
Art Dir: Max Parker

Cast: Humphrey Bogart (Chuck Martin), William Holden (Tim Taylor), Jane Bryan (Peggy), Paul Kelly (Ed Kruger), George Raft (Cliff Taylor)

Ex-con, shunned by society, joins a gang to raise enough money to keep his younger brother – attracted to the criminal life – straight.

With Raft, by this point, leaving behind the best roles of his career, and Bogart soon to experience his, both are seen in parts that would soon disappear for them: Raft in the lead (though here largely uninteresting) role, Bogart as the snarling supporting gangster. What might be described as standard Warner Brothers fare (the director having come off the back of plodding gangster efforts like *A Slight Case of Murder* and *Racket Busters*) actually proves rather engaging. A subject that has remained an evergreen for film-makers – the rejection by society at large of the ex-con and his subsequent wavering towards returning to his life of crime – Bacon's film explores these social and psychological scars (the 'invisible' prison stripes of the title) with some success. As with politically conscious films from the early 1930s, such as the Raft-starring *I Was a Fugitive From a Chain Gang*, the film unrelentingly expresses the desperate social and economic conditions of pre-WWII America, and the pressures faced by the working man. The nature of the judiciary system is also commented upon, Raft complaining that the odds are stacked against people like himself (which, ironically, encourages defiant but foolhardy brother Tim to take to crime after financial pressure from his social-climber wife Peggy). Such commentary does, at times, lead to unsubtlety: Raft bumps into his old prison buddie Bogart on the outside, with the latter tempting him back into a life of crime. With the scene set in a cinema foyer, the film showing is Lewis Seiler's *You Can't Get Away With Murder* (released shortly before, and starring Bogart himself), a warning if ever there was one. Equally, after Raft's death, his brother sets up an automobile garage, with 'Taylor Brothers' printed above it. A passer-by states that the other, absent, Taylor must be a silent partner, and the film ends with this decidedly moral signature literally keeping watch over Tim's activities. Only in death does the criminal achieve respectability.

* Rumour had it that Bogart spent so much time needling newcomer co-star William Holden, that the pair nearly came to blows, an animosity that would resurface 14 years later during the making of *Sabrina*.

See also: *Each Dawn I Die*; *Roaring Twenties, The*.

Italian Job, The

(UK, Paramount Pictures, 1969, 100 mins)

> 'Rhythmically organised set pieces, such as Bridger's triumphant march through the prison, suggest that he [Peter Collinson] might one day direct a good musical.'
> **(Monthly Film Bulletin)**

Credits
Dir: Peter Collinson
Prod: Michael Deeley
Scr: Troy Kennedy Martin
DOP: Douglas Slocombe
Ed: John Trumper
Music: Quincy Jones

Prod. Des: Disley Jones

Cast: Michael Caine (Charlie Croker), Noel Coward (Mr Bridger), Benny Hill (Professor Simon Peach), Raf Vallone (Altabani), Irene Handl (Miss Peach), John Le Mesurier (Governor)

Gold bullion heist in Turin, pulled off by causing a city-wide traffic jam.

Beginning the occasional tradition to cast noted English playwrights as gangsters (*Get Carter* would use John Osborne, while Jez Butterworth's *Mojo* [qqv] would use Harold Pinter), this somewhat xenophobic film ascended to cult status mainly due to the presence of Benny Hill, the use of Mini-Coopers for getaway cars and Michael Caine's immortal 'You're only supposed to blow the bloody doors off!'
Patriotic to the hilt (Bridger's excuse for pulling the heist: he's worried about the country's Balance of Payments), the film marked the transition between the loveable Ealing rogues of *The Ladykillers* (qv) and the imminent arrival of the British villain. Bridger and his crew may be a bunch of crafty cocksure lads, but their threat to face the Mafia and 'drive them into the sea' overshadows the film's lighthearted tone. The final scene, as the bus complete with gold teeters over the edge of the cliff, represents the last bastion of British imperialism – 'The self-preservation society' as the theme song blares.

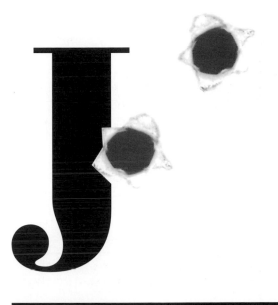

Johnny Apollo

(US, 20th Century Fox, 1940, 94 mins)

Credits
Dir: Henry Hathaway
Prod: Harry Joe Brown, Daryl F. Zanuck
Scr: Rowland Brown, Philip Dunne
DOP: Arthur Miller
Ed: Robert Bischoff
Music: Mack Gordon, Frank Loesser, Alfred Newman, Lionel Newman
Art Dir: Richard Day, Wiard Ihnen

Cast: Tyrone Power (Bob Cain/Johnny Apollo), Dorothy Lamour (Mabel 'Lucky' DuBarry), Edward Arnold (Robert Cain, Snr), Lloyd Nolan (Micky Dwyer), Lionel Atwill (Jim McLaughlin)

A convicted embezzler's son becomes the right-hand man of a local gangster after he is spurned due to his father's reputation.

Twentieth Century-Fox, a studio at the time recognised for its lavish musicals, surprised all with this departure from not only their own favoured material but also the rigours of the genre, as formulated by the first Warner Brothers cycle of gangster films. Moving away from the immigrant image, Apollo is a suave, college-educated man, from a well-to-do family – putting 'his soul in hock' to work for gangster Dwyer in order to secure his father's prison release. Underlying his character though is an empty desire for the fast thrills of the gangster's world, even borrowing his alias 'Apollo' from a tacky neon-lit restaurant sign. The unusual casting of Tyrone Power, in his only gangster film, and musical star Dorothy Lamour – later to go on the road with Bob Hope and Bing Crosby – would also prove rewarding. Lamour, in fact, was the fourth choice for the part of Lucky, gangster Dwyer's girl set to have an affair with Apollo, following Linda Darnell, Nancy Kelly (who had starred with Power in *Jesse James*) and Alice Faye – all deemed unsuitable.

Directed by Henry Hathaway, who would go on to make the original version of *Kiss of Death* (*qv*), the Lamour/Apollo love interest is subdued in favour of the Cain father and son relationship, the elder rejecting his offspring when he discovers he has become 'as big a rat as Dwyer, only smoother'. Touching upon the theme of crime's social stigma (the unemployable Cain Jnr paying for his father's fraud), the film reverses the trend of linking those from poverty-stricken backgrounds with crime; here affluence leads both father and son to corruption. A indictment then of the wealthy classes and the potential harm caused by greed.

See also: *Johnny Eager.*

Johnny Dangerously

(US, 20th Century-Fox, 1984, 90 mins)

Credit
Dir: Amy Heckerling
Prod: Michael Hertzberg
Scr: Norman Steinberg, Bernie Kukoff, Harry Colomby, Jeff Harris
DOP: David M. Walsh
Ed: Pembroke J. Herring
Music: John Morris
Prod. Des: Joseph R. Jennings

Cast: Michael Keaton (Johnny Dangerously), Joe Piscopo (Danny Vermin), Marilu Henner (Lil), Peter Boyle (Jocko Dundee), Griffin Dunne (Tommy), Dom DeLuise (The Pope), Danny DeVito (Burr)

Johnny Apollo: Father to son: Robert Cain Snr (Edward Arnold) lays down the law for Johnny Apollo (Tyrone Power).

Pet store worker recounts his time as big-shot gangster Johnny Dangerously, pursued to the point of arrest by his unsuspecting District Attorney brother.

The fact that the title song was performed by 'Weird' Al Yankovich, and the piece was directed by Amy Heckerling, later to go on to make the teen-Jane Austen satire *Clueless* should indicate what to expect. This odd bag of David Zucker slapstick, gangster spoof and puerile farce, with a wraparound morality tale for good measure, is uneven but shows a passing knowledge of the milieu.

Along with hoods carrying .88 Magnums (that shoot 'through schools'), machine-gun paced dialogue exchange, and recollections of the 'Mother's Day Massacre' Heckerling stuffs in as many nods to the genre as possible. Keaton's apartment block – called 'Gangster's Arms' – contains mail boxes for 'Legs and Shirley Diamond', while Mrs Al Capone pops round to borrow a cup of bullets... you get the idea.

Built around the staple plot points of a 1930s gangster movie, it becomes a crime-doesn't-pay tale, as Lower-East side guy makes good, but repents just in time. From the raping of the Dillinger myth, as a character is to be killed watching a gangster film – *The Roaring Twenties* rather than *Manhattan Melodrama*, to the mother fixation of *White Heat* (*qqv*), specific parallels are drawn – though rarely with any subtlety. Other conventions are also used and abused: the newspaper headline, for example, as top Italian mobster Roman Moronie (bearing an uncanny, and probably intentional, resemblance to

Groucho Marx) is blown up. 'This is fargin' war,' he cries, and the paper repeats the phrase to the letter. Attitudes to women also: 'Dames are put on this earth to weaken us – drain our energy.' Occasionally funny – 'What other gang in New York has a dental plan?' asks Keaton – and sometimes downright odd, as with the short health-awareness film ('Your testicles and you') Johnny shows to his sex-starved brother – the movie is like compass needle held to a magnet, spinning in every direction but the way you want it to go.

See also: *Bugsy Malone*; *Freshman, The*; *I'm Gonna Git You, Sucka*; *Wise Guys*.

Johnny Eager

(US, MGM, 1941, 107 mins)

Credits
Dir: Mervyn LeRoy
Prod: John W. Considine Jr.
Scr: John Lee Mahin, James Edward Grant
DOP: Harold Rossen
Ed: Albert Akst
Music: Broilau Kaper
Art Dir: Cedric Gibbons, Stan Rogers

Cast: Robert Taylor (Johnny Eager), Lana Turner (Lisbeth Bard), Van Helfin (Jeff Hartnett), Edward Arnold (John Benson Farrell), Robert Sterling (Jimmie Lanthrop)

A gangster seeks revenge upon the prosecuting attorney who sent him to prison, by romancing his daughter and setting her up as a 'murderess'.

Like Twentieth Century-Fox's *Johnny Apollo* (qv) a year earlier, MGM's first entry in the gangster film genre was an original attempt to veer away from the norm. Rather like their debut Horror film *Dr Jekyll and Mr Hyde* (with Spencer Tracey and Ingrid Bergman), the production values were above average, casting the seductive pair of Turner and Taylor – the latter deliberately playing down his pretty-boy image. Director Mervyn Le Roy, who had helmed the seminal *Little Caesar* (qv), also lent the film quality.

Acerbically scripted ('You're not exactly Romeo,' Johnny is told. 'You're not exactly Juliet' he quips back), Taylor relishes his atypical role as the once 'notorious' cold-hearted, detached individual eventually melted by a love for Turner, the girl he frames for revenge. Compared to both Machiavelli and Cyrano de Bergerac (with Turner as Roxanne), a vein of Shakespearean tragedy is also injected into the heart of Eager's character. A theme implicit in Le Roy's *Little Caesar*, the gangster and his ambition and avarice can only lead to a downfall, fate – in this case his love for Turner – the sly catalyst. In particular, *Macbeth* is cited – 'no one of women born' could explain the unselfish act of Turner's ex, Jimmy Courtney, who offers money to take Turner away from the City. Van Helfin's alcoholic Jeff, friend, confidante, chronicler and conscience to Eager completes the analogy, quoting 'I can smile, and while I smile cut your heart out with a bloody axe'. If Eager is the twisted incarnation of the deformed Richard III, he conforms to the inherent nobility expected of the tragic figure. As Helfin, the fool to Eager's Lear, states: 'This guy could've climbed the highest mountain in the world if he'd started on the right one.' What negates the image is the closing shot; an officer, at one point wronged by Eager, comments he was 'just another hood'. Unable to quite match up to the potent figures referenced in the film, he dies an ignominious death.

* **Academy Awards:** Van Helfin won for Best Supporting Actor (the first performer to win an Oscar for a role in a gangster film).

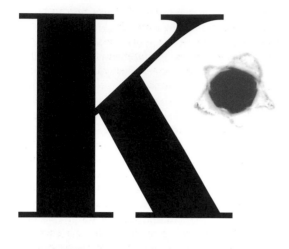

Kansas City

(US, Sandcastle/CiBy 2000, 1996, 115 mins)

*'Kansas City is trademark Altman, a series
of interconnected episodes all linked to one
central theme: the uses and abuses of power.'*
(Todd Boyd, Sight & Sound)

Credits
Dir/Prod/Scr: Robert Altman
Scr: Frank Barhydt
DOP: Oliver Stapleton
Ed: Geraldine Peroni
Prod. Des: Stephen Altman

Cast: Jennifer Jason Leigh (Blondie O'Hara), Miranda Richardson (Carolyn Stilton), Harry Belafonte (Seldom Seen), Michael Murphy (Henry Stilton), Dermot Mulroney (Johnny O'Hara), Steve Buscemi (Johnny Flynn)

In 1934, the laudanum-addicted wife of a presidential advisor is kidnapped, in order to force him to use his influence to ensure the return of the kidnapper's own husband, held captive by a Kansas City black gangster.

Structurally informed by the jazz that flows through the veins of the film, Robert Altman's work transcends the genre features it rigs up by – as he has done since *Nashville* – layering the film with a political conscience. The central kidnap story is the

melody, and connections are woven through a cross section of Kansas City society, from politicians, to white and black racketeers to the maidservant and cleaning lady, with characters flowing in and out, 'performing', as one reviewer noted, 'variations, improvisations and showy riffs'. Circumventing the Richardson/Jason Leigh tale, the sub-strands can free-form chaotically at times in unexpected directions, only drawn together by the statement 'People are consumed by greed... even if they don't need it, they have to have it.'

While Spike Lee's *Mo' Better Blues* and Clint Eastwood's *Bird* put racial issues alongside the music, *Kansas City* goes deeper. Through recreating the jazz milieu, Altman – drawing together a most eclectic choice of contemporary musicians including Joshua Redman, Cyrus Chestnut and Christian McBride – implies that the development of America's highest art form went hand-in-hand with the lawlessness, political corruption and racial problems of the times. Kansas is the conservatory for jazz, but it is the friction of events that inspires the creativity. Hey-Hey Club owner Seldom Seen ('but often heard') is the lynch-pin; in one pertinent sequence, while his venue holds the 'cutting' contest between Coleman Hawkins and Lester Young, Seldom, telling a racist joke, oversees his men brutally murder a cab driver for his part in the duping of Sheepshan Red, a wealthy black government contractor who had come to gamble in the city. Belafonte's Seldom, replete with idiosyncrasies that include transporting his money in a cigar box, is a rare portrayal of a black gangster from the thirties (see also: *Hoodlum*). But with references to Tom Pendergast, vote-rigging and connections to President Roosevelt, Altman's script is careful to indicate that Seldom's influence is localised, and true power exists upon higher levels.

Key Largo

(US, Warner Brothers, 1948, 101 mins)

Credits
Dir/Scr: John Huston
Prod: Jerry Wald
Scr: Richard Brooks, based on the original play by Maxwell

Key Largo: Edward G. Robinson is has-been Johnny Rocco.

Anderson
DOP: Karl Freund
Ed: Rudi Fehr
Music: Max Steiner
Art Dir: Leo K. Kuter

Cast: Humphrey Bogart (Frank McCloud), Edward G. Robinson (Johnny Rocco), Lauren Bacall (Nora Temple), Lionel Barrymore (James Temple), Claire Trevor (Gaye Dawn)

An ex-army major visits the Florida Keys only to find himself held hostage by a one-time big-shot racketeer.

Edward G. Robinson repeatedly confounded critics in the mid-forties by playing a diverse range of characters (in *The Sea Wolf*, *Double Indemnity*, *All My Sons*), but found the ageing, fugitive racketeer Johnny Rocco ('the one and only') a fitting epitaph to his career. Like James Cagney in *White Heat* (*qv*), a return to the gangster genre would provide Robinson with one of his most memorable screen roles, unforgettably introduced to us as he soaks in a luxurious bubble bath, cigar in mouth. Both this, and the scene in which he whispers obscenities into Lauren Bacall's ear, have entered movie gangster folklore. Rocco is the epitome of the gangster on the downslide. He looks back to his heyday, assisted by the ironic Bogart: 'Johnny Rocco was a king, an emperor – his rule extended over beers, slot machines, the numbers racket... when he couldn't corrupt, he terrified; when he couldn't terrify, he'd murder. Welcome back, Rocco... America's sorry for what it did to you.' Dreaming that Prohibition will once more be enforced, but this time uniting the mobs, Rocco (waiting for counterfeit money at the hotel to assist his passage back in the country, after having being exiled) was full of campaign rhetoric: 'When Rocco talked, everyone listened. I'll be back up there one of these days, then you'll really see something.' Huston's film becomes a lament, in part, for the demise of the roaring twenties, a history of the gangster film examined with the residue of cynicism left over from World War II. No longer are easy profits so acceptable.

Key Largo was also the final teaming between Bacall and Humphrey Bogart, following *To Have and Have Not*, *The Big Sleep* and *Dark Passage*. Bogart played the shattered idealist (a war hero who 'won a medal or two') whose disillusionment with the world has made him stop fighting for things – a type that had made his name throughout the forties. Both were somewhat overshadowed here by Robinson's performance and that of Rocco's alcoholic girlfriend (played by Claire Trevor). A postwar melodrama, belonging to the category of 'theatrical cinema', it questions whether the war has been fought simply to allow gangsters, and what they represent, to flourish in the country. Villains are irredeemably bad, the good guys just that.

A reaction to the rise of Nazism, and a message that the good must resist the bad, Huston's direction, while lacking the power of *The Treasure of the Sierra Madre*, is a series of outstanding moments, relying on the fact that characters, not torn flesh, make drama. While death is eventually administered to Rocco, its threat hovers above the cast throughout – just like the hurricane that broods throughout the film.

* **Academy Award:** Claire Trevor won for Best Supporting Actress.

Kid Galahad

(US, Warner Brothers, 1937, 102 mins)

Credits
Dir: Michael Curtiz
Prod: Hal B. Wallis
Scr: Seaton I. Miller, based on the original novel by Francis Wallace
Ed: George Amy
Music: Heinz Roemheld, Max Steiner
Art Dir: Carl Jules Weyl

Cast: Edward G. Robinson (Nick Donati), Bette Davis (Fluff), Humphrey Bogart (Turkey Morgan), Wayne Morris (Ward Guisenberry), Jane Bryan (Marie Donati)

A fight manager comes to blows over a rival crooked fight promoter, after he signs a bellhop as his next champ.

Michael Curtiz's solid direction, the triple force of Edward G. Robinson, Humphrey Bogart and Bette Davis, and a larger-than-average budget made *Kid Galahad* a textbook late Warner Brothers gangster film: unsubtle, visceral and never punch-drunk. Set in the world of professional boxing, a scenario surprisingly unused before, high realism marked the fight footage (bettered only in the likes of *Body and Soul* (qv), *Fat City* and *Raging Bull*). The stark Bogart-Robinson shootout, their second after *Bullets or Ballots* (qv) echoed this, Robinson killing Bogart and bleakly saying: 'You shouldn't've traded in that machine gun.' Contrasting is Tony Gaudio's rich black-and-white photography, Bogart's shadow, gun in hand, famously looming on the wall before he gains entry to the locker-room for the final showdown. In the middle is the eponymous naive boxing bellhop, nicknamed Galahad for being 'clean of heart'. An evidently symbolic figure, he represents the change of mind Robinson's Nick has, as he convinces his bellhop fighter not to throw the fight (Nick has bet on Bogart's rival fighter McGraw). An evident product of the post-Hays Code era, *Kid Galahad* lacked the amoral stance of earlier Warners works, such as *The Public Enemy* (qv), preferring instead to highlight a triumph of good over evil.

* The film was remade in 1962 as a vehicle for Elvis Presley, with the Curtiz version renamed for TV as *Battling Bellhop*.

Kids Return

(Japan, Bandai, 1996, 107 mins)

Credits
Dir/Scr/Ed: Takeshi Kitano
Prod: Masayuki Mori, Yasushi Tsuge, Takio Yoshida
Scr: Noriyasu Sato, based on the novel by Kitano
DOP: Katsumi Yanagishima
Music: Joe Hisaishi
Art Dir: Norishiro Isoda

Cast: Masanobu Ando (Shinji Takagi), Ken Kaneko (Masaru Miyawaki), Ryo Ishibashi (local Yakuza chief), Michisuke Kashiwaya (Hiroshi), Leo Morimoto (Teacher)

Two juvenile delinquent Japanese schoolboys extort money from their peers, before they drift into 'careers', as a boxer and yakuza member.

A closely observed, semi-autobiographical study of how the disenfranchised can slip the net and become undesirables, the structure, as in *Boiling Point* and to an extent *Violent Cop* (qqv), is cyclical as the boys reflect on time past and goof around in the schoolyard they once ran. Far from hopeless, Shinji asks in the final scene 'Are we finished?'. 'Hell, no!' replies Massaru, 'We haven't even started yet!' Unlike Kitano's other work, the protagonists are learning to live, not die. It's a study of failure (offset by the increasing success of a schoolboy comedy duo who appear throughout), made all the more ironic by Massaru's prophetic 'We'll meet again when you're the champ and I'm the boss.' But there is no heavy-handed moralising, apportioning of blame nor a tried-and-tested route to success on offer here. The fact that dishwasher Kazou falls in with the yakuza, while nerd Hiroshi finishes school to become a cab driver, only to wind up dead in a car accident, indicates that working a 40-hour week will safeguard neither your conscience or life expectancy.
Blended with a gritty take on the win-at-all-costs

sport of Asian boxing, Takeshi seemingly parodies the yakuza characters and scenarios; parochial, ineffectual even, they come complete with electric blue shirts and mauve jackets. Ishibashi's cameo, reminding one of his role in *American Yakuza* (qv), allows for a most ignominious demise, at the hands of an assassin on a push-bike. Even the Godfather just wants to call a truce and play golf. But as Kitano, a favourite among the Japanese Mafia, told *Sight & Sound*'s Tony Rayns: as accurate as Massaru's recruitment is, the idea emerges 'that concepts of "family" loyalty and honour are much stronger among the junior members of the gang (shown by the hot-headed Massaru). The higher up the ranks you go, the more "political" they become; they're more into negotiated settlements than crude notions of revenge.'

See also: *American Yakuza*; *American Yakuza II*; *Black Rain*; *Sonatine*; *Yakuza, The*.

Killer, The (Diexue Shuang Xiong)

(Hong Kong, Film Workshop Company, 1989, 111 mins)

'Woo perversely combines the notion of a noble samurai killer with a supercharged Miami Vice camera style and Mills & Boon storyline of moral redemption.'

(Neon, 1997)

Credits
Dir/Scr: John Woo
Prod: Tsui Hark
DOP: Wong Wing-Hang, Peter Pao
Ed: David Wu
Music: Lowell Lowe

Cast: Chow Yun-Fat (Jef), Sally Yeh (Jennie), Danny Lee (Inspector 'Eagle' Lee), Ken Tsang (Sgt. Randy Chung), Kong Chu (Sydney Fung), Lam Chung (Willie Tsang)

After accidentally blinding a singer, an assassin with a conscience is tormented by guilt but persuaded to take on one last job. Betrayed, he is pursued by both a gangland leader and a rogue police inspector, the latter becoming a friend.

'I regard *The Killer* as a romantic poem. I admire the ancient Chinese knights, the loyalty of the samurai spirit and, in the West, the French Romantics. A true 'knight' should be free to come and go as he pleases – he has no need for recognition from those around him because his actions are the most important thing. He will often sacrifice everything, even his life, for justice, loyalty, love and his country, and if he makes a promise to a friend he must keep it,' said Woo in *Sight & Sound*.

Based on one of Woo's favourites, Jean-Pierre Melville's *Le Samourai* (qv) – the protagonists from both are named 'Jef' – but also a homage to Scorsese (the above extract concludes with a dedication to the man), Woo echoes both in terms of underworld codes of honour, fragments of world-weary dialogue about feeling out-of-time and out-of-place, and the conflation of Catholic and gangster elements (the climactic scene is set in a church, as is his third US film *Face/Off*). Woo creates male melodrama, combining passionate violence with passionate suffering. Bonded by a mutual obsession to survive, Yun-Fat's killer and Lee's cop are allegories for the Hong Kong people's uncertainty with the 1997 handover to China. Blurring the boundaries between cop and gangster suggests a common social project – a need to stick together, borne out by an anxiety as to who can be trusted, as gang boss Johnny Weng (Shing Fui-On) pointedly reminds Jef before the latter is set up. Both Jef and Inspector Lee remain outmoded nostalgics: 'Our world is changing so fast. It never used to be like this,' says Jef, later adding 'Honour is now a dirty word.' They are Woo's 'knights' of old; friendship overcomes Lee's 'I uphold the law, you break it' distinction, expressing a need for strong interpersonal relationships in a time of transience.

* A Mandarin-dubbed version exists, 30 minutes longer than its Cantonese counterpart, released in Taiwan four months before the Hong Kong premiere. While Woo regards the latter as the final cut, the extra scenes do have some interest, including a hitman literally stalking Lee and Jef (recalling *Le Samourai*'s image of the tiger) after their vital creek conversation.

The Killer: Face/Off: Jef (Chow Yun-Fat) takes on Inspector Lee (Danny Lee).

See also: *Better Tomorrow, A*; *Driver, The*; *Fallen Angels*; *Hard Boiled*; *Leon*; *Little Odessa*; *Prizzi's Honor*; *This Gun For Hire*.

Killer Meets Killer: See Each Dawn I Die.

Killers, The

(US, Universal Pictures, 1946, 103 mins)

Credits
Dir: Robert Siodmak
Prod: Mark Hellinger
Scr: Anthony Veiller, based on the short story by Ernest Hemingway
DOP: Woody Bredell
Ed: Arthur Hilton
Music: Miklos Rozsa
Art Dir: Jack Otterson

Cast: Burt Lancaster (Ole Anderson 'The Swede'), Ava Gardner (Kitty Collins), Edmond O'Brien (James Reardon), Albert Dekker (Jim Colfax), Sam Levene (Lt. Sam Lubinsky), Vince Barnett (Charleston)

An ex-boxer, resigned to his fate, is killed by two hitman, having betrayed a racketeering outfit that he once assisted in a daring robbery.

Killers, The

(US, Universal Pictures, 1964, 95 mins)

Credits
Dir/Prod: Don Siegel
Scr: Gene L. Coon
DOP: Richard L. Rawlings Snr
Ed: Richard Belding, Stuart H. Pappe
Music: John Williams
Art Dir: Frank Arrigo, George Chan

Cast: Lee Marvin (Charlie), Angie Dickinson (Sheila Farr), John Cassavetes (Johnny North), Ronald Reagan (Browning), Clu Gulager (Lee), Claude Akins (Earl Sylvester)

Two assassins, having whacked a former racetrack driver for his double-cross following an armoured-car heist, decide to trace the $1 million that he supposedly stashed from the theft.

The screenplays for both films start effectively where Hemingway's short story ends, Siegel's version moving the killers to the centre stage, taking Siodmak's film on another tangent. Both films are driven by the need to discover why the victim did not run – Edmond O'Brien's insurance agent and Lee Marvin's killer being the vehicles for this device. The victim himself, in both cases, is an athlete, his sense of fair play unable to survive in a duplicitous society, while the female is the betrayer. Siodmak's film is the perfect expression of *noir*; everything is indoors, even the street scenes are on set, with the exception of one robbery. Darkness and constriction filter into individual shots; black interiors mirroring the internalised feelings of the protagonists. Siegel's version is shot on location in pastels, the killers, as one critic noted, drawn like 'prosperous executives' complete with business-like attaché cases; fear comes in daylight. Both are products of their time. As Stuart M. Kaminsky noted in his comparative essay on the two films: 'The Siegel film [deals] with the problem of stripping away postures, including those of business and economic security, to reveal the shallowness of modern existence which has no foundation in love or morality.' Originally intended, significantly, as the first feature for television – with the director vying for a new title, *Johnny North* – Siegel's film was later pulled from TV in mind of President Kennedy's assassination.

The confusion of values is reflected in the film: good and evil are not so distinct. Marvin's character, unlike O'Brien's, gains his information by force, does not belong to his time (note the repeated mentions of the word) and, in effect, is not a hero. His world is now, in a time when anybody can be killed, one of casual and widespread violence. In control of his feelings, he is an automaton disturbed ostensibly by the victim's apparent ease with his imminent death. The true upset comes in emerging from behind the corporate glaze, facing the real world. While *noir* also came from a need to find the light after the chaos of World War II, Siodmak's film stems from a fear propagated by alienation. Siegel found fear, in contrast, from the mass hysteria, partly fuelled by the Cold War, of his time.

* Ronald Reagan's appearance in Siegel's version was his swansong before moving into politics. He commented at the time: 'I'm kinda sorry my last acting role was a bad guy.'

See also: *Kiss of Death*; *Out of the Past*; *Racket, The*.

Killing, The

(US, Harris-Kubrick Pictures, 1956, 84 mins)

Credits
Dir/Scr: Stanley Kubrick, based on the original novel Clean Break by Lionel White
Prod: James B. Harris
DOP: Lucien Ballard
Ed: Betty Steinberg
Music: Gerald Fried
Art Dir: Ruth Sobotka

Cast: Sterling Hayden (Johnny Clay), Coleen Gray (Fay), Vince Edwards (Val Cannon), Jay C. Flippen (Marvin Unger), Marie Windsor (Sherry Peatty), Ted De Corsia (Randy Kennan)

A gang pull off a heist at a racetrack.

Regarded by himself, as his first true film (see *Killer's Kiss* below), The Killing came at the end of the *noir* cycle, in many ways a companion piece to John Huston's heist thriller *The Asphalt Jungle* (qv). Seen by many, with its elaborate, mathematical time-space structure as a precursor to *2001: A Space Odyssey*, the film, with its cut-up racetrack robbery is akin to the breakdown of technological systems in Kubrick's pioneering space film. Here, the complex structure represents the sense of hopelessness and lost time in a disorientated world order, using the consistent image of the jigsaw puzzle and the chess game to conjure thoughts of fracture and strategy. As Paul Schrader, in his elucidating essay 'Notes on *Film Noir*' said: 'The manipulation of time, whether slight or complex is often used to reinforce a noir principle: the how is always more important than the what.' The use of the narrator, precisely documenting the crime and each participant's role in the heist, backs this theory up, contributing to the semi documentary feel to the film. With additional dialogue provided by hard-boiled writer Jim Thompson, Kubrick draws a comprison between the gangster and the artist as 'the same in the eyes of the masses. They're admired and hero worshiped, but there's always present an underlying wish to see them destroyed at their peak.'

This line recalls *The Asphalt Jungle*'s message that crime is just 'a left-handed form of human endeavour'. In both, the criminal – to succeed – must rely on precise planning, not the brute force employed by their thirties counterparts. Both, as Schrader goes on to say, stand at the end of a long tradition 'based on despair and disintergration', representatives of the disillusionment of the age.

* Kubrick's second film, though officially his first, *Killer's Kiss* (originally titled *Kiss Me, Kill Me*), was a seedy *noir*, an initial exploration into the brooding, forboding world of the City – an element, like contemporary society, that will always swallow up the individual. Costing just $40,000 and shot entirely on location in New York, it was an abstract, absurd even, mixture of the comic and the humdrum, carved with a neo-realist sensibility for the everyday nuances of human behaviour. Thus, prize fighter Davy (Jamie Smith), who whisks dance hall hostess Gloria (Irene Kane) away from her possessive racketeer boss Vince (Frank Silvera), is the doomed hero – represented by the fish in the glass bowl (magnified, alone and vulnerable from all sides).

* While *The Killing* would be emulated many times (not least in *Reservoir Dogs* (*qv*) with its own fractured narrative), the most explicit homage came from Pierre-William Glenn, with *23h58*, in which two ex-motor bike racers (both fans of the Kubrick film) organise a robbery of takings during the 24-hour Le Mans race. Glenn honours the film, rather than stealing from it, inserting stills from the picture at every point – loaded with hope, it's a tribute to the cinema as preserver of perfect memories. As he commented to *Sight & Sound*'s Chris Darke: 'To have no knowledge of the history of the cinema is to have no idea of history.'

See also: *Criss-Cross*; *Face*; *Heat*; *Usual Suspects, The*.

Killing of a Chinese Bookie, The

(US, 1976, Faces Distribution Corporation, 133 mins)

Credits
Dir/Scr: John Cassavetes
Prod: Al Ruban
DOP: Frederick Elmes, Mike Ferris, Michael Stringer
Ed: Tom Cornwell
Music: Anthony Harris, Bo Harwood
Prod. Des: Bryan Ryman, Sam Shaw

Cast: Ben Gazzara (Cosmo), Timothy Carey (Flo), Seymour Cassel (Mort Weil), Robert Phillips (Phil), Morgan Woodward (The Boss), John Red Kullers (The Accountant)

The owner of a cheezy L.A. strip joint, in debt to the mob and forced to murder a Bookie in lieu of the money owed, succeeds in the task, only to discover that he was set up to attempt a near-impossible and kill the biggest Godfather on the West Coast.

Far more Cassavetes material than *Gloria* (*qv*) would prove to be, the director confounded critics yet again (most accused the film of being slow) with this use of the gangster genre to framework his own concerns. Supposedly dreamt up in the course of an evening with Martin Scorsese, the above synopsis is the most redundant part of the film, almost a perfunctory afterthought (producer Al Ruban noted that Cassavetes delayed shooting the scene where the 'Bookie' dies by taking the crew all out to dinner, as if he were trying to avoid any approach towards plot progression).

It takes some 20 minutes of screen time for Cosmo to reach the Bookie's house. As in *Gloria*, where even going to the bank involves a series of complications, events are full of restrictions and friction; Cosmo spends time negotiating differences – arguing on the phone, for example, with his bartender about what act is on stage at his club. Cassavetes shifts action to reaction, organising the film around non-events, and constantly derails the story when we think something will happen – staging the actual killing only to highlight the psychological states of thinking and feeling leading up to the event.

As Ray Carney noted: 'Whereas gangster pictures

are usually about tying narrative knots as tight as possible, *Bookie* presents a series of loose ends, unraveled relationships, and dangling and unresolved encounters.' Cassavetes use of Ben Gazzara (a regular collaborator) may nod towards previous gangster works – Gazzara starred in the title role of *Capone* (qv) – but if anything this proves to be yet another red herring. Cassavetes gangsters are not the Armani-dressed hoods of Brian DePalma's *The Untouchables* (qv), but have hooked noses, bad haircuts and carbuncled faces; even the Bookie himself is an embarrassed old grandfather with fogged-up glasses.

While Cosmo's life is devoted to clarity, harmony and coherence, using his stage acts as an escape to the imagination, Cassavetes pulls in the opposite direction, forcing us to confront the uncertainty and mystery of life. Ultimately, the film is a meditation on the relationship between art and life: Cosmo exists in the sheen, and abstract, Cassavetes in the real.

* At least two versions exist of the film. An original cut in 16mm, which was withdrawn from circulation after a short US run, and a recut (by Cassavetes) in 35mm which included deleted material.

King of New York

(US, Reteitalia/Scena Film, 1990, 103 mins)

'It's 'Top of the world, Ma' stuff. He's [Frank White] got a lot of people who don't think this [everyone in the gang gets equal share] is a good idea. It's gonna be a classical gangster movie.'
(Abel Ferrara, *City Limits*)

Credits
Dir: Abel Ferrara
Prod: Mary Kane
Scr: Nicholas St. John
DOP: Bajan Bazelli
Ed: Anthony Redman
Music: Joe Delia
Prod Des: Alex Tavoularis

Cast: Christopher Walken (Frank White), David Caruso (Dennis Gilley), Larry Fishburne (Jimmy Jump), Wesley Snipes (Thomas Flanigan), Steve Buscemi (Test Tube)

A white drug lord and his black dealers set out to control the New York drug trade by eliminating his rivals.

Abel Ferrara's provocative gangster film, extolling the public enemy as model citizen (a blazing return to form following his adaptation of Elmore Leonard's *Cat Chaser*) is one of the most important works of its type in the last decade.
Ferrara, and regular screenwriter Nicholas St. John, explore the notion of organised crime as naturally socially benevolent. Frank White is the palid Orpheus released from prison who subsequently raises $7 million in drug profits to prevent the closure of a South Bronx hospital. A socially progressive criminal, he offers a pragmatic New Deal – to 'do something good', meaning redistribution of wealth. Ferarra uses White to make the criminal code responsive to social justice and economic morality – people, not profits. His money comes from drugs, viewed as a thriving business in a neighbourhood of economic despair. Unlike the New York of Ferrara's *China Girl*, White transgresses the norm by forming a multi-culturally integrated entourage; his lieutenant Jimmy Jump is black, his contemporaries (Steve Buscemi, Giancarlo Esposito) are multi-racial. His antagonists, such as David Caruso's Irish cop, follow the same pattern. Only his underworld opponents, those he is trying to wash away along with the politically inert system, are segregated – in Chinese, Latin or Italian sects. Ferrara's imagery is the key to understanding his central theme: that of the disintegration of moral distinction. Using colour, White's gang are bathed in blue, while a warm, orange hue celebrates the cops. At the point where the cops raid the club firing, White is lit by both of these colours. This demise of ethical codes, Ferrara, and his altruistic protagonist White, question the very social structure set up to protect us from those like his gangster. Is their behaviour justifiable? Is White's, as a means for social improvement, reprehensible? Reflection takes a great part also. With the city viewed through puddles in the gutter, it is in reach of Frank – but

King of New York: Frank White (Christopher Walken) surveys his kingdom.

his methods will always leave it remote from him. Re-writing the rules, as Scorsese's *Goodfellas (qv)* would in the same year, Ferrara finishes with White expiring quietly in a gridlocked cab. 'There were going to be different things that happened,' said Ferrara. 'Cops and stuff. But Walken said, "It ends not with a bang, but a whimper."' As he dies, the cab's dashboard sports a figure of an angel – angel of mercy, or vengeance? Rather at odds with *White Heat (qv)* and the 'Top of the world stuff' he predicted, Ferrara had his own take: 'The goal is not the film; the goal is to be whole, to be involved as a human being – knowledge, self-knowledge, group knowledge, whatever.'

King of the Roaring Twenties: The Story of Arnold Rothstein

(US, Allied Artists, 1961, 106 mins)

Credits

Dir: Joseph M. Newman
Prods: Sam Bischoff, David Diamond
Scr: Jo Swerling, based on the book The Big Bankroll by Leo Katcher
DOP: Carl Guthrie
Ed: George White
Music: Frank Waxman
Art Dir: Dave Milton

Cast: David Janssen (Arnold Rothstein), Mickey Rooney (Johnny Burke), Dan O'Herlihy (Phil Butler), Dianne Foster (Carolyn Green), Diana Dors (Madge), Jack Carson (Big Tim O'Brien), Mickey Shaugnessy (Jim Kelly)

Biopic of the notorious gambler/gangster.

Light on the facts, largely ignoring Rothstein's involvement in the 'Black Sox' baseball scandal of 1919 (many participants were still alive during filming), Newman's somewhat pedestrian film arrived late in the post, after the first cycle of gangster biopics had been completed. Preferring instead to concentrate upon Rothstein's gradual alienation from friends, lovers and colleagues, Newman shows this in tandem with his subject's increasing use of unscrupulous methods and addiction to gambling. Using this as a metaphorical starting point, his life is seen as ruled by the cards, his language governed by his habit. Blanking long-time partner/friend Burke (a subtle performance from Rooney, already a key figure in the genre having played the title role in Don Siegel's 1957 film *Baby Face Nelson*), he says: 'As far as I'm concerned Johnny, you're no price in my book... a bad risk.' The brief appearance from Diana Dors expands the idea further, as she tells Rothstein's wife (later to be cheated upon): 'When you're married to a gambler the only game you play is solitude.' Gambling takes all of Rothstein's passion for life, it is hinted; his death played out, aptly, at a poker table. In the film's key moment, Rothstein visits his estranged, religiously zealous parents, only wanting recognition for his achievements, but being told he has no faith in anything except money. A flashback to childhood earlier in the film attributed his demeanor to 'an evil spirit in him' but as the film progresses it becomes clear that aggrandisement is the root of all evil. Pursuing the religious theme, his wife-to-be is introduced by the appropriately named press agent Henry Hack as 'an angel', but even she is unable to halt Rothstein's demise, pushing the notion that Capitalism has run over the nation's spiritual and familial beliefs. Self-destructive to the last, his tempestuous partnership with Kelly in the gambling empire (orchestrated by Phil Butler's crooked police detective), crumbles, with Rothstein then pulling judicial strings to convict Butler of the murder of Burke. This ruthless pursuit of personal, sole power shows its vacuous nature as Rothstein's wife leaves him: 'A minute ago I got this town in my back pocket, but if you leave me I've got nothing,' he implores.

Newman does show moments of clarity. While the film, unlike Martin Scorsese's Casino (qv) which precisely details the inner mechanics of such a place, skims over the day-to-day proceedings, one scene leisurely moves the camera up and down a line of Rothstein lackeys as they are working on the telephone. Deliberately lacking the gun-play of other biopics, Newman's work ultimately suggests that Rothstein's success came from two simple attributes: 'a brain and a bank roll'.

* John Sayles' 1988 film Eight Men Out featured Michael Lerner as Rothstein. Based on Eliot Asinof's book, the film explored events surrounding a group of gamblers conspiring with seven members of the Chicago White Sox to throw the 1919 World Series, and the subsequent investigation that followed.

See also: Bugsy; Grifters, The; George Raft Story, The; Mobsters: the Evil Empire; Lepke; Lucky Luciano; Rise and Fall of Legs Diamond, The.

King of the Underworld

(US, Warner Brothers, 1939, 69 mins)

Credits
Dir: Lewis Seiler
Scr: George Bricker, Vincent Sherman
DOP: Sid Hickox
Ed: Frank Dewar
Music: Heinz Roemheld
Art Dir: Charles Novi

Cast: Humphrey Bogart (Joe Gurney), Kay Francis (Carol Nelson), James Stephenson (Bill Forrest), John Eldredge (Niles), Jessie Busley (Aunt Margaret)

A gangster coerces a doctor into coming to his men's aid whenever needed, but after murdering the medic on suspicion of informing, is brought to justice by the physician's wife.

King of the Underworld was the second (and best) of four Warner Brothers gangster films directed between 1939 and 1942 by Lewis Seiler, and starring Humphrey Bogart. Only by the fourth collaboration, the curiosity in Bogart's career The Big Shot, had he become a major star, having appeared in The Maltese Falcon that year.
King of the Underworld was produced by Warners on the back of Racket Busters, also starring Bogart as a gangster tycoon who muscles his way into the trucking business. Directed by Lloyd Bacon – it was their second of three collaborations, following Marked Woman and preceding Invisible Stripes (qqv). Both Bacon – who would go on to work with Edward G. Robinson in Brother Orchid (qv) and Larceny, Inc. – and Seiler were the most competent and successful in their time at producing melodramatic gangster B pictures. Despite clearly viewing them as publicity machines, Bogart produced some fine, solid performances – in particular as Joe Gurney, in King of the Underworld. No run-of-the-mill gangster, but a twisted egomaniac, in the Napoleonic mould, he took sadistic delight in dominating those around him. In particular, the female doctor Carol Nelson and the young writer Bill Forrest, whom he forces to write his biography. Scripted by B movie maestro George

Bricker, and Vincent Sherman, who would go on to direct Bogart himself in *All Through the Night* (qv), the film was lent a certain class by the casting of Kay Francis and James Stephenson.

* Made the same year was Seiler's enormously successful *You Can't Get Away With Murder*, teaming up Bogart with Billy Halop, leader of the Dead End kids, in a virtual re-run of their *Dead End* (qv) roles. Bogart once again is a racketeer whose early life led to a future of crime, while Halop is the impressionable slum kid. *It All Came True* appeared in 1940, months before Bogart would achieve stardom in *High Sierra* (qv). An unusual incorporation of comedy and music with little violence and a distinctly theatrical feel to the film, Bogart's Chips Maguire, a departure from his usual snarling heel, matches this change in style. Taking refuge in a boarding house having killed a policeman with his host's gun, he winds up giving himself up when the police come to arrest the wrong man. Despite the schmaltz it scored well at the box office, Bogart displaying impeccable comic timing. *The Big Shot* was Bogart's last gangster film, until he came back to the genre in 1948 with *Key Largo* (qv). Bearing a resemblance to *High Sierra's* (qv) Roy Earle, his Duke Berne character, a veteran gangster trying to pull off one last heist, is set in scenarios also close to Walsh's film. A lengthy car chase through a mountain pass was the most blatant.

Kiss of Death

(US, 20th Century-Fox, 1947, 98 mins)

Credits
Dir: Henry Hathaway
Prod: Fred Kohlmar
Scr: Ben Hecht, Charles Lederer, based on the story by Eleazar Lipsky
DOP: Norbert Brodine
Ed: J. Watson Webb Jr
Music: David Buttolph
Art Dir: Leland Fuller, Lyle Wheeler
Cast: Richard Widmark (Tommy Udo), Nick Bianco (Victor Mature), Karl Malden (Sgt. William Cullen), Mildred Dunnock (Ma Rizzo), Brian Donlevy (D'Angelo), Coleen Gray (Nettie)

Jewel thief turns in evidence against the underworld, following his wife's suicide, only to be pursued in revenge by an unconvicted thug.

Kiss of Death

(US, 20th Century-Fox, 1995, 101 mins)

Credits
Dir/Prod: Barbet Schroeder
Scr: Richard Price
DOP: Luciano Tovoli
Ed: Lee Percy
Music: Trevor Jones
Prod. Des: Mel Bourne

Cast: David Caruso (Jimmy Kilmartin), Nicolas Cage (Little Junior), Samuel L. Jackson (Calvin), Michael Rapaport (Ronnie), Kathryn Erbe (Rosie), Ving Rhames (Omar)

Ex-convict finds himself trapped between corrupt DA and psychopathic hoodlum, the former wishing to use him to convict the latter.

Barbet Schroeder's remake of Henry Hathaway's film 'had very little to do with the 1947 movie. By the time we started shooting, only the title and one plot point remained', as the director noted. The surviving aspect – a widowed ex-con (the Caruso/Mature character) is pressured into turning evidence against the underworld – is lost amid the self-conscious awareness of the film's place in the crime/gangster genre. More neon than neo-*noir*, it was viewed as 'post-Pulp [*Fiction*]', sharing actors Ving Rhames and Samuel L. Jackson and a delight in trashy shock violence. For example, the death of dealer (and undercover Fed) Omar, shot in the head by Cage's Little Junior, compares to Marvin's equally unexpected death at the hands of Travolta's Vincent Vega in Tarantino's film. This chrome-plated landscape runs against the realism inherent in Richard Price's painstaking script (a year was spent by him researching the multi-billion dollar car theft industry that leads to Kilmartin's early convictions), a fact that unbalances the work.

Hathaway's version was also produced in a transitional period. *Time Out*'s Paul Kerr noted: 'Late forties Fox saw several attempts to conceal the split in the gangster film between *noir* expressionism and 'procedural' authenticity, but few as bizarre as *Kiss*'. While Schroeder's film defined itself through *Pulp Fiction (qv)*, Hathaway achieved redefinition – forging realism and an expressionistic manner through the use of external New York locations, the first gangster film to do so.

Both films cast a critical eye towards the justice system. 'Your side of the fence is almost as dirty as mine', says Bianco to Brian Donlevy's DA, who sets up a fake charge for Bianco to convince the underworld that it was not he who squealed on them. Kilmartin has to tape Stanley Tucci's DA, boasting that his promotion to Federal Judge is more important than prosecuting Junior, in order to secure the conviction. As Junior says, 'The time has come for everyone to clean up their own back yard.' Comparison was also inevitable between Richard Widmark's rendering of the sadistic Tommy Udo and Cage's muscle-bound, asthmatic gangster, Little Junior. Famed for the scene where he pushes a wheelchair-bound lady down a flight of stairs to her death, Udo gained Widmark an Academy Award nomination. Obsessed with gaining recognition from his dying father, Junior is a collection of idiosyncrasies: from his gold medallion and his hatred of the taste of metal in his mouth, to his acronym to help 'visualise' his goals (B.A.D. – Balls. Attitude. Direction.). *Sight & Sound*'s Manohla Dargis argued against the performance, a statement applicable to Schroeder's film as a whole: 'As imposing as Cage is as Little Junior, he never transcends the memory of Widmark's giggling sociopath, or, for that matter, the role's intrinsic blur.'

See also: *Get Shorty*; *Killers, The*; *Out of the Past*; *Racket, The*; *Romeo is Bleeding*; *Things To Do In Denver When You're Dead*.

Kiss Tomorrow Goodbye

(US, Warner Brothers, 1950, 102 mins)

Credits
Dir: Gordon Douglas
Prod: William Cagney
Scr: Harry Brown, based on the novel by Horace McCoy
DOP: Peverell Marley
Ed: Truman K. Wood, Walter Hannemann
Music: Carmen Dragon
Art Dir: Wiard Ihnen

Cast: James Cagney (Ralph Cotter), Barbara Payton (Holiday), Ward Bond (Inspector Weber), Luther Adler (Mandon), Helena Carter (Margaret Dobson), Steve Brodie (Jinx)

A gangster escapes from prison, returning to crime and charming a wealthy heiress in the process, which allows him seemingly to go straight.

Rushed into production following the success of *White Heat (qv)*, *Kiss Tomorrow Goodbye* was a Warner Brothers production in association with William Cagney Productions. Founded by the actor's brother in 1943 (with Jimmy as Vice-President), the company had produced three Cagney vehicles in the mid-forties: *Johnny Come Lately*, *Blood on the Sun* and *The Time of Your Life*. This film, with Cagney portraying one of his most unsympathetic psychopathic hoodlums, marked the first gangster piece from the Cagney brothers. While viewed as an obvious attempt to cash in on James Cagney's resurgent tough guy image, it emerges as a dark melodrama, one of Cagney's most underrated pictures. Exceeding even his brutal treatment of women in *The Public Enemy* and *Lady Killer (qqv)*, Cagney beats Barbara Payton in one scene repeatedly with a rolled-up towel. Matching his dark malevolence was the brooding photography of Peverell Marley, capturing Cagney & co with heavy, thick shadows – a certain influence from the late forties work of Siodmak, Rossen, Polonsky and Hathaway.

* The film was banned from being shown anywhere in Ohio State, being called 'a sadistic presentation of brutality'.

The Krays: Ronnie Kray (Gary Kemp) about to demonstrate the art of giving a Chelsea smile.

Krays, The

(UK, Fugitive Features, 1990, 119 mins)

'The direction does not flinch, as do most other British crime-class-nostalgia movies, from graphic violence, making it impossible to read this film as a wistful lament, like Buster, for a never-never time when crime was simpler and nobody really got hurt.'

(Kim Newman, *Monthly Film Bulletin*)

Credits
Dir: Peter Medak
Prod: Dominic Anciano, Jim Beach, Ray Burdis
Scr: Philip Ridley
DOP: Alex Thomson
Ed: Martin Walsh
Music: Michael Kamen
Prod. Des: Michael Pickwoad

Cast: Gary Kemp (Ronald Kray), Martin Kemp (Reginald Kray), Billie Whitelaw (Violet), Kate Hardie (Frances), Susan Fleetwood (Rose), Stephen Berkoff (George Cornell), Tom Bell (Jack 'The Hat' McVitie)

Biopic of the notorious 1960s London gangster twins,

from childhood to their incarceration for the murders of George Cornell and Jack 'The Hat'.

Philip Ridley's script (self-described as 'Jean Cocteau meets East London') was written with the twins from 1980s New Romantic band Spandau Ballet in mind; the significance of using Martin and Gary Kemp for the roles of London's feared Kray twins is resonant, as Ridley told John McVicar in *Time Out*: 'A lot of what the Krays were putting out in the sixties was almost pop-star PR.' Martin Kemp backs this up: 'They wanted to be famous and they cultivated a look.'

Their clothes throughout, as with so many works from the genre, from *Little Caesar* (*qv*) onwards, becomes an important part of their increasing influence. As Ronnie says in the film 'Clothes are important. Make you what you are', later adding 'Glamour is fear'. But more than that, Ridley uses clothes to express their division. The scene where the boys have got their new togs from Savile Row represents unity; but, as Reggie marries his clothes become more relaxed (he even chooses wife Frances' outfits), while the sociopath Ronnie's become stiffer and heavier.

They consciously pattern themselves on American movie gangsters. Sharp tailor-made suits, manicures, gold jewellery, house calls from the barber, they are vicious Dandies in the mould of George Raft (a personality admired and befriended by the real Krays). As Cornell (who ironically flips a coin, in true Raft style) calls them: 'A pair of movie gangsters. All they care about is what they look like... they walk down the street like kings.' Image is everything.

With a likeness to *The Long Good Friday* (*qv*), in the meeting between the Krays and the American gangster, Medak's film is more akin to a Jacobean revenge tragedy – complete with climactic bloodshed, a cathartic purging some have seen as an echo of *The Godfather* (*qv*).

But the script works overtime to inform us that men 'think they're in control, but they don't know the half of it... [they] stay kids all their lives, and they become heroes or monsters' (symbolised by the toy crocodiles the twins play with, and the brooch Reggie later gives to Frances). 'Women', we are told 'have to grow up. If they stay children they become victims.' Frances falls into this category; the suffocating Kray women do not, becoming the empowering, if subconscious, force behind the Kray's violence. Violet's language, even disregarding her threats to slit her anonymous husband's throat, is full of menace: repeated reference to her sons as 'boys' and her description of the Krays' talk of gangland retribution as 'nattering' treat the Krays' activities as if they are mere games. As with James Cagney's Cody Jarrett in *White Heat* (*qv*), it is the matriarchal figure that represents their true control; the gangster's aggression a direct result of being permanently shackled.

See also: *Villain*.

L

La Scorta (The Escort)

(Italy, Claudio Bonivento Productions, 1993, 92 mins)

Credits
Dir: Ricky Tognazzi
Prod: Claudio Bonivento
Scr: Simona Izza, Graziano Diana
DOP: Alessio Gelsini
Ed: Carla Simoncelli
Music: Ennio Morricone
Prod. Des: Mariangela Capuano

Cast: Enrico Lo Verso (Andrea Corsale), Claudio Amendola (Angelo Mandolesi), Ricky Memphis (Fabio Muzzi), Carlo Cecchi (Richter De Francesco)

A magistrate crusades against the Mafia-infiltrated legal system in Sicily, trusting only his four personal bodyguards.

Set in the Sicilian port city of Trapani, Ricky Tognazzi's film is an unusual yet accurate, one would imagine, depiction of the infiltration of the Sicilian Mafia. Accurate because their appearance is fleeting, unglamorous, mere shadows on the edge of the film. Evidence comes in the form of threats, bullets taped to front doors, potential death, not outright violence (the film only contains two killings).

The eponymous bodyguards are four carabinieri,

members of the militarized national police assigned to provide an escort for Judge De Francesco, who has arrived to replace his assassinated predecessor. Drawing loosely from events experienced by Judge Francesco Taurisano some four years earlier, the film is also a response to the famous murder in 1991 of Judge Giovanni Falcone, his wife and three police bodyguards, via a remotely detonated bomb in a highway tunnel. While Tognazzi – son of comic actor Ugo – claimed the film is 'a great love story between men', the motif is family. Not so much criminal, but certainly surrogate, scenes such as the dinner party indicate a growing bond and solidarity between the judge and his guards. The Mafia – a family based on greed and cruelty – are seen as only part of the problem. As the discovery of the attempt to control the city's water rights (a traditional goal in Mafia politics) is revealed, governmental corruption – the power of words not guns – saturates the plot. De Francesco is transferred from Trapani by local prosecutor Caruso, who contrived the move following the death of a corrupt senator. The truth, as shown by a continuous tracking shot across a number of bureaucrats, is not about the power of the Mafia, but the power allowing it to flourish.

See also: *Black Hand, The*; *Corleone*; *Sicilian, The*.

Lady Killer

(US, Warner Brothers, 1933, 76 mins)

Credits
Dir: Roy Del Ruth
Prod: Henry Blanke
Scr: Ben Markson, Lilli Hayward
DOP: Tony Gaudio
Ed: George Amy
Music: Leo F. Forbstein
Art Dir: Robert Haas

Cast: James Cagney (Don Quigley), Mae Clarke (Myra Gale), Margaret Lindsay (Lois Underwood), Leslie Fenton (Duke), Henry O'Neill (Ramick), William Roberston (Conroy)

Racketeer turns Hollywood movie star, after his gang

double-crosses him following a violent series of New York robberies, only for his past to catch up with him once stardom has beckoned.

A precursor to *Jimmy the Gent*, Warner Brothers' first fully fledged gangster comedy, *Lady Killer* reunited Cagney with Mae Clarke, his co-star (and infamous recipient of a grapefruit in the face) from *The Public Enemy* (*qv*). Once again, the humiliation of Clarke proved the film's talking point, with Cagney (in a rather transparent attempt to recreate the flavour of the grapefruit scene) dragging Clarke by the hair across the room, tossing her out of the door and kicking her down the corridor. In the spirit of the picture, Cagney begins as a cinema usher, the film showing being the Edward G. Robinson starrer *Dark Hazard* – a possible inference of Cagney once more playing second billing to Robinson. This had happened in *Smart Money* two years before (the only picture they ever made together), an ineffectual gangster/gambler film made as a logical step after *Little Caesar* and *The Public Enemy* (*qqv*), when Cagney was vastly underused. Cagney plays in wiseguy mode ('I've been around'), but is man enough to put himself (and the movie business) up for ridicule – making one reviewer literally eat his words, as he forces the copy down his throat.

See also: *Brother Orchid*; *Last Gangster, The*.

Ladykillers, The

(UK, Ealing Studios, 1955, 97 mins)

'The blackest of all English comedies... even Guinness in fangs can't upstage the blithe mettle of Katie Johnson, fulcrum to the fine balance.'
(Stephen Gilbert, *Time Out*)

Credits
Dir: Alexander Mackendrick
Prod: Michael Balcon
Scr: William Rose
DOP: Otto Heller
Ed: Jack Harris
Music: Tristram Cary

Art Dir: Jim Morahan

Cast: Alec Guinness (The Professor), Cecil Parker (The Major), Herbert Lom (Louis), Peter Sellars (Harry), Danny Green (One-Round), Katie Johnson (Mrs. Wilberforce)

A gang planning a daring robbery masquerade as a musical quintet, unbeknown to their befuddled landlady.

Alongside Charles Crichton's *Lavender Hill Mob*, in which Alec Guinness' mild-mannered bank clerk pulls off a daring gold bullion robbery, Ealing Studio's *The Ladykillers* offers an amusing, eccentric and whimsical parody of American gangsterdom. The fact that the gang carry violin cases, not to hide weapons but actually to transport instruments (albeit as part of their cover) simultaneously mocks the Italian-American gangster while laughing out loud at our own inadequacies in creating such mythic figures.

In some ways a macabre farce that reaches an insane but logical conclusion (the gangsters bumping each other off, rather than contributing to the death of the landlady), the criminals and their surroundings were typical of early British mobsters. Richard Attenborough's Pinky aside, these boys – despite their malicious intent – are chaps, a mixture of wideboys, thugs and schemers, whose station robbery exerts only minimal violence. The fact that Mrs. Wilberforce manages to shame them – saying 'Simply try, for one hour, to behave like gentleman' – is all the more laughable, as unreal as her quaint, isolated cottage secreted behind King's Cross Station. The irony that the Ladykillers kill each other while the defenceless lady comes out on top – morality triumphing over immorality – is both an idea of savage absurdity and cruel fantasy, the bumbling gang having endeared themselves to the audience as they chase budgies and sip tea.

See also: *Brighton Rock*.

Last Gangster, The

(US, MGM, 1937, 81 mins)

Credits
Dir: Edward Ludwig
Prod: J.J. Cohn
Scr: John Lee Mahin, based on an original story by William A. Wellman and Robert Carson
DOP: William Daniels
Ed: Ben Lewis
Music: Edward Ward
Art Dir: Cederic Gibbons

Cast: Edward G. Robinson (Joe Krozac), James Stewart (Paul North), Rose Stradner (Talya Krozac), Lionel Stander (Curly), John Carradine (Casper)

A gang leader is betrayed, imprisoned and divorced by his wife, only to emerge from prison ten years later wanting revenge.

Scripted from a story co-written by the director of *The Public Enemy* (qv), the film is typical of the nostalgic yet fatalistic stance taken by gangster films of the late thirties. As the title eagerly suggests, the gangster (in this case Edward G. Robinson's Joe Krozac) is a dying species. Arriving at the back end of the first cycle of the genre, such pessimistic films – *Brother Orchid* (qv) ran a similar plot line – reflected the esteem in which the movie-going public once held the gangster figure, now seen as silver screen idols of the past. Such comparisons are echoed by Krozac's bewilderment once on the outside. The world, like the cinema-going public's fickle tastes, is ever-evolving. Thematically, the film stresses the positive aspects of the family, with Krozac relenting upon his thoughts of revenge once he sees his son will fare better in the care of family man Stewart (his ex-wife's new reporter husband). The individual must sacrifice himself for the good of society – in this case the family. Played out rather too literally (but fitting given the title), Krozac dies at the hands of a rival gang member. It's a recognition of the end of individualism, the gangster being the ultimate expression of rebellion against society's machine.

See also: *Brother Orchid*; *Lady Killer*.

Last Man Standing

(US, New Line, 1996, 101 mins)

Credits
Dir./Prod./Scr: Walter Hill
Prod: Arthur Sarkissian
DOP: Lloyd Ahern
Ed: Freeman Davies
Music Ed: Bunny Andrews
Prod. Des: Gary Wissner

Cast: Bruce Willlis (John Smith), Christopher Walken (Hickey), Alexandra Powers (Lucy Kalinski), David Patrick Kelly (Doyle), William Sanderson (Joe Monday), Ned Eisenberg (Fredo Strozzi)

A stranger drifts into a frontier Texan town, Jericho, to play two rival bootlegging outfits off one another.

Based on Akira Kurosawa's *Yojimbo*, the model for Sergio Leone's *A Fistful of Dollars*, *Last Man Standing*, set in a Prohibition border town, becomes a comic-book product eventually closest to Kurosawa's own inspiration, Dashiell Hammett's 1927 novel *Red Harvest*.
As Hill explained: '*Last Man Standing* is literally a hymn to the tradition of fictional American tough guys.' Bringing gangsters to the leftover Wild West, this ironic hybrid of two touchstones of the Hollywood tradition borrows liberally from such diverse sources as dime novels, the Bible, and, of course, the Samurai movie. Hill's script revels in ridicule: 'I'd seen the real thing and these guys were a long way from it', says Willis' Everyman character. Dealing with the flow of liquor across the Mexican border, Hill's hoods are from another era; their fedoras indicate a longing for the homeland – as Walken's Hickey says: 'I don't want to die in Texas... Chicago, maybe!' Look beyond the generic cauldron, though, and you'll find just a glorified shoot-'em-up.

Lat Sau San Tam: See Hard Boiled.

SOLIHULL S.F.C.
LIBRARY

Leon (US Title: The Professional)

(US, Gaumont, 1994, 110 mins)

Credits
Dir./Prod./Scr: Luc Besson
DOP: Thierry Arbogast
Ed: Sylvie Landra
Music: Eric Serra
Prod. Des: Dan Weil

Cast: Jean Reno (Leon), Gary Oldman (Stansfield), Nathalie Portman (Mathilda), Danny Aiello (Tony), Peter Appel (Malky)

A New York hitman befriends a young girl, after her family are slaughtered by a corrupt cop, and trains her in the ways of his profession.

In what is a wry tribute to Jean Reno's role in Luc Besson's earlier *La Femme Nikita*, as Victor the Cleaner (used to mop up defective assassination attempts), Reno reprised the cold, lonely anti-hero figure – this time in the shape of a hitman himself. One might argue that Nathalie Portman's Mathilda is herself a reflection of hit-woman Nikita, but Luc Besson's portrait of a hitman at home (seen drinking milk and tending his plants) is more a reversal of the oft-told Lolita story, a mixture of teenage heart-throb fantasy and pre-pubescent fairy-tale. Characters are almost cartoon-like in proportions: Gary Oldman's pill-popping, Beethoven-loving murderous police agent, Mathilda's vulgar, abusive father and wicked step-mother, even Leon himself, carrying his machine gun in a violin case, show shades of caricature. Seen, of course, through the eyes of Mathilda, the action and the hero are romanticised. Leon, who opens the film with a silent, impassive execution of orders, is in some ways the perfect gentleman, created from the 12-year-old's lucid imagination. And yet he is in many ways more innocent than his counterpart, a manipulative waif who tells a hotel manager that they are not father and daughter but in fact lovers. Leon's professional alienation from society is paralleled by his bemusement at US culture, unable as he is to recognise Mathilda's impressions of Madonna and Charlie Chaplin. While the gangster (represented by

Leon's mentor and 'employer' Tony) operates within the realms of society – in this case an Italian restaurant – the hitman is forever destined to be the loner who sleeps with one eye open.

The plot itself, finishing with a ludicrous police assault on Leon, is pure Brothers Grimm, allowing love-struck Mathilda, as *Sight & Sound*'s Amanda Lipman noted, to shut 'the book and go back to school' upon Leon's death. Mathilda recalls memories of *Bonnie and Clyde* (qv) and *Thelma and Louise* – but using both examples invokes the films not the myth. Akin to Wesley Snipes' Nino Brown in *New Jack City*, or the characters of *Pulp Fiction* (qqv), it's a self-referential sign that action is no longer governed by environment but intertextual awareness.

* A special edition was released, featuring previously excluded footage. These scenes develop the relationship between Mathilda and Leon further as she initially attempts suicide in front of her mentor, only to be accepted by him as a partner. Mathilda is then used as a decoy to pull off a string of hits, tempting targets to their front doors. One such hit allows her to learn where exactly to shoot the victim (body or head), while Leon laments for the one girl he ever loved (murdered by her father). This ultimately leads to Mathilda getting drunk in a restaurant, and expressing her hormonal desire for Leon.

See also: *Driver, The*; *Fallen Angels*; *Killer, The*; *Samourai, Le*; *Little Odessa*; *Prizzi's Honor*; *This Gun For Hire*.

Lepke

(US, AmeriEuro Pictures, 1974, 110 mins)

'Seemingly more pre-occupied with turning in a Kosher version of The Godfather than with anything else, Menahem Golan manages to muddy his potentially fascinating source material – the establishment of the Syndicate and its offshoot, Murder Inc., and their subtle accommodation of the corporate business ethic and image under pressure from various 'clean-up'

*campaigns – and produces a very stiff and po-
faced mélange of gangster clichés.'*
(Verina Glaessner, *Monthly Film Bulletin***)**

Credits
Dir/Prod: Menahem Golan
Scr: Wesley Lau, Tamar Simon Hoffs
DOP: Andrew Davis
Ed: Dov Hoenig, Aaron Stell
Music: Ken Wannberg
Prod. Des: Jackson De Govia

Cast: Tony Curtis (Louis 'Lepke' Buchalter), Anjanette Comer
(Bernice Meyer), Michael Callan (Robert Kane), Warren Berlinger
(Gurrah Shapiro), Gianni Russo (Albert Anastasia), Vic Tayback
(Lucky Luciano)

**Biopic of the Jewish gangster, who rose from Lower East
Side slum kid to syndicate boss, only to fall foul of DA
Thomas E. Dewey and the electric chair.**

An interesting performance from Tony Curtis aside,
this sluggish, low-budget effort mixed an attempt to
emulate ethnic authenticity with the gangster
tradition. Set-pieces include a shootout in a cinema
showing a retrospective of gangster films, and a
further escapade in a fairground, where Lepke
stands stock-still in the waxworks museum, to
evade detection. Such heavy-handed symbolism
(Lepke seen as a 'dummy') is matched only in
crassness by a scene depicting the death of an
assailant via an exploding bowl of spaghetti.
Further psychological traits are displayed visually:
following the Dewey persecution and pressures
from the Luciano gang, Lepke swaps his natty suit
for a singlet and sweat in his hideout, his image
slowly being demolished.
An attempt to acknowledge Lepke's domestic
nature, in his marriage to a girl, Bernice, of
orthodox Jewish stock, goes some way in indicating
his humanity. But it's about as successful as half-
heartedly intertwining real-life figures into the plot.
The appearance of 'the voice of the Twentieth
Century', broadcaster/columnist Walter Winchell,
who mediates between Lepke and J. Edgar Hoover
to set up a deal concerning his imprisonment, adds
an unusual twist of media interference to
proceedings. But the dispatching of 'Legs' Diamond,

found floating under a pier with an ice pick in his
heart, is just one example of the scant regard for
historical accuracy.

See also: *Bugsy; Enforcer, The; George Raft Story,
The; Hoodlum; King of the Roaring Twenties: the
Arnold Rothstein Story; Lucky Luciano; Mobsters: the
Evil Empire; Rise and Fall of Legs Diamond, The.*

Le Samourai (US Title: The Godson)

(France, Filmel, 1967, 95 mins)

*'Between the ages of 12 and 14, I was formed
and deformed to a great extent by the first
American gangster novels. So I'd be quite happy
to have you say I make gangster films, inspired
by the gangster novels, but I don't make
American films, even though I like American film
noirs better than anything.'*
(Jean-Pierre Melville, *Sight & Sound***)**

Credits:
Dir./Scr: Jean-Pierre Melville
based on the original novel by Joan McLeod
Prod: Eugene Lepicier
DOP: Henri Decae
Ed: Monique Bonnot, Yolande Maurette
Music: François de Roubaix
Art Dir: François de Lamothe

Cast: Alain Delon (Jeff Costello), François Perier (The Inspector),
Nathalie Delon (Jane Lagrange), Cathy Rosier (Valerie), The
Gunman (Jacques Leroy)

**A loner hitman pulls a job and is double-crossed by his
nervous employers, after the police pull him in for
questioning.**

'There is no greater solitude than the samurais...
unless perhaps it is of the tiger in the jungle.' So
opens this 'Japanese' film (as Melville himself called
it), quoting from 'The Book of Bushido', and it is
this urban alienation that proves to be hitman Jeff's
strength, a quality gradually shorn from him in the
film by his relationship with the pianist.
Dialogue is minimal and visuals are everything –

Le Samourai: Jeff Costello (Alain Delon) is the samurai.

none more so than the iconographic snap-brim trilby and trench coat sported by Costello, symbolising rather than verbalising the *noir* homages. Filmed with a non-naturalistic monochrome look, all colour is washed out, as if the film is a photocopy of a 1930s gangster picture. Not unlike his earlier work *Le Deulos*, we have at once – fitting with Melville's above-quoted description of his work – tribute, reinterpretation and disassociation (preferring a mentality closer to a Kurosawa mercenary).

Delon's Jef Costello is the archetypal 1960s nihilistic anti-hero, influenced by Alan Ladd's mercenary Philip Raven in Frank Tuttle's *This Gun For Hire* (*qv*). Cold, indifferent and alone (his canary's cage bars him from contact even with a pet, using it instead as a warning device), he is described as 'the lone wolf' by the crime syndicate who hire him. In love with his own death, from the opening we see him 'laid out' on his bed, as if already dead. As we discover his gun was empty in the denouement, the idea that he had a death-wish is ratified (it was earlier symbolised by the pianist, an inversion of Jean Cocteau's image of Death in *Orphee*). No longer does he wish to kill, but instead commit hari-kiri. As for his employers, they are but briefly glimpsed – 'in a higher league than us' Jef is told, and for the film too, for Melville is out to show the alienation of one man – and to depict any relationship with the gangsters would destroy this. Ultimately, it swings like a pendulum between realism and fantasy, the enigmatic hitman and the logical, law-abiding inspector.

See also: *Borsalino*; *Borsalino & Co*; *Driver, The*; *Fallen Angels*; *Killer, The*; *Leon*; *Little Odessa*; *Prizzi's Honor*.

Little Caesar

(US, Warner Brothers, 1930, 77 mins)

'Its stripped-to-the-bone minimalism gives Little Caesar an obduracy of pace and style that is unique... The most restrained of gangster films, its Spartan efficiency is opportunely functional in defining and displaying its perversely animated central figure.'

(Jack Shadoian, *Dreams and Dead Ends: The American Gangster/Crime Film*)

Credits
Dir: Mervyn Le Roy
Prod: Hal B.Wallis
Scr: Francis Edward Faragoh based on the novel by W.R. Burnett
DOP: Tony Gaudio
Ed: Ray Curtiss
Music: Erno Rapee
Art Dir: Anton Grot

Cast: Edward G. Robinson (Rico), Douglas Fairbanks Jr (Joe Massara), Thomas Jackson (Flaherty), Glenda Farrell (Olga), Stanley Fields (Sam Vettori), Sidney Blackmer (Big Boy)

A petty thug rises to be a big-shot gangster, only to be overthrown by his gang and descend to vagrancy.

As Edward G. Robinson once said: 'When the script was first submitted to me, it was just another gangster story... Finally, I was given a version that made some difference, reading more or less like a Greek tragedy. It's a man with perverted mind, ambitious of a kind, who sets a goal more important than himself – that's what makes him a highly moral character in his perverted way... in his own mind, he thought he was doing the right thing... Rico in his way was like Macbeth and Othello and Richard.' Truly, the closing line – 'Mother of God, is this the end of Rico?' – befits his nickname, awarded by his gang (although early prints changed 'God' to 'Mercy', anticipating objections from the United Council of Churches). A landmark gangster film, despite staid direction from Le Roy, it outlines the pattern for the mobster to come. His career, as we are told, is like a skyrocket – starting in the gutter and finishing

Little Caesar: Rico (Edward G. Robinson) dishes it out but can't take it.

there, so that he becomes the subject of his catchphrase 'You can dish it out but you can't take it'. Rico's ambitions stretch beyond money: 'Be somebody, know that a bunch of guys will do anything you tell 'em, have your own way or nothin''. His uncouth beginnings give way to a taste for the high life, his clothes progressively indicating his status up to the pinnacle; wearing a dinner suit, he presents himself amicably to the press at a banquet in his honour. Fame, respectability and wealth achieve his notoriety, the chief concern for the gangster. But pride (he buys ten copies of the paper), jealousy and inferiority redirect his energies, leading to his eventual ousting from the gang. His death, as with great tragic works, is almost a release. Incensed by the comment that he is 'yella', he emerges from obscurity, a flop house, and dies in a hail of police bullets, rekindling a pathetic sort of self-worth.

* Rico's longtime friend (a relationship filled with latent homo-eroticism), Joe Massara, was based on George Raft, then making his first Hollywood films following his friendship with Owney Madden, the man who organised a taxi racket in New York.

Little Odessa

(US, New Line Cinema, 1994, 98 mins)

Credits
Dir./Scr: James Gray
Prod: Paul Webster
DOP: Tom Richmond
Ed: Dorian Harris
Music Sup: Dana Sano
Prod. Des: Kevin Thompson

Cast: Tim Roth (Joshua Shapira), Edward Furlong (Reuben Shapira), Moira Kelly (Alla Shustervich), Vanessa Redgrave (Irina Shapira), Maximilian Schell (Arkady Shapira)

A hitman for the Russian Mafia returns to his homeland of Brighton Beach to commit an assassination, only to find that he is drawn back towards the family, where his mother is dying of a brain tumour.

Known as 'Little Odessa' because of its large Ukranian and Russian population, the film's integral locale certainly appears as bleak as Siberia – filmed over 26 days during the appalling New York winter of 1994. Described by director Gray as a deliberately 'unhip' film 'about silences and emotional repression', he added to *The Independent*'s Patricia Thomson: 'The film is about a person who is trying to re-establish himself, but, of course, his tragedy is that he can't succeed, because he's gone too far.' This person is Tim Roth's icy contract killer, estranged from his father who calls him 'a street lad. No ambition. No desire. No nothing'. Rather like George Armitage's black comedy *Grosse Point Blank*, the hitman is shown to have a past, albeit one he physically attempts to wipe out as he ritually kills his father – partly for having an affair. An ingrained fatalism in the film, alongside references to Dostoyevsky and Shakespeare ('Since 1980, the film industry has exorcised tragedy from its consciousness' said Gray), the visuals match the dialogue for a gloom-soaked atmosphere. As Roth says to a victim 'Do you believe in God? Wait ten seconds to see if God saves you.' Of course, He doesn't. The reverse of *Pulp Fiction*'s (*qv*) born-again hitman Jules (with his biblical quoting to Pumpkin, ironically played by Roth), a bleak

atheism pervades the film, lifting it beyond mere generic conventions. Unfortunately, this metaphysical approach to the gangster film leaves the audience with the flimsiest of plots. While Gray apparently researched the Russian Mafia (rarely shown on screen with the exception of action fodder like *Maximum Risk*) via newspapers, interviews and local sources, little is noted about their day-to-day operations.

See also: *Driver, The*; *Fallen Angels*; *Killer, The*; *Leon*; *Samourai, Le*; *Prizzi's Honor*; *This Gun For Hire*.

Lock, Stock and Two Smoking Barrels

(UK, HandMade Films/Paragon Entertainment, 1998, 110mins)

Credits:
Dir/Scr: Guy Ritchie
Prod: Matthew Vaughn
DOP: Tim Maurice-Jones
Ed: Niven Howie
Music: David A. Hughes, John Murphy
Prod Des: Iain Andrews, Eve Mavrakis

Cast: Dexter Fletcher (Soap), Jason Flemyng (Tom), Steven Mackintosh (Winston), Vinnie Jones (Big Chris), Sting (JD), P.H. Moriarty (Hatchet Harry)

Four men, owing a rigged gambling debt to a local crimelord, rob their neighbours of a stash, stolen from a trio of yuppie weed-growers.

A roundabout plot and cartoon violence characterise this pacey trip, dripping with laconic humour. Utilizing street language, even subtitling cockney rhyming slang, the film is an exercise in style, using narration, slow-motion and freeze-frames. A *Goodfellas* (*qv*) minus the true malice that lay under that film, it depicts an ethnic-mix of scallywags, that does border on the stereotyped. Witness the two Scousers employed to steal some antique shot-guns, which are later appropriated by Fletcher, Flemyng and co as they rob their neighbours. Described by producer Vaughn as 'a roller-coaster ride...that spirals into fun and confusion', while the director Ritchie noted 'comedy and gangsters are inseparable, the truer they are, the funnier', violence particularly switches from the amusing to the shocking in a moment's notice. A trait found oversees, it would seem, from *Pulp Fiction* and the remake of *Kiss of Death (qqv)* onwards.

The inclusion of British comedy regulars Vas Blackwood and Danny John-Jules, plus Vinnie Jones' stirring appearance as the hard-man-for-hire (complete with foul-mouthed son in tow), indicate a leaning towards the pastiche, initiated in Britain by J.K.Amalou's *Hard Men*. Unlike the recent bloody Irish gangster biopics (*Resurrection Man* and *The General [qqv]*), this Brit-pack effort (complete with rising stars Mackintosh, Flemyng and Frank Harper) moves in the direction of unwanted irony. While it's rich plotting is a joy to watch unfurl, the film is ultimately a little self-satisfied. A mystery, considering most characters are thinly etched at best.

Literate in its appreciation of the gangster film, Ritchie's work pays homage to past British works. The inclusion of P.H.Moriarty as sex impresario and mobster nods towards his role as Hoskins henchman Razors in *The Long Good Friday (qv)*. Sting echoes his club owner in Mike Figgis' *Stormy Monday (qv)*, playing here the bar owner father of Soap, threatened with the loss of his establishment in lieu of his son's debt. Characters themselves are influenced by the genre. 'If you want to know how to do a drug deal, watch *Scarface*' says one. Scenes also echo *The Long Good Friday*: Harper's criminal Dog, in charge of robbing the yuppies, led by Mackintosh, prizes information from one character by aiming golf balls at his body, suspended upside down.

The three-card brag scene, in which Soap ends up owing £500,000 after he is the victim of a con, was even filmed at Repton Boxing Gym, a notorious haunt of the Krays. Equally, actor Harper - who spent a decade working on Smithfield Meat Market - based his character on a composite of gangsters he knew.

Long Good Friday, The

(UK, Calendar Productions, 1980, 109 mins)

'My favourites have always been gangster films. Dangerous films – mostly American, sometimes French. I wondered about why there had been so few English gangster films (this was 1979) to grip me. I thought about Ronnie and Reggie Kray – folk heroes, legends in my part of town.'
(Barrie Keefe, *Sight & Sound*)

Credits
Dir: John MacKenzie
Prod: Barry Hanson
Scr: Barrie Keefe
DOP: Philip Meheux
Ed: Mike Taylor
Music: Francis Monkman
Art Dir: Vic Symonds

Cast: Bob Hoskins (Harold Shand), Helen Mirren (Victoria), Derek Thompson (Jeff Hughes), P.H. Moriarty (Razors), Brian Hall (Alan), Eddie Constantine (Charlie)

London crime boss, with designs on uniting with the US Mafia, is subjected to a series of bombings.

Originally part of a three-picture deal, funded by Lord Lew Grade at ACC/ITC, the film – at his insistence – was cut down to 75 minutes, a main character revoiced and all mentions of the IRA removed – because, in his words, 'it might be a bad influence on young people'. Examining the restored version, we can see that scriptwriter Keefe has simultaneously paid his dues to the American gangster film, while forging a natural successor to British works like *Get Carter (qv)*. After a hiatus of almost a decade in which private eye films like Mike Hodges' *Pulp* and Stephen Frears' *Gumshoe* replaced the gangster, Keffe's creation, Harold Shand (played with fiercesome menace by Bob Hoskins), is the archetypal tragic figure, witnessing the collapse of his empire. Increasingly isolated he brutally slays his Number 2, Jeff, but cradles him father-to-son as he dies. Events have taken a force of their own,

The Long Good Friday: Hooked on Classics: Harold Shand (Bob Hoskins) finds a captive audience.

beyond his control and comprehension, fleshed out
never more powerfully than in the bravura final
scene. Trapped in a car with his assailants, Shand
helplessly watches his wife Helen Mirren taken
away in another vehicle, while director MacKenzie
holds for seemingly minutes on the quiet
frustration and despair that crosses his face. The
crucifixion of the security guard on Good Friday
does not bring the promised Easter Sunday
resurrection, only an ironic gesture towards the
spiritual wasteland that belies the film's religious
title.

Keefe draws increasingly tight parallels between
American and British gangster culture.
Shand's reverence for his mother may echo
Cagney's in *White Heat* (qv) but it also remembers

The Krays' affection for Violet. Just as the Warner
Brothers era spawned films from 'Today's
Headlines', so both Shand and his American
counterpart in the picture reference recent history.
Shand calling the events of the day – in which he
unbeknowingly is targeted by the IRA – 'like
fucking Belfast on a bad night'. Charlie, present to
negotiate a Docklands deal with Shand which will
push England as Europe's leading State, adds later,
events were 'like a bad night in Vietnam'. He feels
the country is a worse risk than Cuba – recalling
Godfather Part II (qv). Harold is the direct
descendent of the old school. Not unlike Coppola
and Puzo's Vito Corleone, he refuses to deal in
narcotics. He sees himself as not a politician but 'a
businessman with a sense of history'. Like a

Roman emperor as he grills his subjects – attached to meat hooks – he is the peacemaker, the patron: 'For more than ten years... I've put money in your pockets, I've treated you well.' Merging the pugnacious but grandiose strain of Robinson's Caesar with the cruel malevolence of Michael Caine's Carter, Harold Shand was the villain for Thatcher's children, a streak that would resonate in subsequent British screen gangsters, not least the Kemp twins' work in *The Krays* (qv). Ambitious, bigoted, patriotic and nostalgic, Shand neither embodies the myth of a Clyde Barrow nor a Ronnie Kray. Believing himself bigger than the Mafia and the IRA, he is a truly British gangster, an empire builder who would trumpet 'Rule Britannia'.

* Over 40 titles were conceived for the film, including *The Last Gangster Show*, *Havoc*, *Harold's Kingdom*, *Citadel of Blood* and *Diabolical Liberty*.

See also: *Mona Lisa*.

Lost Capone, The

(US, Patchett Kaufman Entertainment, 1990, 90 mins)

Credits
Dir./Scr: John Gray
Prod: Eva Fyer
DOP: Paul Elliott
Ed: Karen Stern
Prod. Des: Roy Forge Smith

Cast: Adrian Pasdar (Richard Hart/Jimmy Capone), Ally Sheedy (Kathleen), Eric Roberts (Al Capone), Titus Welliver (Ralph Capone), Jimmie F. Skaggs (Joseph Littlecloud)

Al Capone's estranged brother leaves Chicago to become a small-town sheriff, only to encounter his gangster sibling later in life.

An unusual, and at times forceful, effort to present the Al Capone story, the film is packed with gangland clichés, playing particularly on the theme of the family. John (who changes his name from Jimmy) becomes the white sheep of the clan, told that he turned his 'back on the family' by running away. Proving himself a worthy opponent of his brother, he stops the liquor convoys sent through his State to reach Chicago. It makes it clear that he only ever wanted to be near his father, admitting that where he comes from 'family is everything'. Occasional trite dialogue (the reply to this being: 'You can't choose your family, but you can choose your friends') does rather spoil what is an attempt to analyse the effect of Capone's activities on the people. As Al tells John, 'You fight human nature, I serve it.' The implications are that the masses are inherent law-breakers given their situation; Capone is just operating upon the economic notion of supply and demand.

Closing with a sepia-tinted meeting in 1946 in Miami between Jimmy and Al, his brain now gripped in the latter stages of neuro-syphilis, the ending suggests a certain regret on the part of Al, admitting envy of Jimmy's conscience. Not the whacked-out performance from Ben Gazzara that ends Steve Carver's *Capone* (qv), the film ends with the captions informing us that John died in 1952 in Nebraska, while other brother Ralph continued to play a major part in organised crime until his death in 1974. While these words may be factual, the preceding scene illustrates just how much is supposition in the rest of the picture.

See also: *Al Capone*; *Gangland: the Verne Miller Story*; *George Raft Story, The*; *St. Valentine's Day Massacre, The*; *Scarface Mob, The*; *Untouchables, The*.

Love Me or Leave Me

(US, MGM, 1955, 122 mins)

Credits
Dir: Charles Vidor
Prod: Joe Pasternak
Scr: Isobel Lennart and Daniel Fuchs, based on his own story
DOP: Arthur E. Arling
Ed: Ralph E. Winters
Music: George Stoll
Art Dir: Cedric Gibbons, Urie McCleary

Cast: Doris Day (Ruth Etting), James Cagney (Martin 'The Gimp' Synder), Cameron Mitchell (Johnny Alderman), Robert Keith

(Bernard Loomis)

Nebraskan singer meets a local racketeer and launderer, who becomes her agent and finds her fame and fortune, only to force her into marriage with him – claiming she owes him.

Made during the fashion for the glossy Hollywood showbiz biopic, which paid lip-service to the likes of Glenn Miller and Lon Chaney, this life of famous 1920's torch-singer Ruth Etting ran against the grain, detailing events with complete candour. The relationship between Day and Cagney (who, in his autobiography, lauded his co-star, lamenting her subsequent domestic comedies) is shown as obsessive-compulsive on the part of the singer. A story, then, of independence and creative honesty versus exploitation – economic, sexual and psychological. Scriptwriters Daniel Fuchs and Isobel Lennart were granted permission to utilize all the facts in the story; as a result, with the real-life Etting, Synder and Alderman (Etting's piano accompanist and true love) giving script approval, the players emerge with little nobility. Free of the standard sugar-coated MGM musical stick figures, it is as sordid as it is uplifting.

A successful fusion of gangster and musical genres, the film is shaped in a tradition that harks back to the likes of Paul Fejos' *Broadway*, uniting crime and show business. Structurally, the songs (many sung by or identified with Etting) appear not gratuitously but from dramatic need in the story. Cagney himself, in what would be his last major racketeer role, provides a tour-de-force performance (complete with limp), which ensured that he was nominated for an Academy Award for a third time, one of six the film received.

* **Academy Awards:** Daniel Fuchs won for Best Original Story.

* Co-writer Daniel Fuchs was also responsible for scripting a number of other gangster pictures: *Criss Cross* (qv), *The Big Shot* (See: *King of the Underworld*) and, most interestingly, *The Gangster*. Made in 1947, and directed by Gordon Wiles, this atypical effort dealt with a hoodlum's failure of nerve (played by Barry Sullivan). His desire to go

legitimate ultimately leads not to redemption but a slide into obscurity.

See also: *Bugsy Malone*; *Guys and Dolls*; *Pocketful of Miracles, A.*

Lucky Luciano

(Italy, Films La Boetie, 1973, 115 mins)

'A focus and a channel for the illicit activities of both State and the Mafia... cops and robbers are indistinguishable, and... Rosi's elaborately constructed factual puzzle leaves the impression that the world is an impossible scramble that surpasses all understanding.'

(Richard Combs, The Listener)

Credits
Dir./Scr: Francesco Rosi
Prod: Franco Cristaldi
Scr: Lino Jannuzzi, Tonino Guerra
DOP: Pasqualino De Santis
Ed: Ruggero Mastroianni
Music: Piero Piccioni
Art Dir: Andrea Crisanti

Cast: Gian Maria Volonte (Lucky Luciano), Rod Steiger (Gene Giannini), Edmond O'Brien (Harry J. Anslinger), Charles Siragusa (Himself), Vincent Gardenia (American Colonel)

Biopic of the legendary gangster.

An attempt to unravel the intricate story that lies behind Charles 'Lucky' Luciano, Rosi offers a blend of fact and fiction that circles upon itself. As Edmond O'Brien's Narcotics Bureau Commissioner notes: 'We chase Luciano, Dewey chases us, Kefauver chases us, and in the end everybody will find himself back at the same goddamn place where he started.' With Luciano's death, as *Monthly Film Bulletin*'s Jonathan Rosenbaum noted, 'in the arms of a screenwriter' Rosi may be 'wryly commenting on how any film is largely a matter of chance'. Even the unusual casting of US narcotics agent Charles Siragusa, playing himself – a man who spent 15 years trying to prove Luciano's part in the heroin trade from Italian pharmaceutical

companies to the US underworld black market –
can shed no light on the subject. What is known is
that New York racketeer Luciano, sentenced to
between 30 and 50 years imprisonment in 1936
brought against him by DA Thomas E. Dewey, was
paroled nine years later and deported to Italy for
World War II service. With Dewey orchastrating
the release, the film suggests Luciano contributed
Dewey's political campaigns. He is an 'elusive
martyr' rather than a typical gangster, as one critic
suggested, and the film uses the 1946 dockside
deportation as a pivotal scene, weaving theories
around it. Once more taking the form of an
investigation, Rosi's work attempts to guide us
through the mire, but makes no attempt to
formulate any more than possibilities. Rosi points
to the ironies; that the US released Luciano, gave
him credentials and 'practically gave him a medal';
and that the Mafia in police records are described
as 'persons of good political and civil character'. As
is stated at the end, 'the politician never had any
trouble manoeuvring with racketeers'. The growth
of the Mafia, it is hinted, partly lies at the doors of
Capitol Hill. Luciano's consistent references to
Italy's poverty imply that only with the support,
politically or economically, of a country like the
States could the organisation grow. Rosi's
documentary approach ensures that key historical
scenes – the Apalachin conference, the Valachi
trial, the Night of the Sicilian Vespers – receive
ample coverage, entwining its subject with the
history of the Mafia, if never quite placing him
neatly at its eye.

* The English version originally released
theatrically was 21 minutes shorter than the
final cut.

See also: *Bugsy*; *George Raft Story, The*; *Hoodlum*;
*King of the Roaring Twenties: the Arnold Rothstein
Story*; *Lepke*; *Marked Woman*; *Mobsters: the Evil
Empire*; *Valachi Papers, The*.

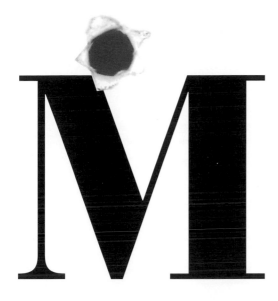

Machine Gun Kelly

(US, American International, 1958, 80 mins)

Credits
Dir/Prod: Roger Corman
Scr: Robert Wright Campbell
DOP: Floyd D. Crosby
Ed: Ronald Sinclair
Music: Gerald Fried
Art Dir: Daniel Haller

Cast: Charles Bronson (Machine Gun Kelly), Morey Amsterdam (Fandango), Susan Cabot (Flo), Wally Campo (Maize), Connie Gilchrist (Ma), Jack Lambert (Howard)

Biopic about the rise and fall of a notorious bank-robber and kidnapper.

Based on a real-life character, although the standard disclaimer adds that other events and characters are fictional, Corman's film provides a rare opportunity to view a serious portrayal of a gangster who never wanted to be Public Enemy No. 1. Played by Charles Bronson, this was his second starring role, following the previous year's *Gang War* in which he played a teacher driven mad with grief following the murder of his pregnant wife after he had witnessed a mob hit. Here, Bronson's Kelly shudders at the sight of wreaths, coffins, and even

has nightmares that girlfriend Flo will be the one to put him in his wooden box.

Strictly small-time, Kelly unwillingly progresses from bank-robbing to kidnapping at the behest of Flo, who claims she has nurtured her man, bequeathing him the reputation, the name and the trademark machine gun (which he can fit together in two minutes 38 seconds, and only 42 secs more blindfolded). What she never achieved was 'the backbone', Kelly only wiping out a rival gang when he was severely pushed. He may have 'wanted the jungle' as Flo notes, but he is unable to 'live in it'. In the finale – as the police call him 'Pop Gun Kelly' – he is a pathetic figure.

One of the film's more curious aspects is the reaction of Flo's parents to Kelly. As the police figures earlier speculate, the gang wants to be known; in a way they want to be caught, for they are of no importance unless people are aware of their crimes. Her parents, rather than condemn their activities, chide them for their lack of headlines; to them, as with Corman's later productions such as *Bloody Mama* and *Big Bad Mama* (*qqv*), bank robbing is a way of life and should be kept in the family.

See also: *Bonnie and Clyde*; *Bonnie Parker Story, The*;

Machine Gun Kelly: Kelly (Charles Bronson) demonstrates while they call him 'Machine Gun'.

Bullet for Pretty Boy, A; Dillinger; George Raft Story, The; Lepke; Lucky Luciano; Rise and Fall of Legs Diamond, The; Young Dillinger.

Mad Dog and Glory

(US, Universal, 1992, 97 mins)

Credits
Dir: John McNaughton
Prod: Martin Scorsese, Barbara DeFina
Scr: Richard Price
DOP: Robby Muller
Ed: Craig McKay, Elena Maganini
Music: Elmer Bernstein
Prod. Des: David Chapman, Deborah Lee

Cast: Robert De Niro (Wayne 'Mad Dog' Dobie), Bill Murray (Frank Milo), Uma Thurman (Glory), Kathy Baker (Lee), David Caruso (Mike)

A gangster presents a cop with a beautiful woman, after his life is saved.

Unsurprisingly, Richard Price's attempt to revive the 'beloved' tradition of Damon Runyon 'cute and quirky cop and crook' fables sat in script form for years at Universal. Director John McNaughton, who made his debut with the brutally cold *Henry: Portrait of a Serial Killer*, was brought in by producer Martin Scorsese, who proclaimed the film the best debut he'd seen in ten years. Reversing the roles usually associated with Robert De Niro and Bill Murray (the former now playing the cowardly cop, the latter the psychotic gangster), the film reads as a critique of movie, and gangster, machismo. Murray has one choice turn of phrase. To Mad Dog: 'I become the expediter of your dreams. But don't disrespect me... underestimate me. If you do, your life becomes a raging sea.' Trouble is, the irony in this tepid film goes no further than that.
De Niro applied his usual diligence to researching his role as the forensics cop. Turning up to a real crime scene, as McNaughton remembers, he saw 'a guy lying on his bed strangled with the phone cord, with his head beat in, the hammer lying next to him, and an ashtray under his head to catch the blood' and promptly started to gag.

Manhattan Melodrama

(US, MGM, 1934, 89 mins)

Credits
Dir: W.S. van Dyke
Prod: David Selznick
Scr: Oliver H.P. Garrett, Joseph L. Mankiewicz, based on an original story by Art Caesar
DOP: James Wong Howe
Ed: Ben Lewis
Art Dir: Cedric Gibbons, Joseph Wright

Cast: Leo Carrillo (Father Pat), Blackie Gallagher (Clark Gable), Myrna Loy (Eleanor), William Powell (Jim Wade), Mickey Rooney (Blackie as a boy)

Two childhood friends grow up to be on opposite sides of the legal fence: one an attorney, the other a big-time gambler, with the former eventually having to prosecute his chum.

A film that gained infamy after John Dillinger was killed emerging from a cinema that was screening it, *Manhattan Melodrama* was the first film to team up William Powell and Myrna Loy, who appeared in *The Thin Man* together that year and would go on to star in another six films together. Originally scripted to follow the lives of three orphans (the third being a priest, later made peripheral), the film was a typical example of a gangster setting and character used to tell a personal drama. In this case, the lifelong friendship between Gable's gambler Blackie and Powell's DA Wade, which is taken to the limits as Blackie is sent to the electric chair (and prosecuted by Wade) for killing a blackmailer intent on ruining his friend's career. Presenting both gangster and lawman sympathetically allows for an intelligent examination of the criminal element. As Wade points out to a jury: 'For years men and women have tolerated racketeers. Because of their own hatred of Prohibition they felt in sympathy with those who broke the law. Crime and criminals became popular. Either we can surrender to the epidemic of crime and violence or we can give warning to the host of other gangsters and murderers that they are through.' But as Blackie says in the final reel: 'If I can't live the way I want, then at least let me die the way I want.' One is asked to question the hypocrisy of a society that at first condones then condemns the criminal, as the law changes.

* **Academy Award:** Art Caesar won for Best Original Story.

Mano Nera, La: See The Black Hand.

Marked Woman

(US, Warner Brothers, 1937, 96 mins)

Credits
Dir: Lloyd Bacon
Prod: Louis Edelman
Scr: Abem Finkel, Seton Miller, Robert Rossen
DOP: Georges Barnes
Ed: Jack Killifer
Music: Bernard Kaun, Heinz Roemheld
Art Dir: Max Parker

Cast: Humphrey Bogart (David Graham), Bette Davis (Mary Dwight), Eduardo Ciannelli (Johnny Vanning), Jane Bryan (Betty Strauber), Allen Jenkins (Louie), Isabel Jewell (Emmy Lou Egan)

A crusading District Attorney persuades the hostess of a high-class clip joint to testify against her racketeer boss, only for one to receive a facial scar (an X) to mark her for life as one who double-crossed.

Based on the conviction of Charles 'Lucky' Luciano in 1936, *Marked Woman* took the testimonies of the prostitutes that helped New York City DA Thomas Dewey put Luciano (known for his collection of brothels) away, and turned them into the basis for, as Karyn Kay said 'one of the best films about women (and therefore, for women) ever to come out of Hollywood'. Although the profession of Davis et al was changed to nightclub hostess, due to the 1934 Motion Picture Production Code, it was

hinted at throughout (Re: the song *My Silver Dollar Man*, sung in the club).

Devoid of sentimentality or glorification, the prostitutes are the unsung heroines. In particular, in the denouement, as the girls drift unnoticed into the fog as Bogart's crusading DA receives all the credit for gangster Vanning's conviction (who gets the same sentence, 30 to 50 years, as Luciano), Bacon directs his camera to follow them, frustrating the melodramatic ending. The girls walk off arm-in-arm, outlaws displaying a sense of female camaraderie; it is they who, in the years of the Depression, have turned to their profession as the only suitable means of employment at this time. As Davis says: 'We've all tried this 12 and a half week stuff. It's no good living in furnished rooms, walking to work, going hungry a couple of days a week so you can have some clothes to put on your back. I've had enough of that for the rest of my life.'

Their work reminds us that they exist as part of a Capitalist society, of which one necessary facet is the 'social and economic repression of women', as Kay puts it, symbolised by the scarring of Davis, as the camera focuses on her friends — each with no choice but to accept this denigration. Not only does *Marked Woman* highlight the necessary plight of the exploited, but also those who exacerbate the situation: the exploiter — namely, the gangster figure Vanning. As club girl Gabby (Lola Lane) astutely points out: 'There'll always be somebody else... The law isn't for people like us!' People like Vanning will always exist and women like those represented will always be used.

See also: *Bugsy*; *Hoodlum*; *Lucky Luciano*; *Lepke*; *Mobsters: the Evil Empire*; *Valachi Papers, The*.

Married to the Mob

(US, Orion Pictures Corporation, 1988, 104 mins)

'Married to the Mob goes from gangster thriller to feminist 'fish-out-of-water' comedy to pop art caper.'

(Graham Fuller, *The Listener*)

Credits
Dir/Scr: Jonathan Demme
Prod: Kenneth Utt, Edward Saxon
Scr: Barry Strugatz, Mark R. Burns
DOP: Tak Fujimoto
Ed: Craig McKay
Music: David Byrne
Prod. Des: Kristi Zea

Cast: Michelle Pfeiffer (Angela DeMarco), Matthew Modine (Mike Downey), Dean Stockwell (Tony 'The Tiger' Russo), Mercedes Ruehl (Connie Russo), Alec Baldwin ('Cucumber' Frank DeMarco), Joan Cusack (Rose)

Recently widowed mob wife tries to resume a normal life, while an undercover cop woos her to bring down her deceased husband's mob boss.

There's only one good line: a cop, on being accused of using mob tactics in his work, says: 'There's a big difference. The mob is run by murdering, thieving, lying, cheating psychopaths. We work for the Presidents of the United States of America.' Intended as a comic glance at the problems inherent in being a mob wife, the cartoon-style credits set the tone – and we're rarely lifted away from ten-second comic strip, the residue, no doubt, from Demme's performance films, that included Talking Heads' *Stop Making Sense* (lead singer David Byrne compiled the soundtrack for this picture). The inverse companion piece to Demme's previous effort, *Something Wild*, it becomes a school, rather than a genre, spanning American Gothic, shopping mall chic and yuppie nightmare movies (such as Scorsese's *After Hours*), the finale shootout a wink to Billy Wilder's *Some Like It Hot* (qv). His hoods are white, lower-class trash, populating the high tack of kitsch Americana: sex-theme hotels, drive-in burger joints and mock-mediaeval restaurants litter the landscape.

As Demme told *Time Out*'s Geoff Andrew: 'It is tricky making a comedy about the Mafia, which in itself is no laughing matter. It's a hideous toxin, a cancer that pollutes, corrupts and destroys everything it touches. So that's why *Married* is less a Mafia movie than a gangster film; I decided not to show the way they operate, and only concerned myself with their general lifestyle, which I read

about in the book *Wise Guy*, which Scorsese is currently making into a film with De Niro [*Goodfellas* (qv)]. Really, my mobsters are just any old gangsters.' That aside, Demme – despite scrapping a truth-based sub-plot about the Mafia running a waste-dumping scam – used the work to demonstrate a sense of anger at the loss of American values. Concerned with presenting a 'cavalier' attitude to violence, it's a film that unfortunately suffers for its stance.

See also: *My Blue Heaven*.

Mean Streets

(US, Warner Brothers, 1973, 110 mins)

'Mean Streets was an attempt to put myself and my old friends on the screen, to show how we lived, what life was like in Little Italy. It was really an anthropological text or a sociological tract.'

(Martin Scorsese, *Scorsese on Scorsese*)

Credits
Dir/Scr: Martin Scorsese
Prod: Jonathan Taplin
Scr: Mardik Martin
DOP: Kent Wakeford
Ed: Sidney Levin
Prod. Des: David C. Nichols

Cast: Harvey Keitel (Charlie), Robert De Niro (Johnny Boy), David Proval (Tony), Amy Robinson (Teresa), Richard Romanus (Michael), Cesare Danova (Giovanni)

The lives of four small-time hoods in Little Italy.

'I was trying to make a kind of homage to the Warner Brothers gangster films... We grew up with *The Public Enemy* and *Little Caesar*. I found *Little Caesar* to be vulgar, very overdone and heavily acted. But even though they were Irish gangsters in *The Public Enemy*, which was a little odd to us, we understood the thinking behind it. I was influenced by the way William Wellman kept popular tunes playing in the background, no score but source

Mean Streets: Charlie (Harvey Keitel) in the climactic crucifixion pose.

music.' As important to the genre as Coppola's *The Godfather* (qv) a year before, *Mean Streets* remains a highly personal film. One of the first movies to utilise popular songs onto a soundtrack, the innovation was 'part of the way we lived... For me, the whole movie was *Jumping Jack Flash* and *Be My Baby*.' Reverberating with the sounds of Little Italy (despite most of the film being shot in Los Angeles), *Mean Streets* is the genuine article – Scorsese even explaining the pool room fight thus: 'That was the main thing in the streets: you had to learn how to kick. Because if you weren't powerful enough with your hands, you'd always kick – kick people in the head, or between the legs, or in the chest to save yourself.' Keitel's Charlie was effectively a re-run of the character J.R. from Scorsese's first (also autobiographical) feature *Who's That Knocking At My Door?* while De Niro's volatile street punk Johnny Boy, the role that shot him to fame, was based on a neighbourhood friend, Sally GaGa, who had undergone a nervous breakdown after accidentally killing a drunk.

An interlocking matrix of honour, trust and friendship, *Mean Streets* dealt with the American Dream in a society where order and violence were twin aspects of existence. For example, the shooting in Tony's bar is to avenge an insult levied at Mario, friend to Charlie's uncle, and local Godfather, Giovanni. Parallel to this is Johnny's insult to Michael, one of their associates to whom he remains indebted. Johnny Boy's killing in the final reel is necessitated by the laws and codes of the street, the mythic structure of the gangland milieu which dictates enforced harmony to achieve economic prosperity. Perversely loyal to Johnny Boy, Charlie is the martyr – 'You don't make up for your sins in the church... you make up for them in the streets, where it counts.' Torn by conscience (suffering guilt in the confessional for his relationship with the epileptic cousin of Johnny Boy, Theresa), Charlie's redemption can only ever see fruition by a conformation to the status quo. A trip to the cinema confirming their heritage, spurning *Borsalino* (qv) for a Western, Scorsese's hoods are the successors to Cagney's Tom Powers or Cody Jarrett, street punks heading for oblivion.

* Roger Corman's *Tomb of Ligeia* is briefly featured

in the film as a tribute to the man who launched Scorsese's career. Corman had offered Scorsese $150,000 to shoot the *Mean Streets* script with an all-black cast at the height of the blaxploitation phenomenon.

* A favourite film of real-life gangster Henry Hill, later to be the subject of Scorsese's *Goodfellas* (*qv*), the story goes that he, along with fellow mobsters, kidnapped Paul Vario (the basis for the Paul Cicero character) and took him to the cinema to watch the film.

Menace II Society

(US, New Line, 1993, 97 mins)

Credits
Dir/Prod: Allen & Albert Hughes
Prod: Darin Scott
Scr: Tyger Williams
DOP: Lisa Rinzler
Ed: Chris Koefoed
Music: QD III
Prod. Des: Penny Barrett

Cast: Tyrin Turner (Caine Lawson), Jada Pinkett (Ronnie), Larenz Tate (O-Dog), Arnold Johnson (Grandpapa), MC Eiht (A-Wax), Marilyn Coleman (Grandmama)

An orphaned black LA teen finds himself increasingly drawn into gang violence.

'We were tired of people thinking *Boyz 'N' the Hood* is the rawest shit they've ever seen. We thought, let's show America the way it really is,' said Albert, one half of the Hughes Brothers' team who burst onto the scene with this nihilistic gangsta rap drama. The most extreme example of this sub-genre, the film grossed $20 million in its first five weeks of release in the US, with the soundtrack album going platinum. Allen commented that the film is 'about cycles of violence in the black community. It takes place in Watts [LA] and moves from the '65 riots to what they bred: victims/criminals or hustlers.' Add to this an examination of how patterns of violence are

mirrored from generation to generation, and a representation of ghetto masculinity – where, as *Sight & Sound*'s Amy Taubin noted: 'not to be a 'menace' is to admit that one is powerless, a victim'. Caine, the film's central and most sympathetic character, is accosted by a woman who claims he is the father of her child: 'You're man enough to take a life, but not man enough to look after one,' he is told. To be a man in this inner-city wasteland is to deny all possibilities of a stable family environment. Drawing from Scorsese's *Mean Streets* and De Palma's *Scarface* (*qqv*) rather than revisiting the Blaxploitation of *New Jack City* (*qv*), the film rejects the profoundly moral (and sentimental) standpoint of John Singleton's *Boyz N' The Hood*, the benchmark for all subsequent Hood films. Offering instead the camera-as-bystander, the film shows no tried-and-tested route out of the hopeless predicaments faced by its characters. The frighteningly indifferent O-Dog, who opens the film by killing a Korean grocer and his wife (stealing the security video to screen ritualistically to his friends later) is 'America's nightmare. Young, black and [doesn't] give a fuck.' Caine spends his time recovering from a gang shooting in hospital 'watching old gangster movies'. The neighbourhood economy itself is founded on drug dealing (Caine's deceased father and mother were dealer and addict respectively). Both social and economic factors are pinpointed, the characters remain unjudged – in the tradition of the best white gangster films. Criticised at its time of release for celebrating not problematising the situation, the film's ghetto population do not offer easy solutions, only adding to the sense of alienation felt by the community's youth. 'Being a black and in America isn't easy,' warns High School Teacher Mr Butler (Charles S. Dutton), 'The heat is on and you're the prey. All I'm saying is survive.' Caine's religiously zealous grandparents, with their hopes for their grandson's respectability, only add to the pressure, in a film that deals candidly with the multitude of directions facing LA's black youth – in a society where no-one is there to point the way.

See also: *Clockers*; *I'm Gonna Git You, Sucka*; *Superfly*.

SOU... ILL S.F.C.

Men of Respect

(US, Central City/Arthur Goldblatt, 1990, 107 mins)

Credits
Dir/Scr: William Reilly, based on Macbeth by William Shakespeare
Prod: Ephraim Horowitz
DOP: Bobby Bukowski
Ed: Elizabeth Kling
Music: Misha Segal

Cast: John Turturro (Mike Battaglia), Katherine Borowitz (Ruthie Battaglia), Peter Boyle (Duffy), Rod Steiger (Charlie D'Amico), Stanley Tucci (Mai D'Amico)

A hoodlum is encouraged by his ambitious wife and a gypsy to kill his way to the top.

Applying Shakespeare's tragedy to the conventions of the gangster genre, William Reilly's film remains textually faithful but falters whenever required to reproduce the metaphysics of the play. And so the witches scene, now set in a basement fortune teller's, appears a surreal episode in an otherwise gritty drama. Morally, the film is also rendered impotent. At no point do we envisage that the elimination of rivals to the existing ruler's power will result in the stable, authorised rule that Shakespeare's play foresees with the final accession of Malcolm. As the opening maxim states: 'There is nothing but what has a violent end of violent beginnings', indicating a perpetual loop of violence. Reilly leaves us with the idea that none of the men, ironically, respect either the organisation's code of conduct or one another. That moral principles, such as respect, cannot prosper in such a capitalist society is Reilly's ultimate conclusion.

* A 1955 film, entitled *Joe Macbeth* and directed by Ken Hughes, was an earlier attempt at merging the Bard's Scottish play with the gangster genre. Paul Douglas plays the eponymous tough guy convinced by his wife (Ruth Roman) to kill his boss.

Miller's Crossing

(US, Circle Films, 1990, 114 mins)

Credits
Dir/Scr: Joel Coen
Prod/Scr: Ethan Coen
DOP: Barry Sonnenfeld
Ed: Michael R. Miller
Music: Carter Burwell
Art Dir: Leslie McDonald

Cast: Gabriel Byrne (Tom Reagan), Albert Finney (Leo), J.E. Freeman (Eddie Dane), Marcia Gay Harden (Verna), John Turturro (Bernie Bernbaum), Jon Polito (Johnny Caspar)

Prohibition tale in which a conniving right-hand man switches allegiances between rival gangs.

The Coen Brothers' ironic antidote to Martin Scorsese's *Goodfellas* (qv), released the same year, drew much of its twisted heart from the works of Dashiell Hammett, namely *Red Harvest* and *The Glass Key*. Gabriel Byrne's 'straight as a corkscrew' Tom Reagan could stand representative of the picture: 'He's a character who sort of throws everything up in the air and intentionally creates confusion', said Joel Coen to *US Premiere*'s John Richardson. 'This is an old Hammett idea – 'If I stir things up, I'll be able to deal with the consequences, whatever they are. Something will emerge that I can exploit."
The Coens subvert, rather than parody; more *film brun* than *film noir*, as one critic noted in reference to the film's earthy, as opposed to inky, palette. Rival boss to Leo, Johnny Casper, says in the opening scene: 'If you can't trust a fix, what can you trust?' and Leo cements this by later wondering: 'Who's a friend, who's an enemy?' It is the right-hand men, Reagan and The Dane, who hold the cards – the men who walk behind the men who whisper in their ears. Significance means nothing, and everything is signified. The death of 'Rug' Daniels, which perpetuates Leo's mistrust of Casper, is briefly explained away in the closing stages as 'just a mix-up', as much a mystery to the characters as the disappearance of his hair-piece. The iconographic fedora hat is seen blowing through Miller's

Miller's Crossing: 'Oh, Danny Boy': Leo (Albert Finney) comes under attack.

Crossing, the patch of forest used for gangland executions, on the opening credits. Reagan later tells Varna (his and Leo's mistress) that he dreamt his hat blew off in the woods. She questions whether he chased it, and if it changed form: 'It stayed a hat... I watched it blow away – nothing more foolish than a man chasing his hat.' Enigmatic and oblique, the references are stirred brazenly into the melting pot. The result is a perverse tribute to the genre.

Leo's surname – O'Bannion – for example, reminds one of the crusading sergeant played by Glenn Ford in Fritz Lang's *The Big Heat* (qv). As Richardson

points out, '*Miller's Crossing* is post-postmodern *Godfather* that rollicks in the silliness of the genre but still somehow plumbs the depths of emotion. This is a movie teaming with caricatures that keep revealing real characters underneath.'

Mobsters: the Evil Empire

(US, Universal, 1991, 104 mins)

Credits
Dir: Michael Karbelnikoff

134

Prod: Steve Roth
Scr: Mike Mahern, Nicholas Kazan
DOP: Lajos Koltai
Ed: Scott Smith, Joe D'Augustine
Music: Michael Small
Prod. Des: Richard Sylbert

Cast: Christian Slater ('Lucky' Luciano), Patrick Dempsey (Meyer Lansky), Christopher Penn (Tommy Reina), Michael Gambon (Don Feranzano), Richard Grieco ('Bugsy' Siegel), Costas Mandylor (Frank Costello)

Account of the lives of gangsters 'Bugsy' Siegel, 'Lucky' Luciano, Frank Costello and Meyer Lansky.

Dubbed 'Young Tommy Guns' due to its similarities to Christopher Cain's *Young Guns* (four bratpackers playing legendary outlaws), Michael Karbelnikoff's film is a cartoon parody of the gangster genre. As Jeff Laffel in *Films in Review* noted, the film 'does not bring to mind Muni, Robinson and Bogart of the great Warner gangster films of the thirties but rather Scott Baio et al in Alan Parker's 1976 spoof *Bugsy Malone*'.

Producer Steve Roth explained his concept to *US Premiere*'s Steve Pond thus: 'What I did was model this picture after *The Roaring Twenties*, with Jimmy Cagney and Humphrey Bogart. They were young guys then. I mean, I think Cagney in *Roaring Twenties* was 24, 25 years old. And he was a hot, tough kid like Slater. Bogart was 27. The sex appeal that they had is the sex appeal that this movie has.' The fact that Cagney and Bogart were both 40 when the film was released does not bode well for the film's authentic representation of the alliance formed between the cocky Italian Luciano and the Jewish mob. Don Feranzano, for example, did not exist. His name was Maranzano. The change was instigated to ensure that the two opposing forces (Don Masseria being the other) didn't both have names beginning with M. Screenwriter Nicholas Kazan admitted to having no time to research his topic, and only one month to rewrite Michael Mahern's screenplay, originally entitled *Gangsters* after Warren Beatty sent him material that would eventually form the basis of *Bugsy* (qv). Thus, Luciano's gang was made smaller, his rise to power simplified and sanitised, and his Russian immigrant girlfriend changed to an American. Costello's advanced years over the others (six years above his master, Luciano) were lost in the desire to make the four contemporaries (and cash in on the exploitative stud farm look to the film). Deliberately aimed at a teen audience, this is not the 'classic gangster film' predicted by Universal president of production Casey Silver, but more a 'rites-of-passage' movie, as the boys, sorry men, come into power.

Weak parallels with *The Godfather* (qv) are made, as Luciano speaks of the Syndicate: 'Corporations have a board of directors, so will we.' Images of war are also brought into play; Tommy receiving a gun once owned by Mussolini, while Rothstein speaks of the tactics of the Prince of Austria in bringing Europe to the brink of war. With the actors barely ageing a day from beginning to end, likening their activities to bloody conflict just seems all the more ludicrous.

See also: Krays, The; Villain

Mojo

(UK, Mojo Films/Portabello Pictures, 1998, 92mins)

Credits:
Dir/Scr: Jez Butterworth, based on his own stage play
Prod: Eric Abraham
Scr: Tom Butterworth
DOP: Bruno De Keyzer
Ed: Richard Milward
Music: Murray Gold
Prod Des: Hugo Luczyc-Wyhowski

Cast: Ian Hart (Mickey), Hans Matheson (Silver Johnny), Andy Serkis (Sidney Potts), Harold Pinter (Sam Ross), Ricky Tomlinson (Ezra), Aidan Gillen (Baby), Martin Gwynn Jones (Sweets), Ewen Bremner (Skinny)

A young singer at the Atlantic Club is kidnapped, and his father severed in two, by the local Rock'n'Roll impresario, only for the club bouncers to discover a traitor in their midst.

Based on the young Butterworth's own play, the film both succeeds and fails because of its heritage. Set, much like the stage version, for the majority in the Atlantic Club itself, the ensemble cast increase levels of bickering to a claustrophobic hysteria. When the treacherous Hart emerges from the secure confines of the club, we almost breathe a sigh of relief as we receive a metaphorical gust of air. While it heightens tensions, one feels too often as if one is in a theatre not a cinema. Although the story was originally conceived for film, before Butterworth was commissioned to adapt the idea for the stage, he is unable to live to his own maxim - 'forget everything and tell the story as a film' - upon converting back for the screen.

This aside, Mojo is a glorious evocation of Soho in 1958. Yet another addition to the Spiv Cycle of films, it harks to a time when Billy Fury and Adam Faith were performing. Naive Presley-lookalike Silver Johnny is their incarnation, actor Matheson even watching videos of Elvis to prepare for the role. Butterworth represents the locale in the same, superficially at least, vibrant manner. Eschewing the seediness of Neil Jordan's Soho in *Mona Lisa* (*qv*), Butterworth depicts (albeit briefly) a society in which trouble brews under the surface. The gangsters are ruthless, but come with smiles.

Pinter's Ross, unlike fellow playwright Noel Coward's gentlemanly Mr Bridger from *The Italian Job* or John Osborne's thug in *Get Carter* (*qqv*), is a gangster on the fringes of the criminal fraternity. Hardly big time, his actions - cutting club-owner Ezra in half - make up for his lack of true respect commanded. Depicted as gay, as he tries to seduce Johnny with cries of 'tickle tickle', Pinter's character borders on cliche, as he skulks in his smoking jacket.

As Butterworth said: 'The characters are not gangsters, but a bunch of kids who think they are and find out very quickly that they're not. The minute they brush very lightly up against that world they turn into children. It's not about violence, it's about the recipients of a violent act and how they cope with it.' True, for Hart's command over his ranks at the Atlantic bar soon crumbles as Ross forces him to kill Ezra. The high-octane pill-popping second-in-command Serkis, who noted the film 'undercuts the American obsession with heroism', also fleshes this out in his character. 'I am a cunt. Everybody knows it. It doesn't make me Al Capone.' Attempting to

dismantle the myth of the gangster, Butterworth has created a work that draws from both the nostalgic loveable rogues of the Ealing comedies and the viscous real-life inspired criminals from works such as *Villain* onwards.

Characterized by some fine ensemble acting, *Mojo* - referring to the lucky charm that is Silver Johnny, and the success that all connected with him are basking in - is an amalgam of styles, a fusion of influences that bursts with pace and energy, but ultimately has little to offer the genre.

Mona Lisa

(UK, Palace Pictures, 1986, 104 mins)

Credits
Dir/Scr: Neil Jordan
Prod: Stephen Woolley, Patrick Cassavetti
Scr: David Leland
DOP: Roger Pratt
Ed: Lesley Walker
Music: Michael Kamen
Prod. Des: Jamie Leonard

Cast: Bob Hoskins (George), Cathy Tyson (Simone), Michael Caine (Mortwell), Robbie Coltrane (Thomas), Clarke Peters (Anderson), Kate Hardie (Cathy), Joe Brown (Dudley)

Goodhearted ex-convict, who served his sentence for an ungrateful Soho vice racketeer, becomes enamoured with a prostitute he is assigned to chauffeur.

After his role as gangland boss Harold Shand in *The Long Good Friday* (*qv*) and his appearance in *The Cotton Club* (*qv*), Hoskins was touted in the likes of *Films and Filming* and *Monthly Film Bulletin* as the East End James Cagney. With the British film industry's limited production system, the potential (desirable to Hoskins or not) was never lived out, and he was left to meander through such trite Hollywood fare as *Mermaids*.

Self-consciously recognising its heritage – the Brighton pier sequence recalls *Brighton Rock* (*qv*) – it simultaneously rejects, through the symbolic art-deco spaghetti served up by Hoskins' soul mate and artist-chum Coltrane, the tradition of Italo-

American gangster pictures. While Nicholas Ray's *They Live By Night* (qv) might appear on TV, a reference no doubt to the Hoskins/Tyson relationship, this too is ironic, for their relationship is as redundant as their escape. Hoskins may be told by the video emporium owner that he is 'one of the family now', but his network of connections is, in fact, limited; he even has to use Thomas to put him up and supply him with arms.

Jordan's trawl through the mire of Soho's strip joints and porno shops is part of the grander picture, a recognition of lapsed human values, personified by Caine's class-conscious vice lord. Hoskins' wry comment that 'Angels are men' and his observation of young Cathy's 'meeting' in the church ('the one place no-one ever goes') indicate too that morals have little place in this world. While Caine says 'the business is different but the rules are still the same', Hoskins is always, as he does with new technology, struggling to comprehend.

Mulholland Falls

(US, MGM, 1996, 107 mins)

Credits
Dir: Lee Tamahori
Prod: Richard D. Zanuck, Lili Fini Zanuck
Scr: Pete Dexter
DOP: Haskell Wexler
Ed: Sally Menke
Music: David Grusin
Prod. Des: Richard Sylbert

Cast: Nick Nolte (Hoover), Melanie Griffith (Katherine), Chazz Palminteri (Coolidge), Michael Madsen (Eddie Hall), Chris Penn (Relyea), Treat Williams (Fitzgerald), John Malkovich (Timms), Andrew McCarthy (Jimmy Fields)

It's 1950s LA, and a dead girl leads the notorious, and virtually autonomous, 'Hat Squad' of the LAPD to uncover a plot involving nuclear testing.

Lee Tamahori's follow-up to *Once Were Warriors* was a luscious exercise in style, a homage to the ferocity of *Kiss Me Deadly* and the LA detective novels of James Ellroy. Delving into the city's postwar secret history, replete with fifties facades and repression, the fictitious screenplay was based on an LA *Times* newspaper article about the untouchable Hat Squad and its leader Max Herman, who became a lawyer after retiring from the force. As four members of the robbery division of the LAPD who wore custom-tailored suits and wide-brimmed hats, Tamahori retains this sartorial elegance, if nothing else, from the role models. As Max is employed with complete jurisdiction to 'get rid of gangsters and criminals' in LA, the script nods to the US's previous 'feared and revered' organisation, the G-Men. Nolte's character, a 'lost hero' straight out of fifties *noir*, received a surname change – from Herman to Hoover, acknowledging their mentor, J. Edgar.

Rather like the film's visual influence, *Chinatown* (production designer Richard Sylbert worked on Polanski's film also), *Mulholland Falls* isn't so much a place, as a way of doing business. As Nolte says, about to unceremoniously eject an out-of-State mob leader down the Falls, 'This isn't America, Jack. This is LA.' He later expounds on this way of life: 'Out here I can burn down your house, rape your wife and kill your dog. LA is my town.'

Having progressed through eight years of development hell (directors, including Michael Mann, and writers came and went), the toll taken on Pete Dexter's script can be seen.

Despite Michael Madsen's increasing resemblance, as one critic noted, to Edmond O'Brien (of *White Heat* and *The Killers* (qqv) fame), both he and the remainder of the cast (Palminteri, Penn, Griffith and old *Class* mates Rob Lowe and Andrew McCarthy) are woefully underused in a convoluted plot that is nevertheless blatantly obvious.

Muskateers of Pig Alley, The

(US, Biograph, 1912, 8 reels)

Credits
Dir: D.W. Griffith
DOP: Billy Bitzer

Cast: Lillian Gish (The Little Lady), Walter Miller (The Musician), Elmer Booth (The Snapper Kid), Harry Carey, Lionel Barrymore, Jack Dillon, Alfred Paget, W.C. Robinson, Robert Harron (Gangsters)

A poor musician loses his money to The Snapper Kid, the head of the Muskateers gang, and subsequently finds himself in the middle of a war between his gang and another.

Seen by many as the first recognisable incarnation of the genre, D.W. Griffith's silent short was based upon several 1912 newspaper reports of a series of gangster killings and vice scandals, climaxing with the shoot-out of a gambler named Herman Rosenthal, that implicated the police. Using actual gangsters like 'Kid' Brood and 'Harlem Tom' Evans on the all-location shoot, Griffith's film introduced several genre characteristics that would set the pattern to come. Elmer Booth's likeably fierce Snapper Kid was a distinct precursor of James Cagney, creating the first sympathetic gangster, but as with Cagney in *The Public Enemy* (qv) as Jean Harlow notes, he takes what he wants. The Lower East Side locale, called 'New York's Other Side' in the film, comprised of dingy rooms, hallways, saloons, narrow streets and garbage-filled alleyways, ensured the genre began in the slums – which would reach a height with the likes of *Dead End* (qv). Other iconographic scenes included the gangster's ball, the feudal gang war and the finale, entitled 'Links in the System', where a hand slides into the left of the picture pushing money into the Kid's hand. While the films of the twenties and thirties would get gaudier, more violent and more complex, the blueprint to work from was done.

My Blue Heaven

(US, Warner Brothers, 1990, 95 mins)

Credits
Dir/Prod: Herbert Ross
Prod: Anthea Sylbert
Scr: Nora Ephron
DOP: John Bailey
Ed: Stephen A. Rotter
Music: Ira Newborn
Prod. Des: Charles Rossen

Cast: Steve Martin (Vinnie Antonelli), Rick Moranis (Barney Coopersmith), Joan Cusack (Hannah Stubbs), Melanie Mayron (Crystal), Carol Kane (Shaldeen)

A New York hoodlum is transplanted to a Californian suburb on the Witness Protection Program, after giving evidence against his bosses.

As screenwriter Nora Ephron commented, there was something absurd about a government programme that relocates hardened criminals to a crime-free area, and then expects them to behave like model citizens: 'The criminals usually come from some ethnic community – not just New York, but also Chicago and Los Angeles – and there they are, suddenly in pineapple-and-cottage-cheese-land.' Picking up where *Goodfellas* (qv) left off (as Henry Hill gets to live the rest of his life 'like a schnook' on the Witness Protection Programme), the film whimsically deals with the notion. Director Herbert Ross (who also used Steve Martin in the US version of *Pennies From Heaven*) again uses popular songs to comment on the action. Fats Domino's *My Blue Heaven* fits well as Vinnie contemplates a bleak future in the bland paradise of suburbia. Structured as a series of vignettes, as Vinnie acclimatises to his new lifestyle, the script at least holds its own against other Mafia satires, notably Jonathan Demme's *Married to the Mob* (qv). The culture clash – as Vinnie tries to pay for his groceries with a $100 bill, never before seen by the cashier – brings sharply into focus the difference between wise guys and the rest of us.

See also: *Cookie*

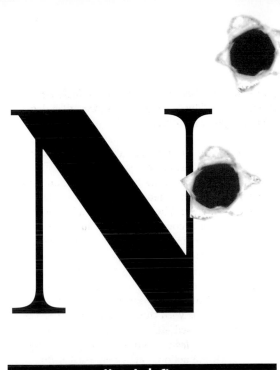

New Jack City

(US, Jarmac Film Inc., 1991, 97 mins)

'One of the first things I thought was that New Jack City read like Little Caesar, Public Enemy, all those great Warner classics. But those were made after Prohibition was over, so [the audience then] could say "Let's enjoy it vicariously. That's how gangsters used to be".'
(Mario Van Peebles, Black Film Review)

Credits
Dir: Mario Van Peebles
Prod: Doug McHenry, George Jackson
Scr: Barry Michael Cooper, Thomas Lee Wright
DOP: Francis Kenny
Ed: Steven Kemper
Music: Michael Colombier
Prod. Des: Charles C. Bennett

Cast: Wesley Snipes (Nino Brown), Vanessa Williams (Keisha), Judd Nelson (Nick Peretti), Ice-T (Scotty Appleton), Mario Van Peebles (Stone)

A New York crack dealer is brought to justice by two maverick cops.

A far more important contribution to the gangster genre than other subsequent black films, namely *Boyz N the Hood* and *Menace II Society* (*qv*), Peebles set out to make a piece of 'edutainment'. Just as his father, Melvin, had inadvertently begun the Blaxploitation trend of the seventies, with *Sweet Sweetback's Baadasssss Song*, so Mario's effort would lead the way for a number of 'unblaxploitation' efforts, promoting a 'Keep the Peace' message. With the film following the traditional 'rise and fall' structure of early Warners films, Peebles intercuts scenes of the bad guys living it up, with cops spouting about the dangers of crack. In many ways, it's comic-book copy, big-time crack dealer Nino Brown's gaudy primary-coloured wardrobe saying it all. The conclusion – a vigilante exacting revenge on Brown despite a plea-bargain finale – adheres disappointingly (yet appropriately) to the death-amongst-the-garbage-cans generic requirements. And yet it's a reshaping of the genre for the time and place; Ice-T replaces Isaac Hayes, we hear rap not soul, crack wars instead of cocaine (or even Prohibition) are the main concern. The inclusion of Ice-T is either an ironic insider joke, or a sell-out, depending on your point-of-view. While he is one of the two 'New Jack' (referring to a style of clothes and music) cops sent undercover to infiltrate Brown's huge crack operation in the Carter apartment building, his work on the soundtrack details his criminal activities. A man who has openly expressed his dislike of cops (and underwent controversy over the tune *Cop Killer*) now blurs the distinction. Such delicate balances are seen throughout: those in the audience likely to be closest to the problems depicted may well respond more to Ice T's rap, not screen image, the Armani clothing and cellular phones more attractive than clean living. Perhaps this is what makes the film so volatile. While the picture's early models were blatantly amoral, *New Jack City* operates from the other side. Openly moralistic, underneath lurks an attraction to the life.

This comes partly from a self-conscious recognition of the gangster heritage, Nino Brown's actions echoing the excess of Al Pacino's *Scarface*. While he is warned not to be as careless as Tony Montana, as he watches *Scarface* (*qv*), he ominously utters the infamous 'the world is mine' quote. References to *The Godfather* and *The Untouchables* (*qqv*) are also made – Nino stabbing a gang member's hand to the table, and then strangling him from behind. George Raft and James Cagney are also invoked as Brown gets high on the lifestyle. As *Sight & Sound*'s Michael Eric Dyson noted, the film 'provides the Cagneyisation of black ghetto life'. But, despite its flaws, the film is more than just a cop/crack action movie. It's a fusion of black culture and social/economic difficulties of the time, symbolised by a nation's increasing addiction to a killer drug. If anything, the film highlights the disenfranchisement of the non-white American population. The result is the inevitable arrival of the Nino Browns of the world. As he says: 'You gotta rob to get rich in the Reagan era.'

See also: *Clockers*; *I'm Gonna Git You, Sucka*; *Superfly*.

New Jack City: Nino Brown (Wesley Snipes, right) spies a killing, watched by 'Gee Money' (Allen Payne) and Kareem (Christopher Williams).

detailed two rival Prohibition gangs, somewhat ineffectually.

See also: *Trigger Happy*.

On the Waterfront

(US, Horizon Pictures, 1954, 108 mins)

Credits
Dir: Elia Kazan
Prod: Sam Spiegel
Scr: Budd Schulberg
DOP: Boris Kaufman
Ed: Arthur E. Milford
Music: Leonard Bernstein
Art Dir: Richard Day

Cast: Marlon Brando (Terry Malloy), Eva Marie Saint (Edie Doyle), Karl Malden (Father Barry), Lee J. Cobb (Johnny Friendly), Rod Steiger (Charley Malloy)

Dock worker with ambitions to become a championship boxer is eventually persuaded to testify to the Federal Crime Commission, following the death of his union lawyer brother at the hands of the racketeers controlling the longshoreman's union.

As *Film Quarterly*'s Peter Biskind suggested, the film 'is a political allegory in the form of a morality play'. Utilizing the documentary techniques popular for the gangster milieu at the time, Kazan's definitive work presented the informer as hero, much as Sam Fuller's *Pick up on South Street* would. Revealing all about criminal associates is the only honourable line. An excuse for action? Perhaps. Kazan, of course, appeared in front of the House of Un-American Activities Committee as a 'friendly witness' in 1952, crusading against Communism. Malloy's testimony before the Commission is shown as a sign of maturity, as he transcends neighbourhood ties to contribute to the greater good. The film is a positive, but idealistic, effort to inspire belief in the notion that justice will prevail. As the opening notes: 'It has always been in the American tradition not to hide our shortcomings, but on the contrary, to spotlight them and correct them. The incidents portrayed in this picture were

Ocean's Eleven

(US, Warner Brothers, 1960, 127 mins)

Credits
Dir./Prod: Lewis Milestone
Scr: Harry Brown, Charles Lederer
DOP: William H. Daniels
Ed: Philip W. Anderson
Music: Nelson Riddle
Art Dir: Nicolai Remisoff

Cast: Frank Sinatra (Danny Ocean), Dean Martin (Sam Harmon), Sammy Davis Sr (Josh Howard), Angie Dickinson (Beatrice Ocean), Cesar Romero (Duke Santos), Richard Conte (Anthony Bergdorf)

An 11-man team, formerly all 82nd Airborne Paratroopers, set out to rob five Las Vegas casinos simultaneously.

Overlong and gaudy Rat-Pack comedy caper, merely a showcase for the likes of Sinatra, Martin and Sammy Davis; their impeccable style and comic delivery on display. Full of quips like 'Wherever I go, people are in dumb admiration' – 'What happens when they speak!', its one conceit (that their past profession means no underworld connections, therefore no stool pigeons) remains the only point of interest. Four years later, the pricipal actors reunited for Gordon Douglas' *Robin and the 7 Hoods*. A musical crime comedy, it true of a particular area of the waterfront. They exemplify the way self-appointed tyrants can be fought and defeated by right-thinking men in a vital democracy.' One may recall the wry disclaimers that opened *Little Caesar* and *The Public Enemy* (*qqv*), but Kazan is approaching the topic in all earnestness, expressing the contradictions in post-war America about the nature of democracy. Brando's Terry Malloy, coerced by the mob to take a fall in a fixed fight, undergoes a spiritual and moral awakening. Through the prompting of Father Barry and girlfriend Edie, Malloy realises he had been 'ratting' on himself all these years through submission to the gangsters. And yet this represents swapping the authority of the mob for that of the three-headed hydra that inhabits society: legal, spiritual and familial. Malloy may have done the right thing, but he is no freer by the end of the picture. The mob, led by racketeer Johnny Friendly, are never seen as a potent force, a substitute family with the dockers their frightened children (they are 'D and D' – deaf and dumb, they do not inform). The mob's tenuous grip is symbolically shown in the final reel: despite Friendly beating Malloy in a fist fight, the former's influence is removed as the workers desert him at the end. Nothing without his 'kickbacks', the film shifts the balance of power away from Friendly. To what, though? Malloy might hold by the 'Do it to him before he does it to you' maxim, but ultimately control rests with the social structures that engulf him.

* **Academy Awards:** Best Picture.
Budd Schulberg won for Best Adapted Script.
Elia Kazan won for Best Director.
Marlon Brando won for Best Actor.
Eve Marie Saint won for Best Supporting Actress.
Richard Day won for Best Art Direction.
Boris Kaufman won for Best Cinematography.
Gene Milford won for Best Editing.

See also: *Valachi Papers, The.*

Once Upon a Time in America

(US, Ladd Company/Warner Brothers, 1983, 227 mins)

'Time is a great character in the film. Above all it is about memory and nostalgia and a grand story of the friendship between two men. It is not the 18th part of 'The Godfather' – it is not so concerned with events as sentiments.'
(Sergio Leone, *Screen International*)

Credits
Dir./Scr: Sergio Leone
Prod: Claudio Mancini, Arnon Milchan
Scr: Piero de Bernadi, Franco Ferrini, Stuart Kaminsky, Enrico Medioli, Franco Arcalli, Leo Benevenuti, based on the novel The Hoods by Harry Grey
DOP: Tonino delli Colli
Ed: Nino Baragli
Music: Ennio Morricone
Prod. Des: Walter Massi, Carlo Simi

Cast: Robert De Niro ('Noodles'), James Woods (Max), Joe Pesci (Frankie), Treat Williams (Jimmy O'Donnell), Burt Young (Joe), Elizabeth McGovern (Deborah)

Complex tale of four Jewish 1930s gangsters, set across three time periods, in which a put-upon gangster alerts the authorities as his colleagues attempt to raid the Federal Gold reserve leading, seemingly, to their deaths.

Sergio Leone's first film for a decade was a sprawling majestic gangster epic, the final part of his American triptych which began with *Once Upon A Time in the West* and continued with *Once Upon a Time, the Revolution*. Conceived as a whole, the films provide three views of a country passing from anarchic heroism to revolution to mob rule. Leone uses the gangster subtext as a pretext for a fairy tale; a homage to the Warner Brothers domination of the genre, a vanished American cinema, it is also a paean to the country itself. As Leone told *Film Comment*'s Elaine Lomenzo: 'America is a dream mixed with reality... in America there is the whole world.'
Based loosely on Harry Grey's novel *The Hoods*, the source was actually autobiographical, the author's name a pseudonym for a gangster named Goldberg

Once Upon a Time In America: Gangsters in miniature: five wannabees.

through their memories; Noodles, believing he caused his comrades' deaths after their foolhardy raid on the Federal Reserve, has lived in purgatory for over three decades. As he discovers, Max pulled the cruellest of hoaxes, covering his own betrayal of the gang by setting up his old friend. As Noodles says: 'You can always tell the winners and losers at the starting gate.' Like the pre-Hays Code gangsters, he is defined by his environment, a slave to both others' wills and the passage of time; a most atypical gangster.

The circular structure, beginning and ending in the 1930s opium den, implies that all following it (the betrayal, the exile, the confrontation) is but a pipe dream, a mixture of memory and fantasy. The impossible youth of Noodles' girlfriend Deborah in the '68 sequence, Noodles' difficulty at recognising a thinly disguised Max and the car of 1920s revellers speeding past all suggest an effort to maintain the dream. As we briefly return to the den, Noodles smiles: his act of betrayal was an illusion – he is now free to pursue his dreams in a world where they often, as in the case of Max's, go awry.

* Three versions of the film exist. Financial backers The Ladd Company released a disastrous chronological recut trimmed down to a mere 144 minutes. Leone, unsurprisingly, threatened to remove his name from the project. The American version, at 227 minutes (which achieved a limited theatrical run in late 1984) is now the most widely accepted of the three, with Leone even taking it to Cannes. A European 250-minute film also exists, containing more information on the Hoffa-based character James Conway O'Donnell, and a 1968 conversation between Noodles and a funeral director.

who had fixed the World Series and written the book while in Sing-Sing prison. Leone noted that the work described the gangsters in terms of pure Hollywood cliché, the myth so prevalent it took over from reality. And the film follows this blueprint, seamlessly cutting between the gang's Lower East Side youth (the early 1920s), a decade later following Noodles' emergence from prison (and Max's self-appointed leadership of the gang at their height), and a final sequence in 1968, as a withered Noodles returns to his old haunts (after a 35-year exile in Buffalo) to confront the supposedly dead Max, who now exists under the guise of a powerful Senator.

As with most of Leone's characters, they only exist

Original Gangstas

(US, Orion Pictures, 1996, 99 mins)

'The people in this film are older, wiser, more human than they were before. [Gangstas] is about the black man coming back to the place he grew up in and taking responsibility for his community and family.'

(Fred Williamson, *UK Premiere*)

Credits
Dir: Larry Cohen
Prod: Fred Williamson
Scr: Aubrey Rattan
DOP: Carlos Gonzalez
Ed: David Kern, Peter B. Ellis
Music: Vladimir Horunzhy
Prod. Des: Elayne Barbara Ceder

Cast: Fred Williamson (John Bookman), Jim Brown (Jake Trevor), Pam Grier (Laurie Thompson), Ron O'Neal (Bubba), Paul Winfield (Reverend Dorsey), Isabel Sanford (Gracie Bookman)

In Gary, Indiana, a group of 'original gangsters' attempt to prevent new inner-city thugs from moving in.

A drab reunion for the 1970s stars of the Blaxploitation genre, the film is a serio-comic triumph of middle-age over youth, reclaiming a little of the legacy left behind with the bell-bottoms and hip-huggers. Featuring Ron O'Neal (*Superfly*'s [*qv*] Youngblood Priest), Pam Grier (star of *Coffy* and *Foxy Brown*), ex-football player Fred Williamson (star of *Black Caesar* and *Hell Up In Harlem* [*qqv*] made by *Gangstas* director Larry Cohen) and even *Shaft* (*qv*) himself Richard Roundtree, the film centres around a post-industrial US town, now overrun by gangs. This bland Mid-West setting automatically neutralises the New York chic of their seventies counterparts. Similarly, the appearance of the once-sexy Grier, for example, now a 40-something gang-basher, doesn't raise the knowing smirk it should from the audience. Living on borrowed time, these veterans, no longer accompanied by the soul-funk fusion of Curtis Mayfield or Isaac Hayes, are given the anthemic Chi-Lites tune '(For God Sake) Give More Power to the People' to strut to. But the irony fails to bite. Claiming that 'only through peace' can prosperity continue, the tragedy of urban decay and the plight of the Afro-Americans is all too true. What place actors – who will forever be associated with characters who were in part responsible for such a decline – are doing telling us this, is mysterious.

* Pam Grier fan Quentin Tarantino was originally slated to make a cameo appearance as an LA cab driver.

See also: *Black Godfather*; *Black Gunn*; *I'm Gonna Git You, Sucka*.

Outfit, The

(US, MGM, 1973, 103 mins)

Credits:
Dir./Scr: John Flynn, based on the original novel by Richard Stark
Prod: Carter De Haven, Jr
DOP: Bruce Surtees
Ed: Ralph E. Winters
Music: Jerry Fielding
Art Dir: Tambi Larsen

Cast: Robert Duvall (Macklin), Joe Don Baker (Cody), Karen Black (Bett Harrow), Robert Ryan (Mailer), Timothy Carey (Jake Menner), Richard Jaeckel (Chemy)

Ex-con and safecracker exacts revenge on a syndicate known as The Outfit, for the death of his brother.

Based on the novel by Richard Stark (aka Donald Westlake), this picks up where *The Hunter*, his work that formed the basis for John Boorman's *Point Blank* (*qv*), left off. Renaming the hero from Parker (in Boorman's film it was Walker) to Macklin, the picture excuses the change from Lee Marvin to Robert Duvall via plastic surgery. Reworking the revenge motive, Flynn's film steps in line with a tradition of gangster pictures from the era. Like Don Siegel's *Charley Varrick* (*qv*) and, of course, Boorman's work, the film pitted the individual, ageing gangster against an anonymous syndicate, whose maxim in Flynn's film runs 'You hit us, we hit you'. One is reminded of corporate takeovers: as Earl Macklin's girlfriend Bett says: 'You know how they are – they act like they own the world.' Earl himself resists attempts to lose identity and be consumed by the monolithic organisation, but a sense of time ebbing away pervades the film. Accused of being small-time – 'Hard guy,' says one of his extortees, 'Think you're Dillinger. You're nothing but a goddamn independent. A heist guy. You go around sticking up banks. What kind of operation is that?' – Earl teams up with ex-partner

Cody to complete revenge upon syndicate boss Mailer. A victory for the 'good guys', as they term it, Flynn's film is a cry for individualism.

See also: *Charley Varrick*; *Point Blank*; *Prime Cut*.

Out of the Past (aka Build My Gallows High)

(US, RKO Radio Picture, 1947, 97 mins)

Credits
Dir: Jacques Tourneur
Prod: Warren Duff
Scr: Geoffrey Homes, based on his novel Build My Gallows High
DOP: Nicholas Musuraca
Ed: Samuel E. Beetley
Music: Roy Webb
Art Dir: Albert S. D'Agostino, Jack Okey

Cast: Robert Mitchum (Jeff), Jane Greer (Kathie), Kirk Douglas (Whit Sterling), Rhonda Fleming (Meta Carson), Paul Valentine (Joe Stefanos), Steve Brodie (Fisher)

Once hired by a racketeer to find his mistress and a missing $40,000 (preferring instead to take flight with her and the money), a private eye is located in hiding yesars later and recalled for one last job to even the score; this time to recover documents to prevent his former boss from being prosecuted for income tax evasion.

By this point the gangster film, in the likes of *The Killers*, *Criss-Cross* (qqv) and this Jacques Tourneur work, became so entangled with *film noir* that the two genres fed off, even relied upon, each other. This involved some transmutation; gone were the larger-than-life heroes and villains of the Warner Brothers Golden Age. Increasingly, James Cagney's return to the genre as Cody Jarrett in *White Heat* (qv) an exception, the protagonist was an ordinary man exploring the darker side of the self, knowing full well that he was working towards self-destruction. As Mitchum's character, an early example of such a man drawn back towards the life he has tried to escape, says 'Even if I have to, I'm going to die last.' The downbeat ending, with this prophecy fulfilled, was a further indicator of change, with redemption denied.

The cause? The economic and sexual liberation of women, following World War II, had led to a paranoia that fed into the portrayal of the female in the late forties; double-crossing beautiful women with hidden motivations, the femme fatale, became a staple of *noir*. And the underworld milieu became the perfect setting for the deadly female pitched against the fearful man. Jane Greer dupes both former lover and racketeer Douglas (absconding with his $40,000) and later Mitchum, who is sent to locate her in Mexico, and falls in love, only to suffer a parallel vanishing trick. Upon returning to her old flame, she sets Mitchum up for the murder she committed of his former partner, who was intent on blackmailing them. Inspiring the line 'They seem to live by night', these characters – like those of the Nicholas Ray film two years later – exist in the darkness, even in the wilderness. As Mitchum throws punches, the fight is seen as a shadow box cast across Greer's face, emphasising her own degradation. In contrast, the gangster, expertly shown here by a slickly dressed Douglas, has become a man of refinement. As with Alexander Scourby's Mike Lagana in *The Big Heat* (qv), good taste is not aspired to, it is already there.

* The film was remade in 1984 as *Against All Odds*, directed by Taylor Hackford, and starring Jeff Bridges. The only noteworthy item was a reappearance of Jane Greer – playing her original character's mother.

* Douglas' character echoed his portrayal of corrupt racketeer Noll Turner in Byron Haskin's Prohibition exercise *I Walk Alone*. Produced by the legendary Hal B. Wallis, the man behind *Little Caesar*, *The Roaring Twenties* and *Kid Galahad*, it was his return to the genre, his first for five years since *All Through the Night* (qqv). Teaming Douglas with Burt Lancaster (to meet again in *Gunfight at the O.K. Corral*), the film was much more downbeat than Wallis' Warner Brothers efforts. Lancaster, playing Madison, Turner's partner sent down for 14 years and rejected upon release by his old friend, also repeated his role in Robert Siodmak's *The Killers*. More cold-hearted and ruthless than ever before, the gangster had changed for the worse.

See also: *Kiss of Death*; *Racket, The*.

Paying the Penalty: See Underworld.

Pepe le Moko

(France, Paris Film, 1937, 93 mins)

Credits
Dir/Scr: Julien Duvivier
Prod: Raymond Hakim, Robert Hakim
Scr: Jacques Costant, Henri Jeanson, based on the novel by Roger D'Ashelbe
DOP: Marc Fossard, Jules Kruger
Ed: Marguerite Beauge
Music: Vincent Scotto, Mohamed Yguerbouchen

Cast: Jean Gabin (Pepe le Moko), Gabriel Gabrio (Carlos), Saturnin Fabre (Grandfather), Fernand Charpin (Regis), Lucas Gridoux (Inspector Slimane)

Jewel thief and hero to the masses dreams of exchanging the Algerian underbelly for Paris.

Finely tuned French gangster picture, which ostensibly mutates into a tragic love tale, as Pepe's long-suffering girl Ines (Line Noro) betrays his dockside whereabouts to the police, partly out of spite at the relationship he's had with his true love, society girl Giselle (bound for Paris, having been led to believe by a conspiracy that Pepe is already dead). The tragic muse is, indeed, invoked, with Pepe lamenting the death of friend Pierrot with a reference to his 'Shakespearean style'.

Though the police see him as a 'hard case', Pepe is the 'king of the jungle', later expanding the metaphor when he is called a 'prince of the underworld' and then 'lion of the alleys'. As he lands in Algiers after a bank raid worth over two million, we discover he cost the lives of five police officers over two years, committed 33 robberies and two bank raids – 'the whole underworld is his accomplice. He is as ready with a smile for his friends as a knife for his enemies.' And yet rarely has the mug shot differed from the man. Unconcerned with money, he respects craftsmanship, dressed as he is in an immaculate black shirt/white tie/grey suit combination. Pepe appreciates style not murder. Hardly brutal, he is 'a man of taste, a great villain', says his nemesis, Inspector Slimane, a man whom Pepe endlessly taunts with death (though an overriding sense of fair play prevents him from despatching it).

Notable for its opening rapid-fire, ten-minute tour of the labyrinth-like Casbah, where the streets have names like 'Futility' and there exists a tempestuous melting pot of Gypsies, Maltese, Chinese, Sicilians and Slavs, the suffocating atmosphere adds to the theme of freedom – never better illustrated than with the enduring parting shot of a distraught Pepe behind the gates of the port, the frame giving an ominous nod to his potential incarceration. The film takes an almost religious stance, preaching against the weakness of the flesh. While Slimane believes his downfall will be ambition, Pepe falls foul of the female, his developing taste for the bottle adding to his loss of control. Swinging from moments of delusion – 'I'll leave when I like' – to those of clarity – 'I'm hemmed in, by hunters in waiting', Pepe finds the top of the pile a very alienating place.

* The film was remade twice. In 1938, Charles Boyer took the role of Pepe in the romantic *Algiers*. Slated to star Mireille Balin (who played Gaby in the French version) and to be directed by Duvivier, neither ended up working on the project. But United Artists ensured verisimilitude in other ways, utilising stock footage from the original and casting according to similarities with the earlier version's

players. Typically, though, Pepe's suicide was changed to his being shot as he tried to escape. Ten years on, a musical version called *Casbah* was made featuring Peter Lorre and Tony Martin.

Performance

(UK, Goodtimes Enterprises, 1970, 102 mins)

'In a way, you could think of this time as an alchemical experiment: we were all very interested in that hocus pocus. It was also about the transforming quality of hallucinogenics on the collective consciousness.'

(Christopher Gibbs, Set Designer)

Credits
Dir/Scr: Donald Cammell, Nicolas Roeg
Prod: Sandy Lieberson
DOP: Nicolas Roeg
Ed: Antony Gibbs
Music: Jack Nitzsche
Art Dir: John Clark

Cast: Mick Jagger (Turner), James Fox (Chas), Anita Pallenberg (Pherber), Johnny Shannon (Harry Flowers), Kenneth Colley (Tony Farrell)

London gangster hides out in a fading rock star's Chelsea basement flat and then assumes his identity.

'The only performance that makes it, really makes it, is the one that achieves madness.' So goes the film's defining quotation. As Donald Cammell was later to say, 'the essence of a 'total' performance is that the playing of a role becomes a transference of identity – a kind of possession'. Chas is possessed by Turner, the gangster movie consumed by the hippie canon. As Roeg, the only man apart from Fox on set with previous film-making experience, put it: 'Turner is like a man who meets a mirror of himself.' True, for Turner becomes fascinated with hard man Chas' masculine armour, just as Chas is frightened initially of Turner's femininity. Both cocoon themselves against their true identity. Turner makes Chas' face up, so he becomes Harry, Chas' mob boss, as he plays 'dress-up'. Individuality

is suspect, existence thus without meaning. Made in 1968, but not released until 1970 (after studio Warner Brothers insisted on 20 minutes of cuts), Cammell and Roeg's film became one of the cultural reference points for the demise of Swinging London, alongside Michelangelo Antonioni's *Blowup*. As *Sight & Sound*'s Jon Savage noted Turner's house is the 'perfect interiorisation of 1966–68: exquisite, hermetic, brilliantly eclectic, [it] freezes time in to everlasting present' or as Marianne Faithfull put it: 'It preserves a whole era under glass.' At the same time it shows pop culture to be not transient but transforming; the soundtrack flashes forward and back into the past and future of R'n'B (plundered by Mods and the Stones).

Drawing upon the period's cross-pollination of criminals, middle-class artists and bohemian aristocrats, Fox became an abstraction of the Krays, while Jagger was the pop icon in the Brian Jones mould (both role models having achieved infamy at approximately the same time). Cammell's poignant casting attempts to make the Stones an enemy of straight people, an enemy to the Establishment, to infuse art and reality in dangerous style.

As much a direct descendent of Vladimir Nabokov and William Burroughs (the cross-cutting techniques echoing the writer's cut-up novels) as Joseph Losey's *The Servant* and the works of Jean-Luc Godard, *Performance* drew its main inspiration from two areas. The works of Jorge Luis Borges appear prominently. Apart from *A Personal Anthology* being read by Turner and Rosenbloom, a picture of the writer appears as Chas fires a bullet into Turner. Referencing Borges' story *The South* (concerning a man who experiences his ideal death) can only mean that Turner's death, his merging with Chas, is the ultimate ending. The legend of Hassan-i-Sabbah, the Old Man in the Mountain who rewarded his assassins by drugging them with hashish and permitting them into his Garden of Delights, is also present. His last words, reportedly, were the Turner-spoke phrase 'Nothing is true. Everything is permitted' – a concept preached by 1950s demonologist Aleister Crowley in his motto 'Do What Thou Wilt'. Crowley was championed by one-time Hollywood brat and underground film-maker Kenneth Anger, who spent much time on the set. His films, such as *Scorpio Rising*, contained the same mix of sex, violence and occult that informed *Performance*. The hippie and the assassin, love and death, join in union through the power of the hallucinogenic. Similarly, other offset activities fuelled the film. Jagger's pregnant girlfriend Marianne Faithfull was replaced by Pallenberg (who'd appeared with Jane Fonda in *Barbarella*), a previous partner of Rolling Stone Brian Jones and, at the time, linked with fellow band member Keith Richards. While Cammell also claimed to be seeing her, the sex scenes involving Jagger were not faked (out-takes winning an award at the Amsterdam Porn Festival months later). Such tension prompted Richards to refuse to collaborate with Jagger on the soundtrack. Cammell had also recruited two hoods for bit-parts, one being John Binden who played Moody, and it was reported that James Fox was taken down to Brixton and the Old Kent Road and (according to 'Spanish Tony', the Stones' underworld connection) sent on housebreaking missions. So disturbed was he by the role that he gave up acting for the following decade.

Petrified Forest, The

(US, Warner Brothers, 1936, 82 mins)

Credits:
Dir: Archie Mayo
Scr: Charles Kenyon, Delmer Daves, based on the play by Robert E. Sherwood
DOP: Sol Polito
Ed: Owen Marks
Music: Bernard Kaun
Art Dir: John Hughes

Cast: Humphrey Bogart (Duke Mantee), Leslie Howard (Alan Squier), Bette Davis (Gabrielle Maple), Genevieve Tobin (Mrs. Chisholm), Dick Foran (Boze Hertzlinger)

In the Arizona desert, a disillusioned writer is held hostage in a diner by a vicious gang, and begs for his life to be taken.

Performance: Turner (Mick Jagger) turns gangster.

A relatively unknown cinematic commodity at the time, Humphrey Bogart – despite playing the role sensationally on Broadway in 1935 – was not originally considered to repeat his role of hunted gangster Duke Mantee on film. Edward G. Robinson was to be drafted in, but was dropped in favour of Bogart only when co-star Leslie Howard (who was signed to replay his stage role) threatened to quit the project unless his theatrical opposite was brought in on the project. Ironically, despite Howard repeating the quality of his stage performance (with dialogue from the play retained for the film), it was Bogart who drew the notices. The most nihilistic of gangster movies, Howard's Alan Squire quotes from T.S. Eliot's *The Hollow Men*, the Petrified Forest his *Wasteland*. A wilting flower in a harsh desert, he lives in a world of outmoded ideas; a romantic, he wants to be buried in the forest to preserve his immortality as an artist who died before his time – and he recognises a kindred spirit in the shape of Mantee. The gangster here is 'the last great apostle of rugged individualism' but he sees him as a relic of a lawless age. Mantee is allegorical in construction; seen by Gramp Maple (Charley Grapewin) as inheriting the mantle of Billy the Kid, he is an irrational, elemental force who represents the destructive and power-mad low-brow aspects of civilisation, a primitive product of a materialistic society. By contrast, Squire is the rational, sensitive evocation of high culture, that is, ineffectual intellectuality. *The Petrified Forest* can be read as a cultural clash, or at base level, the relationship of mind and body.

* Some 20 years later, Bogart played Mantee again in a television adaptation of *The Petrified Forest*, in which the parts of Alan and Gabrielle were played by Henry Fonda and Lauren Bacall. The film was also remade in 1945 as *Escape in the Desert*, directed by Edward A. Blatt.

See also: *Funeral, The.*

Pocketful of Miracles, A

(US, Franton Productions, 1961, 136 mins)

'Whereas in the old days the most shameless element in a Capra film might be the change of heart in some crusty old capitalist, 'Pocketful of Miracles' tries to revive a whole, dead world of sentimental gangsters and ultimately sympathetic socialites in the grand Runyonesque manner.'

(Monthly Film Bulletin)

Credits
Dir/Prod: Frank Capra
Scr: Hal Kanter, Harry Tugend, based on the original story by Damon Runyon
DOP: Robert Bronner
Ed: Frank P. Keller
Music: Walter Scharf
Art Dir: Hal Pereira, Roland Anderson

Cast: Glenn Ford (Dave the Dude), Bette Davis (Apple Annie), Hope Lange (Queenie Martin), Arthur O'Connell (Count Romero), Peter Falk (Joy Boy)

Kindly gangsters help a poor apple seller convince her visiting daughter that she is well-to-do.

Frank Capra's last feature film, and it showed. A Technicolor remake of his 1933 effort *Lady For a Day*, it was based on a story by Damon Runyon entitled *Madame La Gimp*. While Capra, in his autobiography, blamed Glenn Ford's autocratic and self-serving on-set behaviour, and his demand to (mis)cast current lady friend Hope Lange, not all can be attributed to him. At an overlong 136 minutes (*Lady For a Day* ran all-but 90) Capra's film loses touch with brevity, scenes running well past their value in this, as one character notes, 'Cinderella story'.

Full of Runyon eccentrics, the central crux proves, even by Capra's standards (here maudlin rather than honest sentiment), difficult to swallow. The idea that a sizeable chunk of the New York underworld would postpone carving up their crime empires to ensure an old Broadway derelict's reunion with her long-lost daughter is somewhat laughable. The difference between such old tosh and more successful gangster-filled whimsies is in the removal of all menace from Glenn Ford's Dave the Dude. 'Luck is an art I got', he says (it is indeed why he superstitiously carries an apple from the barely recognisable Bette Davis in his pocket). And it is this, in comparison to the murderous Darcey who wants to set up a National Syndicate with himself as Il Duce, that reduces the film's impact. Consider the limping Cagney in the musical biopic *Love Me or Leave Me* (qv) as Martin 'The Gimp' Synder, the unscrupulous racketeer who forces nightclub singer Ruth Etting into marriage. While finishing on a positive note (the repentant Synder building his own club and hiring Ruth as his singer), Cagney's unflinching performance never fails to remind us that he got there by a devious route. Just so for Edward G. Robinson as the reformed monk in *Brother Orchid* (qv). Even in the most feel-good of endings, a path of deviance must be shown.

See also: *Bugsy Malone; Guys and Dolls.*

Point Blank

(US, MGM, 1967, 92 mins)

Credits
Dir: John Boorman
Prod: Judd Bernard, Robert Chartoff
Scr: Alexander Jacobs, David Newhouse, Rafe Newhouse, based on the novel The Hunter by Richard Stark
DOP: Philip H. Lathrop
Ed: Henry Berman
Music: Johnny Mandel
Art Dir: George W. Davis, Albert Brenner

Cast: Lee Marvin (Walker), Angie Dickinson (Chris), Keenan Wynn (Yost), Carroll O'Connor (Brewster), Lloyd Bochner (Carter), Michael Strong (Stegman)

A gangster, left for dead by his partner and wife after a profitable heist, tracks them down.

Briton John Boorman essayed precisely the American scene in this fractured account of retribution. Obliquely commenting on West Coast life, as did Don Siegel's *The Killers* (qv), we see lives built around self-deception: Carter's wallet, full only of credit cards; the destruction of the Cadillac, the apartment with its multitude of appliances. Walker and the landscape he walks through become a symbol for the times, not dissimilar to the Chelsea milieu shown in *Performance* (qv). With the scene involving Walker dusting off some Syndicate hoods, he is framed by the discotheque backdrop projections – thus becoming absorbed into contemporary electronic popular art, in much the way that Chas becomes Turner in the Cammell film.

Much futile speculation has surrounded the unresolved details of the film. Chiefly, how does Walker, having received gun shots to the stomach, swim back across the Bay from Alcatraz island in waters so strong and cold that no prisoner has, for certain, ever made it across? *Film Quarterly*'s James Michael Martin suggests two alternatives. Walker is either 'A restless reviving spirit, an exterminating angel brought back by the gods, returned to the living to stalk his betrayers and avenge his own death' – or he is 'lost in a labyrinth of troubled memories, dreams and wish fulfilment at the moment of death', a more satisfactory theory with the repeated gun shots and Walker musing 'Cell. Prison cell. How'd I get here?... Did it happen? Was it a dream?' Walker is an allegorical figure of truth. Unconcerned with the $93,000 owing to him, all he pursues is justice in a world of false values; he is our saviour, offering to crush those, like the bewildered car salesman, who cheat throughout their lives.

See also: *Charley Varrick*; *Outfit, The*; *Prime Cut*.

Pope of Greenwich Village, The

(US, MGM/UA, 1984, 122 mins)

Credits
Dir: Stuart Rosenberg
Prod: Gene Kirkwood, Howard W. Koch Jr
Scr: Vincent Patrick, based on his own novel
DOP: John Bailey
Ed: Robert Brown
Music: Dave Grusin
Prod. Des: Paul Sylbert, Joseph M. Caracciolo

Cast: Mickey Rourke (Charlie), Eric Roberts (Paulie), Daryl Hannah (Diane), M. Emmet Walsh (Burns), Burt Young (Bed Bug Eddie), Kenneth McMillan (Barney)

Two small-time hoods in New York's East Side become embroiled with the Mafia after stealing from them.

'But it ain't the old days. Wise guys rat people out now', Paulie's uncle tells him, wanting his nephew to do the deed on friend Charlie for the warehouse safe job of which they were both part. Set in the apt location of Little Italy for a re-run of *Mean Streets* (qv), these wise guy wannabes wouldn't dare. Breaking into Italian and saying 'capisch' occasionally, owning a few flash suits and part of a racehorse, does not make a mobster. As Diane points out to Charlie, he's 'one inch away from becoming a good person' but is caught up in 'tribal loyalty'. Their activities are at best impish – spiking the drinks of a traffic warden, or playing baseball (to the sound of Frank Sinatra, naturally) in their suits. What makes Vincent Patrick's script noteworthy is the dual effect of organised crime. The locale may have its own policing, the only neighbourhood where children and old ladies can walk the streets safely at night. But step out of line, and it's no trial by jury as Paulie discovers, just the horrific loss of a thumb – a scene much lingered upon.

* Rosenberg's film comes as part of a long tradition in low-rent hoodlum movies. A more recent addition would be Nick Gomez's *Laws of Gravity* (who would go on to make *New Jersey Drive*, another desperate gangster movie). Again, in debt considerably to *Mean Streets*, the inexperienced cast, improvising their dialogue inside an urban mise-en-scène, are caught by hand-held, grainy images as the camera jostles to catch its subject. Drawing from the Keitel/De Niro relationship, the older and more responsible Jimmy (Peter Greene) hastens inevitable tragedy with his confused loyalty to the wired, impulsive Jon (Adam Tree). Anti-dramatic, the film positively defuses the image of the gangster as hero. Even the volatile Frankie (Paul Schulze) says: 'I'm just trying to live my life... to do what I like to do.'

The Professional: See Leon.

Prime Cut

(US, National General, 1972, 86 mins)

Credits
Dir: Michael Ritchie
Prod: Michael Borofsky, Joe Wizan
Scr: Robert A. Dillon
DOP: Gene Polito
Ed: Carl Pingitore
Music: Lalo Schifrin
Prod. Des: Bill Malley

Cast: Lee Marvin (Nick Devlin), Gene Hackman ('Mary Ann'), Sissy Spacek (Poppy), Janet Baldwin (Violet), Angel Tompkins (Clarabelle), Gregory Walcott (Weenie)

Hired to retrieve a debt in the heartland of Kansas, the collector discovers a prostitution racket, in the guise of a meat farm, and subsequently sets about bringing down the operation.

'Chicago's crumblin'. Nothing left there 'cept kids and old men... Chicago's a sick old sow... someday they're gonna boil that town down for fat', says Gene Hackman's 'Mary Ann', owner of the meat factory-cum-whore ranch ('Cow flesh, girl flesh – all the same to me', he adds). *Prime Cut* is a neatly packaged joke; from the opening scene, the title plays on not only the percentage profit of an operation but the fleshy remains of Lee Marvin's predecessor. In a jump-start credit sequence, we're given a detailed tour of the factory, only to discover the sausages produced and sent to the Chicago bosses have a human quality to them. This is rural vs. city, Kansas – 'the heartland' – is seen as the new frontier for gangster activity, while Chicago is dead meat. Even the President doesn't visit the city anymore, we are told. Eventually, of course, the film has to give up the gag and relent to convention: the 12-bore rifles belonging to the overawed inbreds prove no match for Marvin's sub-machine gun.

Populated by either the bizarre (stoned, naked girls on display in the straw-filled animal pens), or tension-induced sequences (the drive through the thunderstorm, leading to the shootout in the sunflower field) Robert Dillon, whose work would again be reunited with Gene Hackman in *French Connection II*, created a script that used 'meat' as a symbol to explore man's indifference to his fellow creatures.

While Hackman and Marvin both may be effectively gangsters, the former views man as beast (and as a result will die like one). To him, a human being is a trading tool, and the film unusually plays on the emotional effect of a mobster's wake, through Sissy Spacek, making her film debut, as the doped-up orphan Lee Marvin rescues from the meat-rack.

See also: *Charley Varrick*; *Outfit, The*; *Point Blank*.

Prizzi's Honor

(US, ABC Motion Pictures, 1985, 129 mins)

Credits
Dir: John Huston
Prod: John Foreman
Scr: Janet Roach, Richard Condon, based on his own novel
DOP: Andrzej Bartkowiak
Ed: Rudi Fehr, Kaja Fehr
Music: Alex North
Prod. Des: Dennis J. Washington

Cast: Jack Nicholson (Charley Partanna), Kathleen Turner (Irene Walker), Robert Loggia (Eduardo Prizzi), John Randolph (Angelo 'Pop' Partanna), Angelica Huston (Maerose Prizzi)

A hitman falls for a hit-woman, only to be set up to kill each other by the Mafia princess wronged years before.

John Huston's satirical study of the Mafia casts a cynical doubt as to the true worth of the religion of family and its values from the very beginning. The prologue, set in a tacky church far removed from the opulent wedding that opens *The Godfather* (*qv*), depicts a boy being asked to swear to uphold the Prizzi's honour. His disinterested 'Yeah' says it all; the film explores the multiple interpretations of the word 'honour', and how, depending upon the moral standpoint, it can be used. Nicholson's enforcer Charley, complete with Bogart upper-lip, is the centre of the piece, with a neat family joke thrown in for good measure: his real-life love of the time, Angelica Huston (John's daughter), plays the Don's love-stricken offspring, in love with none other than Charley. Nicholson spends the film attempting to find a language to cope with increasingly complex perceptions of his own identity and his emotions, blossoming for fellow assassin Kathleen Turner who is targeted after being suspected of skimming from a casino. For Charley it comes down to 'Do I ice her? Do I marry her?' He is told: 'You will always put the family before anything else in your life. She is your wife. We are your life.' His conclusion that 'Family is the only place I can be' is a sly dig at the rigidity of such seemingly all-embracing organisations which stifle the senses (an oblique reference to the Catholic Church, possibly?)

* *Film Comment*'s Michael Walsh gave an unusual but enlightening reading, believing the film a gloss on Puccini's masterpiece *Gianni Schicchi*, the third in a triptych of operas called *Il Trittico*. The eponymous Gianni was a Florentine rascal who swindles the recently deceased Donati's inheritance from his conniving relatives. Music being used as a commentator on the action, we hear the opera's only aria sung by Schicchi's daughter Lauretta on the radio, in the scene where Maerose confronts her father. An oblique comment, Lauretta's words indicate that Maerose is suggesting how much she likes Charley. Other musical jokes include the kidnapping scene scored to Rossini's overture to *La Gazza Ladra* ('The Thieving Magpie') and Don Corrado listening to 'Questo O Quella', from Verdi's *Rigoletto*, the opening aria of the unscrupulous Duke.

Public Enemy, The

(US, Warner Brothers, 1931, 83 mins)

Credits
Dir: William A. Wellman
Prod: Darryl F. Zanuck
Scr: Harvey Thew
DOP: Dev Jennings
Ed: Edward M. McDermott
Music: David Mendoza
Art Dir: Max Parker

Cast: James Cagney (Tom Powers), Edward Woods (Matt Doyle), Beryl Mercer (Ma Powers), Jean Harlow (Gwen Allen), Joan Blondell (Mame), Mae Clarke (Kitty)

The rise and fall of two Prohibition-era gangsters.

Interchangeable in many ways with Mervyn Le Roy's *Little Caesar* (*qv*), both were produced in the pre-Hays Office days (hence the sexual undercurrent and violence), with the unknown leads subsequently catapulted to stardom, at the formative stage of Warner Brothers developing their heightened urban melodramas. In structure (the rise and fall), the moral order (*Public Enemy*

SOLIHULL S.F.C.
LIBRARY

The Public Enemy: The original poster for William Wellman's influential work.

glorify the hoodlum or the criminal.' Whether this ambition was ever realised is debatable. Powers' behaviour is accounted for in a series of vignettes, rather than continuous narrative, as we see his development from child to man. His gangster is something of a 'teenage rebel', as *Monthly Film Bulletin*'s Richard Combs pointed out; his lack of a caring father (his real one, a policeman, beat him) leading him to pass through a series of substitute father figures, such as Putty Nose and 'Nails' Nathan. Only his upright brother can exert control over him (knocking him down twice without reprisals) – as if Tom desires to be under the wing of the family, even looking for approval by bringing some of his ill-gotten gains home for mother. Wellman, from the opening scenes, sets up a bevy of images (the man with his pails of beer, the Salvation Army band, the boys' mischief) that mesh the characters with their environments, heavily underlining the point that the social conditions were as much to blame as those who acted upon them. A definitive portrayal of the gangster, *The Public Enemy* contained all the quintessential elements that would sum up the gangster genre: the clothes, the cars, the guns, the myth of success.

Cagney's infamous abuse of women, pushing a grapefruit into Mae Clarke's face, and his demise (returned to his mother's house as a mummified corpse) became instant cinema folklore   often imitated, never bettered.

providing Tom with a brother to counterpoint his values, *Little Caesar* using Rico's best friend), and aspirations (the American Dream as viewed through the only avenue open to them – crime), the films remained the same. More complex than its cousin, *The Public Enemy* ambiguously sways between condemning and condoning Tom's actions, presenting the psychological reason for his behaviour as childishness, a reaction to the inadequacy of the adult world. Criticised, along with *Little Caesar*, for glorifying the criminals, a decidedly uncertain forward was added, 'It is the ambition of the authors of *The Public Enemy* to honestly depict an environment that exists today in a certain strata of American life, rather than

Pulp Fiction

(US, Miramax, 1994, 153 mins)

> *'The idea was to use these really old stories... the sort of thing you've seen a zillion times before... to take these genre characters and put them in a life situation.'*
>
> **(Quentin Tarantino, *UK Premiere*)**

Credits
Dir/Scr: Quentin Tarantino
Prod: Lawrence Bender
Scr: Roger Avary
DOP: Andrzej Sekula

Pulp Fiction: 'I'll lay my furious vengeance upon thee': Vincent (John Travolta) and Jules (Samuel L. Jackson) do a hard day's work.

Ed: Sally Menke
Music Dir: Karyn Rachtman
Prod. Des: David Wasco

Cast: John Travolta (Vincent Vega), Samuel L. Jackson (Jules), Bruce Willis (Butch), Harvey Keitel (The Wolf), Ving Rhames (Marsellus Wallace), Pumpkin (Tim Roth), Honey Bunny (Amanda Plummer), Rosanna Arquette (Jody), Eric Stoltz (Lance)

Three 'pulp' crime stories closely intertwine: a hitman taking the boss's wife on a date, a boxer throwing his fight and a bloody assassination.

Conceived and largely written by Tarantino on a sojourn to Amsterdam, *Pulp Fiction* was the deserved phenomenon of 1994, a neatly woven tapestry of pop-cultured protagonists. Originally entitled *Black Mask*, Tarantino and co-writer/friend Avary (who contributed to the Gold Watch segment), drew, apart from the aforementioned pioneering crime anthology magazine, from the spirit of hard-boiled novels 'containing lurid subject matter', the likes of Spillane, Thompson and even Leonard. To champion this, Vincent (hitman and supposed brother of *Reservoir Dogs*' (*qv*) Mr Blonde) carries a Modesty Blaise novel, appropriately read on the toilet. While composing the work, Tarantino himself read *No Good From a Corpse* by Howard Hawks' preferred screenwriter Leigh – *The Big Sleep, Rio Bravo Bracket*. The complexity of influences, conscious or otherwise, increase when one considers the film's own medium: Robert Aldrich's *Kiss Me Deadly*, for the unseen contents of the briefcase, Robert Rossen's *Body and Soul* (*qv*), with the boxer manoeuvred into throwing the fight, John Boorman's *Deliverance*, for the anal rape, Jean-

Luc Godard's *Bande à Part* for Vincent and Mia's dance scene and less specifically the Blaxploitation genre for Jules' persona.

Tarantino allows for contradictions, a maelstrom of style surrounds characters cut-out of their genres and merged with everyday LA. Hitmen au fait with foot massages, TV trivia and the Bible, tuxedoed 'cleaners' attendant at functions before 9am, and the gangland boss who carries his minion's coffee to the stakeout, we see 'a bunch of gangsters doin' a bunch of gangster shit' in the home, not the office. This humanisation (read even humiliation as the two hitmen, at one point dressed in Hawaiian shirts, look like 'dorks'), prepares us for the denouement, Jules' spiritual conversion.

His 'Divine intervention' frustrates the pot-boiler ending, the destiny laid out for him (death, as with Vincent). In a world of casual violence, moral dilemmas are present, and choice is everything.

* **Academy Awards:** Quentin Tarantino and Roger Avary won for Best Original Screenplay.

* Cannes Film Festival: *Pulp Fiction* won the Palme D'Or.

See also: *Get Shorty*; *Kiss of Death*; *Romeo is Bleeding*; *Things To Do In Denver When You're Dead*.

Quick Millions

(US, 20th Century Fox, 1931, 72 mins)

Credits
Dir./Scr: Rowland Brown
Scr: Courtney Terrett
DOP: Joseph H. August
Ed./Art Dir: Duncan Cramer

Cast: Spencer Tracy ('Bugs' Raymond), George Raft (Jimmy Kirk), Marguerite Churchill (Dorothy Stone), Sally Eilers (Daisy de Lisle), John Wray (Kenneth Stone)

A truck driver turned protection racketeer falls for a society girl and hopes to achieve respectability.

From the opening shot – a train hurtling towards Chicago through the surrounding countryside – the film draws us towards the concerns voiced by the public at large.

Brown, later to write the screenplay for *Johnny Apollo*, conveys a strong sense of social classes in America, as *Dead End* and *Bullets or Ballots* (qqv) later would. Structured in places as a debate on the real problem, a radio reformer tells his audience: 'Fellow suckers, since we are permitting the racketeer and the gangster, who you all know is a direct by-product of the bootlegger, they are

threatening our safety, menacing our government, raising our rent, increasing the price of everything from the vegetables we eat to the milk our children drink.' A society lady later tells a Citizens' group: 'We'll no longer have a republic. We'll have a gangster-governed kingdom. Why!? Why can't we do something? We've got the laws and we've got the officials sworn to enforce them.' The District Attorney answers this at a further point in the film, by addressing the leading citizens, blaming businessmen for shielding racketeers: 'We're becoming hoodlum-minded. We're becoming a race of underdogs tearing at the entrails of society, a society based upon wealth instead of intellectual attainment... Now all crime is based on money.' As the DA admits, judges are weak and he himself has been unable to gain indictments – Bugs' demise emphasises this; as with *City Streets* (qv), his own gang, and not the mechanics of justice, take him for a ride to dispose of him.

Eugene Rosow called the work: 'a subtle denial of the promise of social mobility in Depression America, and a frank expression of the upward mobility of those willing to be criminally ruthless in their pursuit of success.' Unlike the Warner Brothers vehicles of the time, *Quick Millions* has a moral centre – and condemns those Rosow talks of.

* Director Brown was also responsible for the original stories that inspired Michael Curtiz's *Angels With Dirty Faces* (qv) and Archie Mayo's *The Doorway to Hell*. Made in 1930, the film (originating from Brown's *A Handful of Clouds*) stressed the gangster's identification with Napoleon. Other, more conventional, elements included a takeover scene, a machine-gun slaughtering, and bootlegging rivalry.

Racket, The

(US, Paramount Famous Lasky, 1928, 60 mins)

Credits
Dir: Lewis Milestone
Prod: Howard Hughes
Scr: Harry Behn, Del Andrews, based on the play by Bartlett Cormack
DOP: Tony Gaudio
Ed: Tom Miranda

Cast: Thomas Meighan (Captain McQuigg), Marie Prevost (Helen Hayes), Louis Wolheim (Nick Scarsi), John Darrow (Ames), Lucien Prival (Chick)

Bootlegger who brazenly defies the law is captured, but a politician – needing the votes he controls – ensures his release, only for the gangster then to be hunted down by an incorruptible police captain.

Racket, The

(US, RKO Radio, 1951, 88 mins)

Credits
Dir: John Cromwell, Nicholas Ray

Prod: Howard Hughes
Scr: W.R. Burnett, William Wister Haines
DOP: George E. Diskant
Ed: Sherman Todd
Music: Paul Sawtell
Art Dir: Albert S. D'Agostino, Jack Okey

Cast: Robert Mitchum (Capt. McQuigg), Robert Ryan (Scanlon), Ray Collins (Welch), Robert Hutton (Arnes), Don Porter (Connolly), Lizabeth Scott (Irene)

Racketeer with the city officials in his pocket attempts to corrupt scrupulous police officer only for a nightclub singer to turn upon him.

Originally a popular play on Broadway, starring Edward G. Robinson, it created such a sensation it was banned in Chicago for being too explicit about gangster involvement in political corruption. Cormack, a Chicago journalist and friend of *Scarface* (qv) screenwriter Ben Hecht, modelled Nick Scarsi (Robinson) on Al Capone and his political bedfellow on Chicago Mayor Big Bill Thompson. The 1928 silent picture was ordered by the New York Picture Commission to delete scenes involving bribery, and a state official phoning to have a gangster released from jail. Gangsters, we were shown, traded votes (or campaign contributions) for protection from the law that politicians could offer. Such censorship arose from a belief that the public must be prevented from viewing the law as corruptible, and the film was an important transitional point for the genre, sowing the seeds for the 'social realism' works that dominated the 1930s.

The remake, again produced by Howard Hughes and ushering in the new generation of gangster actors (Mitchum and Ryan), was updated to include references to Estes Kefauver's Senate Crime Investigating Committee. The Crime Commission meets with the State Governor in the prologue to assure us that it is no longer a question of local crime, but of the national syndicate's moving in – in this case run by the omnipotent (and unseen) figure known only as 'The Old Man'.

While he views physical violence as outmoded, Scanlon prefers things 'a little rougher'. Repeatedly asserting 'This is my city', he comes complete with pretensions (an English butler), catchphrases ('Blow, Shyster') and dramatic death scene. Burnett and Haines' screenplay lifted not only dialogue but the spirit straight from Cormack's work. As Mitchum says, in his closing speech: 'Justice – a slow machine. People like Welch [the corrupt assistant DA] always throwing sand in it... Tomorrow it starts all over again.'

See also: *Killers, The*; *Kiss of Death*; *Out of the Past*.

Reservoir Dogs

(US, Miramax, 1992, 100 mins)

'Making the greatest Western is a pretty tall order. But if you set out to make the greatest heist movie, you'll probably get in the top 15 if you make a good one.'

(Quentin Tarantino)

Credits
Dir/Scr: Quentin Tarantino
Prod: Lawrence Bender
DOP: Andrzej Skeula
Ed: Sally Menke
Music: Karyn Rachtman
Prod Des: David Wasco

Cast: Harvey Keitel (Mr. White), Christopher Penn (Nice Guy Eddie), Tim Roth (Mr. Orange), Michael Madsen (Mr. Blonde), Steve Buscemi (Mr. Pink), Lawrence Tierney (Joe Cabot)

The aftermath of a diamond-store heist gone wrong, with one member of the gang suspected of being a traitor.

The sensation of the 1992 Sundance Film Festival, *Reservoir Dogs* was the film that revitalised the crime movie, spawned a host of imitations, thrust US indie cinema into the light and gave us the media-coined soundbite – 'post-Tarantino'. Largely gaining a reputation across Europe based on misconceptions about its most notorious scenes (the infamous ear shot is cutaway from in an ironic joke), its blend of rapid-fire pop culture diatribes, male posturing, seventies kitsch soundtrack and designer violence struck a note.

The gangsters (known only by colour-coded pseudonyms), from their analysis of Madonna's *Like a Virgin* to an appreciation of Pam Grier shows, were megaphones for the media-saturated nineties. Mr Pink, who remains 'tortured' in the TV-trivia discussions, believes himself the true 'professional', repeatedly admonishing the others for their lack of professionalism. And yet it is within a world defined by their own moral order. Pink being the only escapee (so it appears) at the end, it remains a universe where emotional ties cause downfall. Orange/White/gang-leader Joe Cabot (Tierney also appeared in *Dillinger* [*qv*] in 1945) and his son Nice Guy Eddie, all are drawn together through human feeling. Asked if he has killed anybody, Mr Pink replies that he 'tagged a couple of cops'. 'No real people?' comes Mr White's blunt question. Their world is 'cops and robbers' – an underbelly where sensibilities do not exist, a game with its own rules (Blonde even refers to White and Pink fighting as 'kids' playing rough). The parameters of their environment are also defined by language.

Using words like 'exposure' and 'ice', Tarantino recreates a criminal network that evolves across his work. Figures such as Vic Vega (Madsen's Mr Blonde) is the brother of *Pulp Fiction*'s Vincent. Vic's prison officer, Scagnetti, recalls Tom Sizemore in *Natural Born Killers*, while Mr White's partner, Alabama, refers to Patricia Arquette's character in *True Romance*. Drawing us to its own artificiality, Tarantino structures through a complex series of flashbacks, revealing each criminal's integration into the gang, and subsequent escape after the unseen robbery. As we see the undercover cop Orange rehearsing his role in front of the mirror (being 'Marlon Brando'), he has to learn the 'rules' if you wanta be in their gang. Their world, like the theatrical stage of the rendezvous warehouse (the film's chief setting) is a play enacted in front of us, recognisable and yet distanced.

Costing just $1.5 million, Tarantino's script borrowed liberally from the classics of the heist movie: Kubrick's *The Killing*, Huston's *The Asphalt Jungle* and Sargent's *The Taking of Pelham* 123 (*qqv*). Ringo Lam's *City on Fire* proved an even greater source, while the infamous opening slow-motion stroll to 'Little Green Bag' was borrowed from fifties caper movie *Ocean's 11* (*qqv*). Fitting with

Reservoir Dogs: Mr Orange (Tim Roth) reveals his true colours.

Tarantino's 'artificial stage', he juggles with cinema's heritage, reshapes the gangster genre, its characters and concerns, for an audience brought up on *The Fantastic Four*.

* The film was delayed in receiving a video certificate for several months (along with Abel Ferrara's *Bad Lieutenant*) in the UK by the British Board of Film Classification, allowing it to remain in the cinemas (and considerably boosting its cult reputation).

* *Pulp Fiction* co-writer Roger Avary wrote and directed his own take on the heist movie in 1994, *Killing Zoe* (executive produced by Tarantino and his producer Lawrence Bender). Set in Paris, it involved safe-cracker Zed (Eric Stoltz) coming together with childhood friend and heroin addict Eric (Jean-Hugues Anglade) for a bank robbery. With Zoe meaning 'life' in Greek, Avary explained his concept: 'I wanted to write an extreme example

of what my generation is about – people who are living for the moment.' Sharing Tarantino's obsession with the banal, Avary thought of his criminals more as marauding Vikings (despite Zed's belief, à la Mr Pink, in professionalism).

See also: *Criss-Cross*; *Face*; *Heat*; *Usual Suspects, The*.

Resurrection Man

(UK, Revolution Films, 1997, 101 mins)

'The film leaves you with a feeling of having been on an occasionally unguided tour of an abatoir.'
(Richard Falcon, Sight & Sound)

Credits
Dir: Marc Evans
Prod: Andrew Eaton
Scr: Eoin McNamee, based on his own book

DOP: Pierre Aim
Ed: John Wilson
Music: David Holmes, Gary Burns, Keith Tenniswood
Prod. Des: Mark Tildesley

Cast: Stuart Townsend (Victor Kelly), John Hannah (Darkie Larche), Brenda Fricker (Dorcas Kelly), James Nesbitt (Ryan), Geraldine O'Rawe (Heather Graham)

Mid-seventies Belfast set tale of a Cagney-obsessed charismatic Loyalist gangster pursued by a local journalist.

Based loosely on the antics of the Loyalist gang, the Shankhill Butchers, the film is a brutal, cold-hearted depiction of gangsterdom at its most bloody and motiveless. While director Evans wished, and succeeded in this desire, to eschew the politics in order to avoid being 'stifled by the responsibility of the subject matter', Kelly is left depicted as an almost psychopathic figure, randomly slaying gang members and public alike. Townsend's Kelly, son to a Catholic father and Protestant mother, begins the film watching the conclusion to *The Public Enemy* (*qv*), Cagney's fate prefiguring his own gunning in the final reel. In the same way Bertrand Tavernier's anti-heroes of *The Bait* remain obsessed by Al Pacino's Tony Montana, Kelly is a movie gangster's gangster. As Townsend said in an interview, Victor's 'like an outsider, something higher and more evil in his own world. Here's this guy who thinks he's a film star but at the same time he's pure evil. Young guys in Belfast in the seventies did want to emulate Cagney. He was a folk hero. He was the Irishman who went to Hollywood to make movies; he was tough, he was gangster.'
With a devotion to his mother (they trade Cagney quotes), a subtextual homoerotic relationship with mentor McClure (Sean McGinley) and an increasing addiction to cocaine, Kelly is a blend of the Krays and *Goodfellas'* (*qv*) Henry Hill. Like all of those characters, Kelly - self-styled leader of the 'Resurrection Men' – lacks a respectable father figure, seeking out a surrogate as he imposes his almost mythic quality upon Belfast residents. More a series of terrifying vignettes and stylised moments (Victor emerging from his from door in

the opening; shaving his hated stroke-ridden Pa with an open razor, the concluding Bathhouse scene), the film is at times a very dangerous piece of cinema. Relentless in its depiction of violence, the film broods with menace, but often irresponsibly has no moral reference point. Nesbitt's drunk, wife-beating journalist just becomes a counterpoint to Kelly. A man seen as a hero to the end, Kelly is lionised by one and all (shown as his Ma is interviewed after his death), offering up little comic relief in the process.

Rise and Fall of Legs Diamond, The

(US, United States Pictures, 1960, 101 mins)

Credits
Dir: Budd Boetticher
Prod: Milton Sperling
Scr: Joseph Landon
DOP: Lucien Ballard
Ed: Folmer Blangsted
Music: Leonard Rosenman
Art Dir: Jack Poplin

Cast: Ray Danton (Legs Diamond), Karen Steele (Alice), Elaine Stewart (Monica), Jesse White (Leo Bremer), Simon Oakland (Lt. Moody), Robert Lowery (Arnold)

Biopic of the hoofer-cum-gangster.

Like *The St. Valentine's Day Massacre* and *The George Raft Story* (*qqv*) respectively, Legs Diamond was suffused with a nostalgia for a lawless age, using the biographical method to recreate a hallowed period of gangsters in the 1920s and thirties. Presenting itself sternly as the official chronicler, the opening caption tells us: 'Jack 'Legs' Diamond was spawned in the 1920s; an era of incredible violence. This is the way it happened.'
In fact, little is made of the period of his life in which he worked for 'Little Augie', or the antipathy between him and Dutch Schultz. A character sketch is preferred. Portrayed as a devil with the ladies, Legs sees himself as above the law, even immortal ('I'm never going to jail'; 'The bullet hasn't been made that can kill me', proving it later

when he is shot but survives). Hardly all talk, his rise to narcotics, protection rackets and bootlegging is carefully documented by the progressive number of people he steps on. His sick brother Eddie, whom he eventually spurns; Arnold Rothstein, big-time gangster for whom Legs becomes the chief bodyguard and then begins dating his girl Monica; Alice, the girl he courts at a dance hall (even setting an opponent's dress alight so they will win the prize trophy), and marries so she can't testify against him. She eventually walks out on him, saying: 'A lotta people loved my husband, but he never loved anybody; that's why he's dead', after he has said to a gunman 'You go right ahead and kill her; it won't stop me getting what I want.' His vulnerability is revealed when he is left alone, unprotected because of a lack of love.

His fall is pre-empted by the newsreel he sees in Europe, telling of Al Capone's incarceration and the lifting of Prohibition. As he is told when he returns to the States, discovering a National Syndicate has taken over during his sojourn, bodies everywhere is 'bad PR'; 'The world is changing and it's time you left it.' Legs is set to die the gangster's lonely death. An old-fashioned gangster, his inability to adapt and the inevitable alienation caused by the individual's drive for success lead to his demise. As with so many generic pieces, the film is as much about the shifts and currents of US history, as about the individual's need for companionship.

See also: *Bonnie and Clyde*; *Bonnie Parker Story, The*; *Bullet For Pretty Boy, A*; *Dillinger*; *George Raft Story, The*; *King of the Roaring Twenties: the Arnold Rothstein Story*; *Lepke*; *Lucky Luciano*; *Machine Gun Kelly*; *Young Dillinger*.

Roaring Twenties, The

(US, 1939, Warner Brothers, 105 mins)

Credits
Dir: Raoul Walsh
Exec. Prod: Hal B. Wallis
Scr: Richard Macaulay, Jerry Wald, Robert Rossen, based on an original story by Mark Hellinger
DOP: Ernest Haller

Ed: Jack Killifer
Music: Milo Anderson
Art Dir: Max Parker

Cast: James Cagney (Eddie Bartlett), Priscilla Lane (Jean Sherman), Humphrey Bogart (George Hally), Gladys George (Panama Smith), Jeffrey Lynn (Lloyd Hart), Frank McHugh (Danny Green)

The paths of two World War I veterans cross once again during Prohibition, when they discover they are rival racketeers. After a brief partnership, the repeal of the law ensures one's fortunes dwindle, while the other expands his criminal activities.

'He used to be a big shot': the closing words to Raoul Walsh's film (who would go on to makes *High Sierra* [qv] with Bogart), the most lavishly romantic of the 1930s, and the last great Warners effort of the decade. And with its extensive use of newsreel footage historically charting the previous decade, the emphasis is on what once was: 'Guys just don't go tearing things up like we used to. You and me just don't belong', says Cagney, playing the once-honest racketeer who sinks to skid row, to Bogart, opposite each other again after Michael Curtiz's *Angels with Dirty Faces* (qv).

This idea is borne throughout, from the opening prologue when returning soldiers are treated as if they've taken a holiday. Just as the Hughes' Brothers' film *Dead Presidents* would show for Vietnam veterans, the prevailing social and economic conditions (Eddie returns from WWI to find mass unemployment and raised rents) will ensure the honest man (called 'geraniums') is forced into choosing a life of crime; as the voice-over says, Eddie 'becomes part of a criminal army – born of a marriage of an unpopular law [Prohibition] and an unwilling public.'

The narrator, used in conjunction with the footage which takes us from 1918 to 1933, prefigured the likes of the semi-documentary works, such as Fritz Lang's *The Big Heat* and Roger Corman's *The St. Valentine's Day Massacre* (qqv). Providing pertinent, almost disapproving, comments upon the events documented, social change ('Women's skirts get shorter', 'The hip flask in now an integral part of a national scene') is juxtaposed to the Volstead act, which attempts to guide us to the belief that America's 'era of madness' has been brought about partly by the disintegration of moral values; the bootlegger is 'a modern crusader' and 'cares nothing about tomorrow as long as there is money today'. With this highly structured 'pageant' approach, *The Roaring Twenties* can be seen as the stern chronicler. Distanced by years from actual events and less 'moral' works like *The Public Enemy* (*qv*), it provides a retrospective 'What went wrong' operation.

* Mark Hellinger, from whose original story the script came, went on to produce several gangster films of note in the late 1940s. Apart from Robert Siodmak's *The Killers* (*qv*), he began a fruitful relationship with Jules Dassin. Dassin, who made the heist movie, *Riffifi*, following exile to Europe after his denouncement as a Communist by director Ed Dymtryk in front of the House of Un-American Activities, was responsible for two important contributions to sub-genres of the gangster movie. *Brute Force*, made in 1947, was a condemnation of the prison system, along the lines of *I Am a Fugitive of a Chain Gang*. A year later saw *Naked City*. Narrated by Hellinger – who tells us 'There are eight million stories in the Naked City' – the film was a pioneer for location shooting, entirely filmed as it was in New York. Oscars went to William Daniels' stark cinematography and Paul Weatherwax's editing. Pursuing a murderer through the city, the film emphasised more than most the documentary approach, first established in *The Musketeers of Pig Alley* (*qv*).

The Roaring Twenties: Eddie Bartlett (Jimmy Cagney) and George Hally (Humphrey Bogart) hear the roar.

Romeo is Bleeding

(US, Gramercy Pictures, 1994, 108 mins)

> '*A film about the lies women tell men, and the lies men tell themselves, Romeo is Bleeding takes its inspiration from Chandler and the old hard-boiled school.*'
>
> **(Manohla Dargis, *Sight & Sound*)**

Credits
Dir: Peter Medak

Prod: Tim Bevan, Eric Fellner, Michael Flynn, Paul Webster
Scr/Prod: Hiliary Henkin
DOP: Dariusz Wolski
Ed: Walter Murch
Music: Mark Isham
Prod. Des: Carl Clifford, Stuart Wurtzel

Cast: Gary Oldman (Jack Grimaldi), Juliette Lewis (Sheri), Lena Olin (Mona Demarkov), Roy Scheider (Don Falcone), Anabella Sciorra (Natalie Grimaldi)

Corrupt police sergeant, in the employ of the Mafia, comes unstuck over a female key witness.

Once touted as one of the ten best unmade scripts in Hollywood, this perfectly confused neo-*noir* receives inspiration only from Gary Oldman's narrator, retelling the tale for cathartic purposes, while affecting a Phillip Marlowe lilt to his voice. Accidentally showing a scene further down the narrative strand, he quips 'I'm getting ahead of myself' but the joy of breaking up the linear progression is sadly explored no further.
Roy Scheider's brief but considered appearance as mob boss Don Falcone is the other saving grace; his speech to Grimaldi has all the hallmarks of a Boss' words. Set on the veranda of a vast mansion while a bathrobed Scheider is taking breakfast, he appears a man of culture, questioning Grimaldi on twentieth-century poets, while the subtext suggests a concern not with death but succession, as if he were royalty. 'Eventually I'll be destroyed. The next generation of barbarians are ready to take over... but why open the door to them?' Falcone wants to extend his power from beyond the grave, hand-picking those who will take over his kingdom. This image, though, is later disastrously undermined – with Falcone's simplistic capture and demise. Unsurprisingly, in a world where a police sergeant has taken over $500,000 in Mafia pay-offs, morality is low on the agenda. Falcone again: 'A life's a life. Moral distinctions can paralyse you,' and adds that pacifists are 'the morally bankrupt elite'. A fine protestation of the transient nature of life, not just in the underworld.

See also: *Get Shorty*; *Kiss of Death*; *Pulp Fiction*; *Things To Do In Denver When You're Dead*.

Ruby

(US, Propaganda Films, 1992, 110 mins)

Credits
Dir: John Mackenzie
Prod: Sigurjon Sighvatsson, Steve Golin
Scr: Stephen Davis
DOP: Philip Meheux
Ed: Richard Trevor
Music: John Scott
Prod. Des: Rob Wilson King, Ken Hardy, David Brisbin

Cast: Danny Aiello (Jack Ruby), Sherilyn Fenn ('Candy Cane'), Arliss Howard (Maxwell), Tobin Bell (Ferris), David Duchovny (Officer Tippit), Marc Lawrence (Santos), Richard Sarafian (Proby)

Biopic of the strip club owner and former mobster who shot Lee Harvey Oswald.

Rather like Harold Shand, East End gang boss in John MacKenzie's first film, the seminal gangster picture *The Long Good Friday* (*qv*), Danny Aiello's Jack Ruby becomes aware as the narrative progresses that he's in way over his head, but finds himself unable to draw back. Ironically, the film opens with Ruby watching Joe Valachi give evidence at the Senate hearings against the Cosa Nostra; he calls him a 'scumbag,' indicating his loyalties. Ruby is then seen passing information, as a paid informant, to the FBI, about a suspected communist agitator in the unions. A self-described 'small time club owner with a sense of the past', he is the man of old-time values at America's disposal – as ready blindly to assassinate Castro as he is Oswald 'so one day everything would have to be brung out in the open'.
Revealed as a gangster himself – involved in gun-running, slot machines, narcotics, race track scams – his crimes are born of naiveté, a yearning for a time before everything was 'connected up wrong'. Like Oliver Stone's vast *JFK*, the film sheds its own light on the shooting, claiming Oswald let an assassin into the book depository, and like that film it is about the complex interconnections between the underworld, CIA and the White House. As its epigraph says: 'Drama is a lie that tells us the truth'. Draw your own conclusions.

163

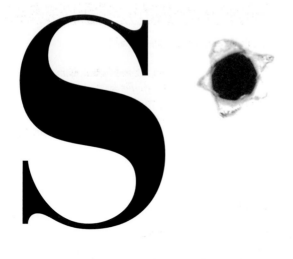

S

St Valentine's Day Massacre

(US, 20th Century-Fox, 1967, 99 mins)

'The result is fascinating: a cool, dispassionately logical narrative which makes complete sense of the intricate quarrel between Capone and Moran, and also portrays very graphically the way rackets were run as respectable big business while open warfare was waged in the streets.'
(Monthly Film Bulletin)

Credits
Dir/Prod: Roger Corman
Scr: Howard Browne
DOP: Milton Krasner
Ed: William B. Murphy
Music: Fred Steiner
Art Dir: Jack Martin Smith, Philip M. Jefferies

Cast: Jason Robards (Al Capone), George Segal (Peter Gusenberg), Ralph Meeker (Bugs Moran), Jean Hale (Myrtle), Clint Ritchie (Jack McGurn)

Detailed depiction of events leading up to the Massacre.

Written by Howard Browne, an authority on 1920s era Chicago, Roger Corman's film revives the semi-documentary biopics popular a decade before. With his first comparatively big budget film, Corman

St Valentine's Day Massacre: the gang's all here.

rarely takes risks, preferring a straightforward explanation of the Massacre. While not his most innovative production, it was one of the most consistent, disentangling the complex set of relationships pertinent to 'one of the most violent days in American history', usually glossed over or ignored by previous films. Setting out its factual representation from the beginning, we are told by the narrator (who documents, never sensationalises) that 'every character and event herein is based on real characters and events'. For the most part, Capone's murder of Joseph Aiello being an exception, it does just this, a brief resumé of each man's career included. Only when venturing into the participants' psyches – as we are told several characters' mundane thoughts on their last day alive – do we stray from the matter in hand. Neither does Corman neglect the film's heritage; while avoiding the moral demise imposed on Capone in Richard Wilson's *Al Capone* (beaten savagely to death by prison inmates), Corman returns to Pre-Hays code values, as *Bonnie and Clyde* (qv) would. Both films represented the pinnacle of the two strains of gangster film being made at the time; the semi-doc and the mythic biopic, but – with Corman's Segal character rubbing a lettuce sandwich into harlot Jean Hale's face – we cannot help but think of the gloriously amoral *The Public Enemy* (*qv*). Racial origins – words like 'Wop', 'Mick', 'Kraut' – are also not shied away from.

Setting the Massacre in a context wider than previous gangster films, we are told that on 14 February 1929, Mickey Mouse was about to make his screen debut and Herbert Hoover was due to be inaugurated. The Wall Street Crash and Lindbergh's Paris flight are mentioned in the same breath; as an audience we are allowed to recognise the gravity of this cataclysmic event. As we are told towards the end, the Massacre outraged the public and brought a temporary halt to gang warfare; but bringing the film some topical relevance by the 1960s, gangsters would reform to become even more powerful than 40 years previously. Capone and Moran are viewed not as renegades but as businessmen, in league with the corrupt society they run – a precursor, as Martin Ritt's *The Brotherhood* (*qv*) would be, to *The Godfather*'s (*qv*) use of the gangster as a metaphor for America.

See also: *Al Capone*; *Capone*; *Gangland: the Verne Miller Story*; *George Raft Story, The*; *Lost Capone, The*; *Scarface Mob, The*; *Untouchables, The*.

Scarface: Shame of a Nation

(US, United Artists, 1932, 95 mins)

'Do it first, do it yourself, and keep on doing it.'
(Tony Camonte, *Scarface*)

Credits
Dir: Howard Hawks
Prod: Howard Hughes
Scr: Ben Hecht
DOP: Lee Garmes, L.W.O'Connell
Ed: Edward Curtiss
Music: Adolph Tandler, Gus Arnheim
Prod. Des: Harry Oliver

Cast: Paul Muni (Tony Camonte), Ann Dvorak (Cesca Camonte), Karen Morley (Poppy), Osgood Perkins (Johnny Lovo), Henry C. Gordon (Ben Guarino), George Raft (Guino Rinaldo)

The rise and fall of an Italian-American hoodlum.

Scarface

(US, Universal Pictures, 1983, 170 mins)

'Edward G. Robinson, Cagney, Paul Muni – none of them could hold a candle to Pacino when Pacino's playing a gangster. He's like a male Bette Davis on a rampage.'

(Lawrence J. Quirk)

Credits
Dir: Brian De Palma
Prod: Martin Bregman
Scr: Oliver Stone
DOP: John A. Alonzo
Ed: Jerry Greenberg, David Ray
Music: Giorgio Moroder
Prod. Des: Ed Richardson, Ferdinando Scarfiotti

Cast: Al Pacino (Tony Montana), Michelle Pfeiffer (Elvira), Mary Elizabeth Mastrantonio (Gina), Robert Loggia (Frank Lopez), F. Murray Abraham (Omar)

Exiled Cuban criminal begins working for a Miami drug lord, only to usurp him and, inevitably, to fall from grace.

Originally billed as 'the gangster film to end all gangster films', Howard Hawks' *Scarface* was created straight out of contemporary headlines: the killing of Big Jim Colisimo in a Chicago phone booth is echoed in the opening scene; the siege and capture of 'two-gun' Crowley akin to Tony Camonte's finale, and, of course, the exploits of Al Capone, known to all as Scarface. Encouraged by producer Hughes to pump up the action (Hawks tells of creating 20 car wrecks), the film was typical Hughes bombast, employing over 1,500 extras in just one scene, and using 62 different sets in three separate studios. Little wonder that Brian De Palma's 1983 overblown, cartoon-like remake was dedicated to Hawks and one-time Chicago newspaperman-cum-screenwriter Ben Hecht, in an obvious attempt to exceed the excess of the original, meant in part by Hecht as a rebuttal of Sternberg's *Underworld* (*qv*), a film he scripted but did not like. And just as Hawks' film is based on truth, so De Palma's updates the Italian protagonists to Cuban immigrants, exiled by Castro in 1980. The remake's screenwriter, Oliver Stone, ensures the 'rise and fall' structure, along with the implied incestuous relationship between Camonte/Montana and his sister, remain intact. An absence of detailed scenes depicting Montana's drug deals nevertheless feels conspicuous in comparison to Hecht's step-by-step account of Camonte's rise. Both are products of their time – De Palma's a garish, synthetic tribute to the American Dream, swapping booze for drugs. Its analogy is found in the $100 billion a year coke industry in Miami, the need for consumption, epitomised by Pacino's ever-increasing habit. While Camonte has pretensions of high-class (his bumbling secretary), the vulgar Montana craves only quantity – his downfall is as much due to bad taste as it is down to immorality and paranoia. Yet both these anti-heroes are innately infantile, Camonte (a strangely anti-Hawksian hero) lovingly caressing his new Tommy gun as if it were a toy. Both have few illusions of the supposed innate honour of the gangster, the Simian-like Camonte (Muni even studied ape photographs in preparation) rising to the top only because he is more willing to use violence.

As for the symbolism, De Palma exchanges Hawks's expressionistic visuals (such as the bowling alley assassination with its X strikes and tumbling pins) for tack. The airship displaying 'The World is Yours' (also seen in the original as a neon sign) inadvertently suggests the film's gross inflation and hot air, the paradise-like sunset painting behind Montana in Lopez's office representing not just aspiration but the life of this trash prince.

* De Palma's version was submitted five times in the US to the MPAA board to reduce its X certificate to an R, developing its reputation as a violent movie. Equally, Hawks' *Scarface* was banned in several states, condemned by the Hays Office (which imposed the film's subtitle and moralising preface) for its sympathetic portrayal of a gangster, and delayed for two years by censors before achieving release (it featured 28 killings, a record for the time). Hawks was also forced to shoot a new ending, using a double for Muni who had returned to the New York stage, in which Camonte was tried in court and hanged. After Hawks left a further scene was added, set in a publisher's office,

Scarface: Tony 'Scarface' Camonte (Paul Muni) goes down in a blaze of glory.

depicting a group of citizens expressing outrage with gangsterism. Upon screening the 'approved' version, Howard Hughes, generating enormous publicity with the censorship battle, decided to return to the original – keeping only the subtitle and preface as compromises. Speculation became rife as to what had been cut, some critics claiming non-existent scenes between Camonte and his grandparents had been excised. According to Hawks, only an exchange between Camonte and his sister was cut, the censors believing it 'was too laudatory for a gangster'.

The Scarface Mob

(US, Desilu Productions, 1962, 96 mins)

Credits
Dir: Phil Karlson
Prod: Quinn Martin
Scr: Paul Monash
DOP: Charles Straumer
Ed: Robert L. Swanson
Music: Wilber Hatch
Art Dir: Ralph T. Berger, Frank T. Smith

Cast: Neville Brand (Al Capone), Robert Stack (Eliot Ness), Walter Winchell (Narrator), Keenan Wynn (Joe Fuselli), Barbara Nichols (Brandy La France)

The story of The Untouchables and their attempt to bring Al Capone to justice.

Narrated by the voice of authority, Walter Winchell, Phil Karlson's semi-documentary pilot (leading to the *Untouchables* TV series) is a tough, risqué B movie. Attempting to glamorise Ness' role (and relegating Oscar Farley's), it's a film full of arresting moments. In particular, the funeral procession for Ness colleague Joe Fuselli, led under Capone's window and consisting of a number of confiscated trucks – which, according to the script, led a number of people to inform on Capone, allowing the US Treasury Department to compile an income tax evasion case against him. The Mafia ritual of the Kiss of Death is also unusually shown. Chosen to murder Fuselli, Jimmy Napoli (Frank De Kova) receives a kiss from each member of Capone's mob. Napoli himself is raided by Ness and co., who find him asleep in bed with gun in hand, ready to wake and shoot at will. As a result the picture downplays the role the Treasury had in his arrest, preferring to examine the effect on Ness' personal life.

Very much of its time, Karlson's film also employs 1930s techniques; particularly the montage sequence, used to show Ness' wipeout raids on Capone's breweries, 'the heart and Achilles heel of [his] empire'. Attempting to impress by its detailed analysis of events (right down to a meeting time Ness had), authenticity is created, partly through the use of Sicilian dialect with no subtitles. Neville Brand's portrayal of Capone (a role he reprised briefly in *The George Raft Story* (*qv*) a year later), complete with scar and cigar, adds to the effect.

* Links between this work and Brian De Palma's crack at the Capone story, *The Untouchables* (*qv*), can also easily be seen; the end shot of Ness and his men assembled on the courthouse steps following Capone's conviction, and the rapport Capone has with reporters are seen again in De Palma's work.

* Karlson also made two other important contributions to the genre. Based on the Georges Simenon novel, *The Brothers Rico* saw perennial gangster actor Richard Conte as Eddie, ex-accountant for the mob whose brother has been marked for death. Two years earlier, in 1955, was *The Phenix City Story*. Containing a prologue of documentary footage, (optional to theatre owners!), the film exposed the Alabama city – along the lines of *The Houston Story* and *Kansas City Confidential* - for the wicked locale it was reported to be.

See also: *Al Capone*; *Gangland: the Verne Miller Story*; *Lost Capone, The*; *St. Valentine's Day Massacre, The*.

Shaft

(US, MGM, 1971, 100 mins)

Credits
Dir: Gordon Parks
Prod: Joel Freeman
Scr: John D.F. Black, Ernest Tidyman, based on his own novel
DOP: Urs Furrer
Ed: Hugh A. Robertson
Music: Isaac Hayes
Art Dir: Emanuel Gerard

Cast: Richard Roundtree (John Shaft), Moses Gunn (Bumpy Jonas), Charles Cioffi (Vic Androzzi), Christopher St. John (Ben Buford), Gwenn Mitchell (Ellie Moore)

A private eye is hired to find the kidnapped daughter of a Harlem gangster.

The film that sparked the wave of 1970s Blaxploitation films, *Shaft* was part of a new post-Civil Rights mood that presented blacks in a positive light; not the isolated minor character nor the Sidney Poitier-style social martyr – for once characters were not derogatory or embarrassing. Uncompromising and frank – 'I gotta couple of problems. I was born black and I was born poor', says Shaft – the film was awash with seventies style and funk. Hot on the heels of Ossie Davis' *Cotton Comes to Harlem*, both films transposed the white genre (New York private eye thriller) into an all-black context. Director Gordon Parks Snr (father to *Superfly* (qv) director Gordon Parks Jnr) claimed no didactic pretensions to the film, saying 'It's just a Saturday night fan picture which people go to see because they want to see the black guy winning.' And yet he gave a nod to the racial problem; his damsel-in-distress was rescued by a band of black militants who spring her from the Mafia, exchanging 'wop' and 'nigger' insults as they do.

* Numerous sequels were spawned. Gordon Parks' *Shaft's Big Score* (1972) and John Guillermin's *Shaft in Africa* (1973) saw Richard Roundtree slip on the leather coat twice more. In *Big Score*, he finds himself in the middle of a territorial gang war; in *Africa* he battles modern-day slave traders.

* **Academy Award:** Isaac Hayes won for Best Score ('Theme From *Shaft*').

See also: *Black Caesar*; *Black Godfather*; *Black Gunn*; *Hell Up In Harlem*; *I'm Gonna Git You, Sucka*; *Original Gangstas*.

Shanghai Triad
(Yao A Yao Yao Dao Wai Pe Qiao)

(China, Shanghai Film Studios/Alpha Films/UGC/La Sept, 1995, 112 mins)

Credit
Dir: Zhang Yimou
Prod: Jean Louis Piel, Yves Marmion, Wu Yigong
Scr: Bi Feiyu, based on the novel Gang Law by Li Xiao
DOP: Lu Yue

Ed: Tu Yuan
Music: Zhang Guangtian
Art Dir: Cao Jiu Ping

Cast: Gong Li (Xiao Jinbao), Li Baotian (Tang), Li Xuejian (Liu Shu), Shun Chun (Song), Wang Xiao Xiao (Shuisheng), Jiang Baoying (Cuihua)

Seen through the eyes of a young serving boy, set to work in 1930s Shanghai, a powerful mob boss is betrayed by his own men and takes refuge on a deserted island.

Zhang Yimou and Gong Li's personal parting at the time of the film's creation adds all the more resonance to the key image of the film: the eye. Shot through young Shuisheng's eyes, much of the film is viewed literally through a crack in the door as the bumpkin boy progresses from innocence to experience. While Yimou uses Shuisheng to allow us a glimpse of the boss Tang (based on a synthesis of real-life characters), so he himself is voyeuristically casting a gaze over his former lover through his character's eyes. This teasing structure, set over eight days, also ensures death (the massacre of Tang's servants) is as a shadow play – never seen, and only the consequences felt. Honour, sexuality and youth are also all 'seen' through the eye. 'Your uncle died defending me,' Shuisheng is told by the enigmatic Tang: 'His eyes are crying out for vengeance.' Tang's mistress Bijou sings (to Tang's disgust) *Moonlight*; symbolic of her affair with the right-hand-man-turned-traitor Song, it is full of references to eyes wandering over her body. Even the island peasant girl is noted for her 'pretty eyes'.

But Yimou also finds himself watching his own country, describing the film as a warning to the Chinese people: 'In effect I just wanted to say to my countrymen and to others that there is something more important than power and mere material possessions. What counts most in life is man's capacity for love and generosity. That is also why I did not want to make a traditional Mafia film.' A parable of greed, the city represents corruption, while the rural setting stands for honest, simple values. Bijou, once a country girl, now 'Queen of Shanghai', is the bridge between Shuisheng and

Tang, the festering city dweller. Allegorically, Shanghai and Tang represent the moral vacuums of present-day China and their government respectively. Many Chinese now refer to Party rule as *liumang zhengfu* ('government by gangsters') and Yimou draws the comparisons, using history as a smokescreen. Even so, the Chinese government, suspicious of his work, delayed production in 1994, and pressured Yimou to cancel his trip to the New York Film Festival, where his film was to open the gala.

Sicilian, The

(US, Gladden Entertainment, 1987, 146 mins)

Credits
Dir/Prod: Michael Cimino
Scr: Steve Shagen, based on the original novel by Mario Puzo
DOP: Alex Thomson
Ed: Françoise Bonnot
Music: David Mansfield
Prod. Des: Wolf Kroeger

Cast: Christophe Lambert (Salvatore Giuliano), Terence Stamp (Prince Borsa), Joss Ackland (Don Masino Croce), John Turturro (Aspanu Pisciotta), Richard Bauer (Professor Hector Adonis)

Biopic of the famous Sicilian bandit, known for robbing the Mafia, and fighting Church and State.

Highly praised in some quarters (being compared to Visconti's *The Leopard*), but venomously derided in others ('see it... and have a good hoot' said *Time Out*'s Geoff Andrew), Cimino's epic portrait of the notorious figure Giuliano concentrates on the mythic proportions of the story. Giuliano, a member of the Separatist Movement from 1943 who campaigned for Sicily to be taken over by President Truman as the 49th State of America, is seen as part Robin Hood, part Christ figure. A bandit by 'profession', the subject of Cimino's complex and layered film is a fitting protagonist for a film-maker ever concerned with the problems of the 'hero'. As critic Robin Wood states, the film 'develops the inquiry into the validity of the individual hero'. The 'people' are the heroes, but also seen as Communist and thus discredited. Giuliano, increasingly distanced from human relationships as he defines himself as a godlike figure, eventually – following a final massacre at Porta della Ginestra – orders people to 'get out' of his car. Consistently motivated by visions of personal glory, claiming he wants recognition, he even compares himself to Alexander the Great, ever fighting his image as 'just a bandit'. His hope is to share land among the peasants, but is opposed by church, aristocracy and the Mafia (who also opposed his hope of US integration) – in a parallel to the problems faced by the immigrants in Cimino's earlier *Heaven's Gate*. Giuliano eventually marries all three, symbolically so to the Mafia as he meets shrouded behind a lace curtain (read bridal veil) with Don Masino (already told he looks like a 'bridegroom'). Ironically, he unites these diverse parties in one aim – seeing him dead.

In keeping with Cimino's themes, the film is about America, the promised land viewed from afar ('like every Sicilian, you'd like to go to America and start up a pizzeria'), as part of a career-long attempt to define what it is to be an American. Fate (history rests on a pistol misfiring twice), symbolised by a circling bird, also plays a part. The circular structure, with scenic and linguistic echoes, ensures that we realise history is a process of repeated events, the Capitalist society a closed circle and inescapable. The questions 'What else?' and 'What next?' are frequently asked, but the possibilities of change are never fulfilled. At best, Cimino's film is a study in failure, from Masino's nephew (the university denying him a place as a surgeon) to Giuliano himself. As Professor Adonis (Giuliano's go-between to the Don) says in the final reel, 'the people only ever wanted bread not land.'

* Salvatore Giuliano was already the subject of a quasi-documentary in 1966 by Francesco Rosi, who shot the film entirely on location in Sicily partially using non-professional actors. Chronicling his life in flashback, following the opening scene detailing his funeral and wake, it details Giuliano's guerrilla-related activities in post-war Sicily, leading eventually to his own men deserting him.

See also: *Black Hand, The; Corleone; Scorta, La.*

Some Like It Hot

(US, United Artists, 1959, 120 mins)

Credits
Dir/Prod/Scr: Billy Wilder
Scr: I.A.L. Diamond
DOP: Charles Lang Jr
Ed: Arthur P. Schmidt
Music: Adolph Deutsch
Art Dir: Ted Haworth

Cast: Marilyn Monroe (Sugar Kane), Tony Curtis (Joe/Josephine), Jack Lemmon (Jerry/Daphne), George Raft (Spats Colombo), Pat O'Brien (Mulligan)

Two musicians witness the St. Valentine's Day Massacre, and, to evade the mob, disguise themselves and join an all-girl band.

Billy Wilder's second picture to come from his second great collaborator I.A.L. Diamond, following his split with Charles Brackett after *Sunset Boulevard*, went on to be the most successful comedy up to 1959. Claimed to be based on a once-popular German silent film entitled *Heaven and Earth* (his picture *Love in the Afternoon* was also a distant adaptation of a work from the same country), the film is both cynical and romantic, challenging the notion of sexual identity a decade before it would become an issue.
Curtis comes complete with perfect Cary Grant accent, as he impersonates a tycoon to seduce the never-better Marilyn Monroe, while Joe E. Brown is fed immortality with the 'Nobody's Perfect' pay-offline.
Appearances by Pat O'Brien, George Raft – who encounters a coin-flipping gunman recalling his role in *Scarface* (qv) and later fingers a grapefruit à la James Cagney, and Edward G. Robinson who is reduced to bursting from a cake to gun down Spats and his boys –provide the heritage.

* **Academy Award:** Orry-Kelly won for Best Costume Design.

See also: *St. Valentine's Day Massacre, The*.

Sonatine

(Japan, Bandai, 1993, 93 mins)

'Often baffling but always, somehow, exactly right.'

(John Wrathall, *UK Premiere***)**

Credits
Dir/Scr/Ed: Takeshi Kitano
Prod: Masayuki Mori, Hisao Nabeshima, Takio Yoshida
DOP: Katsumi Yanagishima
Music: Joe Hisaishi
Art Dir: Osamu Sasaki

Cast: Takeshi Kitano (Murakawa), Aya Kokumai (Miyuki), Tetsu Watanabe (Uechi), Masanobu Katsumura (Ryoji), Susumu Terashima (Ken), Ren Ohsugi (Katagiri)

Sent to Okinawa to assist in a territorial feud, several killings provoke the yakuza member to lay low with his cohorts on a lonely stretch of beach.

As director and star Kitano said of his masterpiece: 'There are times when we ought to think seriously about how to die instead of how to live. I wanted to show what a person does when they come to terms with death.' In the crucial scene to the film, 'Beat' Takeshi's yakuza underling Murokawa, a world-weary figure ('We've led the tough life for too long') informs his female admirer, who adores tough guys: 'If I were tough I wouldn't carry a gun... if you're dead scared too long it's like a death wish.' It's Murokawa's reckoning – something he has been preparing for since he killed his father in High School, for preventing him having sex.
The central beach scenes represent a song for innocence, as the gang don fluorescent shirts, play games and pull practical jokes on each other, a yearning for a time before the killings began. This naturally proves impossible and violence does, of course, prevail.
Strangely calming, melodic and beautifully sentimental, this is the freshest and most considered of Far East gangster films, thankfully lacking John Woo's hyperactivity in favour of a surreal, philosophical tinge. Akin to the director

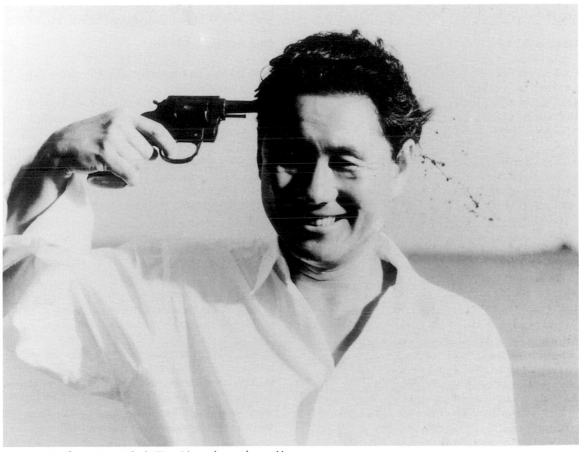

Sonatine: Murakawa ('Beat' Takeshi Kitano) learns how to die, quickly.

himself (who, with his implacable face, brings an inner peace to the role that few actors could) *Sonatine* is a misfit within the system. Bending the generic form to the limits – in a manner comparable in the West only to something like Abel Ferrara's *The Funeral* (qv) – the gangster is perceived as a wholly mortal person.

See also: *American Yakuza*; *American Yakuza II*; *Black Rain*; *Boiling Point*; *Kids Return*; *Yakuza, The*.

So No Otoko, Kyobo Ni Tsuki: See Violent Cop.

Spin of a Coin: See The George Raft Story.

State of Grace

(US, Orion Pictures Corporation, 1990, 134 mins)

Credits

Dir: Phil Joanou
Prod: Ned Dowd, Randy Ostrow, Ron Rotholz

Scr: Dennis McIntyre
DOP: Jordan Cronenweth
Ed: Claire Simpson
Music: Ennio Morricone
Prod. Des: Patrizia Von Brandenstein, Tim Galvin, Doug Kraner

Cast: Sean Penn (Terry Noonan), Ed Harris (Frankie Flannery), Gary Oldman (Jackie Flannery), Robin Wright (Kathleen Flannery), John Turturro (Nick), John C. Reilly (Stevie)

Irish-American cop infiltrates a Hell's Kitchen gang, led by his best friend's brother who is attempting to make a deal with the Italian Mafia.

Released in close proximity to *Goodfellas (qv)* in the US, Phil Joanou's take on the true story of the Westies (a gang who underwent police investigation in the mid-eighties) was always going to suffer by comparison. The film's as much about the change of New York's social, geographical and racial structure as anything else – 'The neighbourhood's disappearing in a tide of yuppies and dog shit', says older brother and gang-leader Frankie, who ironically lives in 'a Laura Ashley suburban mutation'. At an earlier point, property developers are seen to kick out the Irish tenants from an apartment block, prompting Penn to enquire, upon blowing up the building, 'So we're like Robin Hood?' They incorrectly see themselves as robber barons, folklore heroes who give to the poor, recalling the roots of the mythic gangster of the pre-Warner Brothers age, the only nod to the film's generic heritage provided by script or direction.
At most an exercise in style, Joanou merges Peckinpah with leather-clad rock'n'roll (backtracking through his CV by including U2, the subject of his rockumentary *Rattle and Hum*, on the soundtrack and using songs like 'Streetfighting Man' to represent psychological angst).

Stormy Monday

(UK, Moving Picture Company, 1987, 93 mins)

Credits
Dir/Scr/Music: Mike Figgis
Prod: Nigel Stafford-Clark

DOP: Roger Deakins
Ed: David Martin
Prod. Des: Andrew McAlpine

Cast: Sean Bean (Brendan), Sting (Finney), Tommy Lee Jones (Cosmo), Melanie Griffith (Kate), James Cosmo (Tony)

US industrialist attempts to take over a Newcastle jazz club.

With the exception of *The Krays (qv)*, the gangster film in the late eighties and early nineties became infected with club culture. Most notably, Danny Cannon's *The Young Americans* and Ron Peck's *Empire State* using the neon-lit milieu of the clubber scene as the foothold for the modern gangster. Along with Figgis' *Stormy Monday*, the films employed the use of token American stars (Harvey Keitel and Martin Landau for Cannon and Peck's films respectively; Tommy Lee Jones and Melanie Griffith for Figgis's) to indicate the increasing saturation of Stateside values into our culture. As one character says, the 'America Week' being celebrated throughout the film by the locals is 'a new era of transatlantic co-operation and prosperity'. Griffith, as a Monroe-type stranded on Tyneside, is the ultimate dream girl, while Jones' Texan businessman/gangster, attempting to buy The Key club from owner Sting in an effort to launder money, is a symbol for the political and cultural invasion suffered by the UK. Twirling batons, bouncers with NYPD uniforms, all, ironically, add up to an attempt by our people to emulate the style and glamour of the States – proving, if anything, it's as much our fault as theirs.
Try as it might (even setting the film in Newcastle), *Stormy Monday* is no *Get Carter (qv)*, replacing grit with retro-chic and a sultry jazz score in an attempt to appropriate the American thriller into the British crime drama. The film – as Figgis commented to *City Limits*' Amanda Lipman – was destined for US audiences: 'The Americans took it, and found a way of looking at themselves.'

Street War: See Black Godather.

Street With No Name, The

(US, 20th Century Fox, 1948, 93 mins)

Credits
Dir: William Keighley
Prod: Samuel G. Engel
Scr: Harry Kleiner
DOP: Joseph MacDonald
Ed: William H. Reynolds
Music: Lionel Newman
Art Dir: Chester Gore, Lyle Wheeler

Cast: Mark Stevens (Cordell), Lloyd Nolan (Inspector Briggs), Richard Widmark (Alec Stiles), John McIntire (Cy Gordon), Barbara Lawrence (Judy Stiles)

Detective infiltrates gang to help concoct a robbery and leads them straight to the authorities.

Sourced from the FBI files, and filmed in actual locales with FBI personnel (so the opening caption tells us), the 'street' in question is an analogy for organised crime sweeping across America, according to a displayed typewritten note from J. Edgar Hoover. Pre-empting the likes of Fritz Lang's *The Big Heat* and Joseph H. Lewis' *The Big Combo* (*qqv*), its semi-documentary style delivers its information like a lab analysis as the script dissects the reasons for increasing syndicate crime – chiefly, the juvenile delinquents of yesterday springing up as gangsters of today.
Director William Keighley came to the project with high credentials, having helmed some of the finest second-league gangster pictures – *G-Men*, *Bullets or Ballots* and *Each Dawn I Die* (*qvv*), and added two gripping silent sequences, a technique to be emulated in Jules Dassin's *Rififi* in 1955. Of equal note is Richard Widmark's gangster Alex Stiles, as affecting but less infamous than his Tommy Udo from *Kiss of Death* (*qv*). A hypochondriac, he's a blend of misogynistic tendencies and intelligent refinement, beating his wife and threatening to throw a girl out of a window if she opens it again, after gracefully

playing the piano. His aim: 'to build an organisation along scientific lines'.

* The film was remade in 1955 by Samuel Fuller as *House of Bamboo*.

See also: *Big Combo, The*; *Big Heat, The*; *Frightened City*; *Force of Evil*; *Underworld USA*.

Superfly

(US, Warner Brothers, 1972, 98 mins)

'The only thing is, Superfly rings so hollow that one could find more Black Power in a coffee bean.'
(**Philip Strick, *Monthly Film Bulletin*)**

Credits
Dir: Gordon Parks, Jr
Prod: Sig Shore
Scr: Kurt Baker
DOP: James Signorelli
Ed: Bob Brady
Music: Curtis Mayfield

Cast: Ron O'Neal (Youngblood Priest), Carl Lee (Eddie), Sheila Frazier (Georgia), Julius Harris (Scatter), Charles McGregor (Fat Freddie)

A Harlem drug dealer wants to pull one final large deal off to quit the life.

'Eight-track stereo, color TV in every room, and can snort half a piece of dope every day. That's the American dream, nigga', Priest is told by friend Eddie. With much of the dialogue improvised, the budget a mere $150,000, the style-conscious *Superfly*, along with *Shaft* (*qv*) and Melvin Van Peebles' *Sweet Sweetback's Baadasssss Song*, allowed black people briefly to touch the dream and live like 'black prince'(s), Cocaine dealer Priest, who wants to shift $300,000 worth of coke in four months to make the million and quit, was the epitome of cool; the black 'gangsta' and the precursor to Wesley Snipes' crack-dealing Nino Brown in *New Jack City* (*qv*). Figures such as he

and John Shaft, regardless of which side of the law
they took, were for the first time representing
blacks with a sexual screen presence, and usurping
traditionally white-dominated roles (cops and
gangsters).

Superfly emphasises that crime is the only way out
of the ghetto and, like the bootleggers of the
twenties, the drug-dealer has the respect and envy
of the community for his activities. It continually
asserts the black gangster's stylistic assertion of
individual worth and the black junkie's continued
oppression in a corrupt world dominated by whites.
Producer Sig Shore told *Black Film Review*'s David
Mills that he based his observations on what he
saw growing up in Harlem. 'What fascinated me
was the way [Black men] got into being hustlers on
the street. In the Jewish ghetto, or the Irish or the
Italian, the way a guy became a mob leader was
that he was stronger than the other guys, or he
was less reluctant to use a gun. It was different in
the black ghetto. They did it with style. It was a
competition of style.' As with other Blaxploitation
films, *Superfly* develops the myth of the Urban
Black Warrior, a man who speaks with the idioms
of the street and dresses like his people in a
collective search for identity.

* A 1990 sequel, *The Return of Superfly*, directed by
Shore, was made. Returning from Paris after a 20-
year self-imposed exile to avenge the death of
Eddie, Priest (now played by Nathan Purdee)
discovers the huge change in the drug peddling
business. It recouped merely $1 million of its $4
million budget, a misconceived attempt at cashing
in on the resurgent Funk Aesthetic.

See also: *Clockers*.

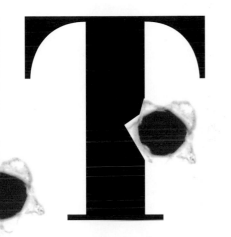

3-4x Jugatsu: See Boiling Point.

2499 Antapan Krong Muang: See Dang Bireley's and the Young Gangsters.

Taking of Pelham One, Two Three, The

(US, Palomar Pictures/Palladium Productions, 1974, 104 mins)

Credits
Dir: Joseph Sargent
Prod: Gabriel Katzka, Edgar J. Scherick
Scr: Peter Stone, based on the novel by John Godey
DOP: Owen Roizman
Ed: Jerry Greenberg, Robert Q. Lovett
Music: Bruno Robotti
Art Dir: Gene Rudolf

Cast: Walter Matthau (Lt. Garber), Robert Shaw (Blue), Martin Balsam (Green), Hector Elizondo (Grey), Earl Hindman (Brown)

A gang hijack a New York subway train, demanding $1 million for the release of the passengers.

This is the film that gave *Reservoir Dogs* (qv) its inspiration for naming its participants after colours, and Joseph Sargent himself borrowed liberally from others' work. Namely, *High Noon* (for the clock-watching co-extensiveness of filmic and 'real' time) and *The Third Man* (for the pursuit through the subways reminding us of Harry Lime's Viennese sewers). Scripted with a cynical eye, the film uses the hijack as a telescope to focus on man's cold indifference to man. The Mayor is pointed at as an ineffectual puppet, only interested in people as voters; Frank, an attendant at the Control Centre, shouts under duress: 'Screw the goddamn passengers. What do they expect for their 35 cents to live forever?'; the hijackers themselves have no qualms about ending human life: 'Well, either you live or you die.' Along with using the crime as a catalyst to explore wider concerns (as Antonia Bird's recent *Face* (qv) does), *The Taking of Pelham 123* fits rigidly within heist movie parameters. Namely, each gang member achieves a defined identity (here, as in *Reservoir Dogs* (qv), through tag-name and uniform/disguise) linking them to the group. Gang members' individual motivations for taking part are always outlined (here Blue is merely a mercenary, while Green was sacked from driving a subway train) and success is foiled ultimately through either greed, betrayal or power (Blue kills Grey when he won't adhere to his plans). As seen here, the heist movie concentrates all values and expectations on one last crime, which if successful, will put all the participants on easy street – a feature prominent in the likes of *The Killing* and *The Asphalt Jungle* (qqv).

See also: *Criss-Cross; Heat; Usual Suspects, The.*

They Live By Night

(US, RKO, 1948, 95 mins)

'I do not feel that [one of the constant themes in my work] is man against society that is trying to crush him. That would be indulging in self-pity, and it's man's responsibility to himself to adjust to the world around him.'

(Nicholas Ray, *Movie*)

Credits
Dir./Scr: Nicholas Ray
Prod: John Houseman

Scr: Charles Schnee, based on the novel Thieves Like Us by Edward Anderson
DOP: George E. Diskant
Ed: Sherman Todd
Music: Constantin Bakalienkoff
Art Dir: Albert S. D'Agostino, Al Herman

Cast: Farley Granger (Bowie), Howard Da Silva (Chicamaw), Cathy O'Donnell (Keechie), Jay C. Flippen (T-Dub), Harry Harvey Snr (Hagenheimer)

A young couple in love become fugitives-on-the-run.

Integral to that curious sub-genre of the gangster film, the lovers-on-the-run, Ray's debut picture, originally named *The Twisted Road*, emerged from the post-war chaos that categorized many films of the time. Alongside Joseph H. Lewis' *Gun Crazy*, William Witney's *The Bonnie Parker Story*, Arthur Penn's *Bonnie and Clyde* (qqv) and Fritz Lang's precursor to these, *You Only Live Once*, Ray's film showed ostensibly innocents, manipulated by environment that supersedes the fundamental goodness in their characters. As the opening titles note: 'This boy and girl were never properly introduced to the world we live in.' Our role as viewer becomes subjective, we are automatically begged to elicit sympathy, a rarity in gangster cinema (even if we often secretly admire them), typified by Ray's unusually paternal and understanding policemen. While crime in the 1930s was a way of survival, a response to the harsh economic realities, the post-war arena searched for explanations for such unruly behaviour, society being deemed as superficially healthy. Ray, however, presents his couple, Bowie and Keechie, as victims: of society, bad influence, circumstance and themselves.

While overtly displaying certain shades of *film noir*, not least the titular reference indicating that the protagonists will never break into daylight, the film is never at ease in the city, Bowie is confronted by an urban gangster at one point and told he does not belong there. Bowie, and his prison buddies T-Dub and Chicamaw, are country thieves. Ray also softens the role of the woman. Keechie is not the gold-digging schemer of *The Postman Always Rings Twice*, but a tag-along girl. 'If you want me to,' she

They Live By Night: Bowie (Farley Granger) and Keechie (Cathy O'Donnell), their impending doom foreshadowed by a bedstead.

responds to the question of marriage – the ceremony held underneath a dingy neon 'Marriages Performed' sign. Not tragedy, the characters lacking the stature to fall from grace, but – as many have noted – a 'romantic pessimism', the couple are intruders on the world. Unlike the Warner Brothers gangsters that preceded them, or the *noir* anti-heroes that developed concurrently, Bowie and Keechie are rarely at home in their environment. 'Some day I'd like to see some of this country we've been travelling through,' says Bowie, his words tinged with the irony. There is no repulsive, perverse attraction to their characters, just heartfelt sadness. Says Bowie in the final reel: 'The only wrong you ever did was to marry me.'

* Robert Altman also committed Anderson's novel to film in 1974, naming it after the original, with Keith Carradine and Shelley Winters as the lovers.

Things To Do In Denver When You're Dead

(US, Miramax, 1995, 115 mins)

'It's really unfair both to the genre and to Quentin [Tarantino] to say he now owns the gangster movie.'

(Scott Rosenberg, Empire)

Credits
Dir: Gary Fleder
Prod: Cary Woods, Cathy Konrad
Scr: Scott Rosenberg
DOP: Elliot Davis
Ed: Richard Marks
Music: Michael Convertino
Prod. Des: Nelson Coates

Cast: Andy Garcia (Jimmy the Saint), Gabrielle Anwar (Dagney), Treat Williams (Critical Bill), Christopher Lloyd (Pieces), Steve Buscemi (Mr Shhh), Christopher Walken (The Man with the Plan)

Ex-hoodlum takes on a final job for his former boss – scaring the new boyfriend of his retarded son's ex-girlfriend – with disastrous results.

Compared to Sam Peckinpah's *Pat Garrett and Billy The Kid*, Jimmy and his crew being men of honour stranded in the harsh glass frontier of modern-day Denver, Gary Fleder's directorial debut was influenced by the death of writer Scott Rosenberg's father, from cancer. Despite what Rosenberg said (see above), comparisons to Quentin Tarantino are inevitable. The presence of Christopher Walken and Steve Buscemi 'talking the talk', career resurrections (Treat Williams), casting against type (after *Back to the Future* and *The Addams Family*, Christopher Lloyd as the leprosy-suffering Pieces). But what this smugly hip film avoids is an accusation of amoral indifference to death by confronting it full on. Ex-hoodlum Jimmy now runs an Afterlife Advice centre, making videos for the nearly-departed to offer pearls of wisdom to their loved ones. The philosophy may be cold – 'One life is just a mustard burp in the air' but mortality, and the precious gift of being alive, is at least acknowledged. Death overshadows the gang, as Walken's wheelchair-bound mob boss, The Man With The Plan, labels

them all 'Buckwheats' (meaning to be killed in the most painful way possible) after the job in hand goes awry. Mental and physical deformity is also commonplace. The aforementioned Pieces and the aptly named psychotic Critical Bill are not the culture-savvy gangsters of Tarantinoland. Fleder and Rosenberg's mobsters are of a new breed. Jimmy's girlfriend, played by Gabrielle Anwar, asks him if he's a gangster. In return, he questions whether 'they still have gangsters'. His nickname, sharp suit and slicked back hair may belie this, but the gang are men of another world. Pieces is a projectionist in a porn cinema, Bill states 'I am what I'm always – the back of beyond', while Franchise (Bill Forsythe) lives in a trailer-park. Even deadly assassin Mr Shh, sent by Walken to eliminate the boys, is the antithesis of what one would expect for such a character, as indeed are Walken's own somewhat literate henchman. Perversity for the sake of it? Perhaps, but it is difficult to place the film within strict generic conventions. One can easily argue that these offbeat characters are antidotes to Tarantino's hard men, regaining a sense of realism. A wry example of the way the gangster film must go to survive post-*Pulp Fiction* (qv).

See also: *Get Shorty*; *Kiss of Death*; *Romeo is Bleeding*.

This Gun For Hire

(US, Paramount, 1942, 82 mins)

'Not since Jimmy Cagney massaged Mae Clarke's face with a grapefruit has a grim desperado gunned his way into cinema ranks with such violence as does Mr Ladd.'

(Bosley Crowther, New York Times)

Credits
Dir: Frank Tuttle
Prod: Richard Blumenthal
Scr: Albert Maltz, W.R. Burnett, based on the novel *A Gun For Sale* by Graham Greene
DOP: John Seitz
Ed: Archie Marshek
Music: Frank Loesser, Jacques Presse
Art Dir: Hans Dreier, Robert Usher

This Gun For Hire: Cold as ice: Willard Gates (Laird Cregar) shares breakfast with the deadly Raven (Alan Ladd).

Cast: Alan Ladd (Philip Raven), Veronica Lake (Ellen Graham), Robert Preston (Michael Crane), Laird Cregar (Willard Gates), Tully Marshall (Alvin Brewster)

A professional killer sent to execute a blackmailer seeks revenge on his employers, poison gas developers the Nitro Chemical company, after they pay him off in hot money to ensure his capture.

Pre-empting the protagonists of *Leon* and *Le Samourai* (qqv), Alan Ladd's cold-hearted angel-of-death ('I don't go soft for anybody') Phillip Raven ensures the film is responsible for blueprinting all entries to the 'hitman' sub-genre from then on. Ladd himself, until then acting only bit-parts, including *Citizen Kane*, was chosen by Paramount who were looking for an unknown to play the role, and went on to develop an on-screen chemistry with co-star Veronica Lake in three more films, including *The Glass Key* (qv).

Living in sparse surroundings with just a cat for company, he is efficient and unemotional – 'I feel fine' is the blunt reply when asked how he reacts to killing someone – Ladd is the tormented outsider, killing to catharticly purge the murder of his abusive step-mother.

A proximity between the screenplay and Graham Greene's source novel is suggested with the credits rolling over a picture of the book, although Raven's deformity (caused by his mother in the film) mutated from a hairlip to a smashed wrist. Screenwriters Albert Maltz and W.R. Burnett, the latter later to adapt the 1928 silent film *The Racket* for RKO, as well as providing the source novels for *The Asphalt Jungle* and *High Sierra* (qvv), ensure that

SOLIHULL S.F.C.
LIBRARY

commerce and gangsterism are never far apart. Wheelchair-bound Chemicals boss, Alvin Brewster, is the Godfather of the piece, a hoarse whisper telling us that his employees are his 'family', at once weakened by his disability and empowered by the authority he holds over his workers. Intermediary Gates, and even Brewster's nurse, fear him – just as Christopher Walken's crew respect his incapacitated character in *Things to Do in Denver When You're Dead* (qv), and both films show that the gangster's manipulation of others is a mental, not physical, strength.

Made during World War II, this is paranoid patriotism film-making, as Nitro Chemicals sell their formula to the Japanese, just as Sam Fuller's *Pickup On South St* would, in the next decade, highlight McCarthyite anti-Communist witch-hunts.

* The film was remade in 1957 as *Short Cut to Hell*, directed by one James Cagney (his only behind-camera effort).

See also: *Driver, The*; *Fallen Angels*; *Killer, The*; *Little Odessa*; *Prizzi's Honor*.

Trigger Happy

(US, United Artists, 1996, 93 mins)

> 'When I was a kid growing up, I used to think God must be the greatest gangster of them all.'
> **(Larry Bishop)**

Credits
Dir./Scr: Larry Bishop
Prod: Judith Rutherford James
DOP: Frank Byers
Ed: Norman Hollyn
Music: Earl Rose
Prod. Des: Dina Lipton

Cast: Gabriel Byrne (Ben London), Richard Dreyfuss (Vic), Ellen Barkin (Rita Everly), Jeff Goldblum (Mickey Holliday), Gregory Hines (Jules Flamingo), Kyle MacLachlan (Jake Parker), Burt Reynolds ('Wacky' Jacky Jackson)

Underworld boss, released from a mental hospital, returns to discover plots of betrayal against him.

Slick, retro-gangster chic, Larry Bishop's enjoyable effort to emulate the stylistics of the 1960s posse known as 'the Rat Pack', led by Sammy Davis Jnr and Dean Martin, resulted in a pleasing enough pastiche. Hardly a re-invention of the genre, more an affectionate toying with conventions, its Western cousin might have been Sam Raimi's quick-draw contest *The Quick and the Dead* as the plot revolves around a number of shootouts at hot-spot The Rough House, eliminating the high-calibre cast one by one.

Bishop, whose father Joey was also a member of the clan that produced and starred in the mob comedies like *Ocean's Eleven* (qv) and *Robin and the Seven Hoods*, was at school with star Dreyfus, who plays the deranged Vic, and director Rob Reiner, who took a small part as Albert the Chauffeur. The film also reunited Bishop with Richard Pryor and Christopher Jones, all of whom began their careers in the satirical LSD film *Wild in the Streets*.

Appearances from Burt Reynolds, Diane Lane and Billy Idol complete the star-studded line-up, with a supporting actor from *Ocean's Eleven*, Henry Silva, playing the mercurial Sleepy Joe. While it has been rightly earmarked as a project of staggering narcissism, an extended in-joke between friends, it proves more than just a feast of cameos. An eerie mixture of off-beat comedy, pat philosophy and Mexican stand-offs, the film looks at life and death in a quirky way. 'I judge a man's life by the way he dies', says Byrne, forever advocating the message of 'My Way' – a tune repeatedly played throughout. Not just in memory of 'Rat Pack' member Sinatra, those who survive life's trigger-happy quality are perhaps the ones who live closest to this maxim.

place for the genre to develop. The landscape, as with Griffith's work, would also set the standard locales to be used: the ballroom, where the 'Underworld's annual armistice' is held, the courtroom, the prison, banks and jewellery stores all featured.

Ben Hecht's script drew from his days as a reporter on the *Chicago Journal*. He noted in his autobiography *A Child of the Century*: 'An idea came to me. The thing to do was to skip the heroes and heroines, to write a movie containing only villains and bawds. I would not have to tell any lies then... As a newspaperman I had learned that nice people – the audience – loved criminals, doted on reading about their love problems as well as their sadism. My movie [was] grounded on this simple truth... It was the first gangster movie to bedazzle the movie fans and there were no lies in it – except half a dozen sentimental touches introduced by its director.' This romantic air would be swept away a year later when Lewis Milestone's *The Racket* (*qv*), a precursor to the 1930s social realism gangster pictures, would detail political corruption in Chicago.

Sternberg himself went on to duplicate the formula in two more films. *Dragnet* starred Bancroft again, as ex-cop and alcoholic Two Gun Nolan ironically battling bootleggers. *Thunderbolt*, made in 1929, saw Bancroft as the eponymous bank robber, who crosses swords with a young banker for the affections of Fay Wray.

* **Academy Awards:** Ben Hecht won for Best Original Screenplay.

Underworld (UK Title: Paying the Penalty)

(US, Paramount, 1927, 8 reels)

Credits
Dir: Josef Von Sternberg
Prod: Hector Turnbull
Scr: Charles Furthman, Robert N. Lee, from a story by Ben Hecht
DOP: Bert Glennon
Art Dir: Hans Dreier

Cast: George Bancroft ('Bull' Weed), Evelyn Brent ('Feathers' McCoy), Clive Brook ('Rolls Royce'), Larry Semon (Slippery Lewis), Fred Kohler Snr ('Buck' Mulligan)

Bank robber and jewel thief is caught and condemned to death – but escapes to hunt down his best friend and former lover, now in love with each other.

According no doubt to apocryphal accounts the film ran all night when it opened in New York. Often regarded as the first gangster film, discounting D.W. Griffith's short *The Musketeers of Pig Alley* (*qv*), it paints the gangster, 'Bull' Weed as a sympathetic, jovial character (well-liked except by rival Mulligan and the police), strong enough to bend a silver dollar in half. While generous to a fault, the closing scene, where he recognises the loyalty 'Feathers' and 'Rolls Royce' have shown him (despite falling in love), shows that he values true friendship above all else: the themes of trust and betrayal already in

Underworld USA

(US, Globe Enterprises, 1960, 98 mins)

Credits
Dir./Prod./Scr: Samuel Fuller
based on the story by Joseph Dineen
DOP: Hal Mohr
Ed: Jerome Thomas
Music: Harry Sukman
Art Dir: Robert Peterson

Cast: Cliff Robertson (Tolly Devlin), Beatrice Kay (Sandy), Larry

Gates (Driscoll), Richard Rust (Gus), Dolores Dorn (Cuddles), Robert Emhardt (Connors), Allan Gruener (Smith), Paul Dubov (Gela), Gerald Milton (Gunther), Peter Brocco (Vic)

Embittered ex-con, searching for the killers of his father, ingratiates himself with mob boss to flush out the guilty man.

While typical of Samuel Fuller's own canon, the film is an unusual manipulation of generic convention. Presenting the common federal agents-versus the syndicate scenario, Fuller saw the battle as a metaphor for war, symbolised by the trophies in the detective's office, the close-up of Tolly's clenched fist, and the posters championing an All-American aggressive nature. As special investigator Driscoll, in charge of the Federal Crime Commission, notes: 'The syndicate bosses in the field command the rackets like Generals in the field command the divisions.' It is of these field marshals (Gunther – labour, Smith – prostitution, Gela – drugs) whom Tolly is in pursuit, and success can only come through using both the FBI and the syndicate's Chief of Staff, Connors. Tolly himself, resolutely committed to his solitary obsession of avenging his father's death, is in a perpetual state of war in the film. His vigilante attitude leads him to deliberate imprisonment in order to question the dying Vic, partly responsible for the death of Devlin Snr. Unable to relate to anyone except in connection to his ultimate goal, his demise at the hands of a bodyguard, is certain, coming after he has succeeded in eliminating all principal members of the gang. His actions, now defined only by the syndicate, ensure he has lived beyond his limits as a human being. Fuller saw his country in a constant

Underworld USA: Cuddles (Dolores Dorn), overlooked by Tony Devlin (Cliff Robertson).

state of discord; the war could be civil, inter-racial, or criminal – but it always involved the loss of this humanity, an individualism extinguished by a subjugation to a mass movement.

In a piece of gangster journalism crossed with German expressionism, Fuller blended romanticism and hard-nosed realism in what resulted as a bleak cousin to Fritz Lang's *The Big Heat* (qv). Based on a series of articles in *The Saturday Evening Post*, the film was released shortly after the infamous mob convention in Apalachin, New York, brought to the world's attention the existence of organised crime. On a less metaphorical level, Fuller displayed an honest pessimism towards such activities. As Gus says: 'There'll always be people like Driscoll and there'll always be people like us.' The syndicate itself – 'a beehive of concealed activity' – is under the respectable guise of a charitable group called 'National Projects'. Recruiting schoolgirls for prostitution rings runs concurrently with encouraging underprivileged kids to use the syndicate's rooftop swimming pool. Again one can turn this around and view this legitimate face as that of the US itself, fighting Communism in the Cold War, while underneath lies a maelstrom of unscrupulous methods for doing so.

See also: *Big Combo, The*; *Big Heat, The*; *Force of Evil*; *Frightened City*; *Street With No Name, The*; *Valachi Papers, The*.

Untouchables, The

(US, Paramount, 1987, 120 mins)

'I don't like to make my criminals family men who are only in it because their father's dying. I love The Godfather, but it's not my image of mobsters.'

(Brian De Palma, *Film Comment*)

Credits
Dir: Brian De Palma
Prod: Art Linson
Scr: David Mamet
based on the original books by Eliot Ness, Oscar Fraley and Paul Robsky

DOP: Stephen H. Burum
Ed: Jerry Greenberg, Bill Pankow
Music: Ennio Morricone
Art Dir: William A. Elliott

Cast: Kevin Costner (Eliot Ness), Sean Connery (Jim Malone), Robert De Niro (Al Capone), Andy Garcia (George Stone), Charles Martin Smith (Oscar Wallace)

Special Agent for the Treasury Dept. assembles unlikely law enforcers and attempts to bring down Al Capone.

David Mamet's screenplay takes enough liberties with the Eliot Ness story to accommodate De Palma's fantasy. Ness had no Italians or anyone over 30 in his team (ruling out the Garcia/Connery characters), he never dropped an assailant from a roof, nor did he shoot it out with Capone's men, and most importantly he never encountered Capone or exchanged a word with him – setting eyes on the Chicago gangster only when he was already on trial for tax evasion. His part in the conviction was small; accountant Frank Wilson (bearing a resemblance to Martin Smith's character) and his painstaking analysis of Capone's income and expenditure deserve the praise. Ness, in fact, picked nine men to smash Chicago's 20,000 illicit breweries – their uncharacteristic honesty coining them the nickname 'The Untouchables'. Nevertheless, it was the top grossing at the box office for the year, taking over $76 million in the US. Like his *Scarface* (qv), the film is an allegory about power and America (Capone literally bloated with corruption). Sergei Eisenstein's *Battleship Potemkin*, in the well-crafted climactic set-piece in the railroad depot, is borrowed liberally from. As is Hitchcock: witness Ness's murder of Nitti as his 'fall' from grace and innocence, having earlier been framed in the camera lens by a stained glass dome. De Niro, who took the role (effectively an inflated cameo) originally designated for Bob Hoskins, gained 30lb for the role, echoing the work he did for *Raging Bull*. He also reportedly insisted on seeking out Sulk & Sons on New York's Park Avenue (which Capone once frequented) to purchase the same kind of silk underwear.

The Untouchables: Robert De Niro inherits the Capone mantle.

* **Academy Awards**: Sean Connery won for Best Supporting Actor.

See also: *Al Capone*; *Capone*; *Gangland: the Verne Miller Story*; *George Raft Story, The*; *Lost Capone, The*; *St. Valentine's Day Massacre, The*; *Scarface Mob, The*.

Usual Suspects, The

(US, Blue Parrott/Bad Hat Harry, 1995, 105 mins)

'I saw this as an opportunity to take the conventional ideology that narration is true and is an indicator of exactly what happened, and play with that a little. So often in films you know exactly what's happening and where the story will lead. I'd rather an audience feel like they've learned something, that something new has been revealed in every scene, every shot and every composition. If it doesn't inform, it doesn't belong in the picture.'

(Bryan Singer)

Credits
Dir./Prod: Bryan Singer
Scr: Christopher McQuarrie
DOP: Newton Thomas Sigel
Ed./Music: John Ottman
Prod. Des: Howard Cummings

Cast: Stephen Baldwin (McManus), Gabriel Byrne (Keaton), Chazz Palminteri (Detective Dave Kujan), Kevin Pollack (Hockney), Pete Postlethwaite (Kobayashi), Kevin Spacey ('Verbal' Kint), Benicio Del Toro (Fenster)

A gang of criminals are manipulated into pulling off a dangerous heist worth $91 million at the San Pedro docks.

A shaggy dog story of a heist movie for the post-*Reservoir Dogs* (qv) age, Singer's mythological crime drama placed the gangster – in this case the unseen Keyser Soze – as a figure of unimaginable, quasi-religious, power – 'a myth, a spook story to frighten your kids with', as we are told.
The theological imagery is potent. Centring for the most part around a head-to-head between Special Agent Kujan and Verbal, only one of two survivors of the heist, the film toys with the post-modern idea of the unreliable narrator, negating all that has

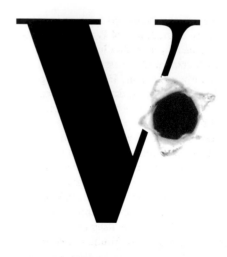

preceded in the story. Yet it also feels like a confessional, Kujan the beguiled Priest. Soze himself is integral to Verbal's account of the heist, an omnipotent arch-criminal who supposedly orchestrated events from the initial police line-up of 'the usual suspects' that brings the gang together to the final raid on the boat. Little is what it seems in what is an immaculate exercise in the art of story-telling, allowing the film to pose the evergreen question 'What is truth?' What starts as a plan to intervene on a drug deal that would harm Soze's own empire mutates into an assassination attempt upon the one person who could identify him, a man repeatedly referred to as 'the devil'. Yet, with the final reel revealing the inspiration for Verbal's tale, the myth may be truth or the story just part of the legend.

McQuarrie's jigsaw of a script draws more from the likes of Arthur Penn's *Bonnie and Clyde* (qv) than the culture-specific works of Tarantino, inflating the image of Soze beyond the life of the film itself (note that, apart from the proliferation of names beginning with 'K', Kevin Spacey's initials match those of the Keyser). Here, as with Penn's work, the gangster's prowess is dependent more upon the power of our imagination (be it hero-worship or pure fright) than his actual deeds.

* Academy Awards: Kevin Spacey won for Best Supporting Actor.
Christopher McQuarrie won for Best Original Screenplay.

See also: *Asphalt Jungle, The*; *Criss-Cross*; *Face*; *Heat*; *Killing, The*; *Reservoir Dogs*; *Taking of Pelham 123, The*.

Valachi Papers, The

(US, Dino De Laurentiis, 1972, 127 mins)

'It seems that just about every major studio turned it down. I was very ashamed of Hollywood over that. This was well before the time of The Godfather and, as is so often the case, film people were more concerned with today's trend than tomorrow's. The Mafia was not an OK subject, but more important, they were afraid. One studio executive told me that he would have loved to have made the movie, but he didn't want to go through the rest of his life worrying about starting his car in the morning.'
(Peter Maas, *Films Illustrated*)

Credits
Dir: Terence Young
Prod: Dino De Laurentiis
Scr: Stephen Geller, based on the original work by Peter Maas
DOP: Aldo Tonti
Ed: John Dwyre
Music: Riz Ortolani
Art Dir: Mario Garbuglia

Cast: Charles Bronson (Joe Valachi), Mario Pilar (Salerno), Fred Valleca ('Johnny Beck'), Giacomino De Michelis (Little Augie), Arny Freeman (Warden)

True story of the Mafia operative who turned informant.

Outgrossing even *The Godfather* (*qv*) in some territories, Terence Young's film of Peter Maas' best-seller had as strained a production history as the book itself, which came under pressure to stop publication even from the White House. Lacking finance and then an American distributor, it was a film – as Maas suggests above – that few people wanted to make.

Based on the testimony of a Mafia lieutenant, who sang for his own safety against his boss Vito Genovese to a Senate Crime Committee, the film combines a series of flashbacks with a semi-documentary style, popularised over a decade before. Neither improving on these biopics – star Bronson himself was in one, *Machine Gun Kelly* (*qv*) – nor Coppola's epic of the same year, Young's film revels in its murky history.

Scenes of the greatest interest are those depicting Cosa Nostra ritual. As Valachi is sworn in, he utters with upmost solemnity: 'This is the way I will die. If I betray the secrets of the Cosa Nostra I will burn like the fires of hell.' Betraying the organisation is death without trial, as is a violation against any member's wife. While it's the story of Valachi, his rise from driver to drug-dealer, it's also an examination of the Luciano-Genovese era, encompassing events such as Apalachin and the anarchic collapse of his organisation. As Genovese notes: 'Before I went away we had an organisation, a structure. Everybody had a place... a position. Everybody was responsible to everybody.' The overriding (and rather grandiose) metaphor is the collapse of the Roman Empire, Julius Caesar invoked by a former Valachi boss. Again, a film that raises gangsters to the status of leaders.

* Dino De Laurentiis was responsible for another gangster biopic a year later. Carlo Lizzani's *Crazy Joe*, with Peter Boyle in the title role, focused on the famous Brooklyn mobster Joey Gallo who was gunned down in Umberto's Clam House in New York's Little Italy in 1972. A gangster who read Sartre, his cult status was assured as he threatened the Mafia hierarchy.

See also: *Big Combo, The*; *Big Heat, The*; *Force of Evil*; *Street With No Name, The*; *Underworld USA*.

Villain: 'I'm Vic Dakin!': Richard Burton tells it like it is.

Villain

(UK, Anglo-EMI, 1971, 98 mins)

'Villain's superficial nastiness (largely a matter of louder and better synchronised punches) conceals a relatively old-fashioned approach to the genre.'
(Nigel Andrews, *MFB*)

Credits
Dir: Michael Tuchner
Prod: Alan Ladd, Jr, Jay Kanter
Scr: Dick Clement, Ian La Frenais, adapted from the novel The Burden of Proof by James Barlow
DOP: Christopher Challis
Ed: Ralph Sheldon
Music: Jonathan Hodge
Art Dir: Maurice Carter

Cast: Richard Burton (Vic Dakin), Wolfie Lissner (Ian McShane), Nigel Davenport (Bob Matthews), Donald Sinden (Gerald Draycott), Fiona Lewis (Venitia), Colin Welland (Tom Binney), Joss Ackland (Edgar Lowis), T.P.McKenna (Frank Fletcher)

Homosexual gangster from London's East End carries out an armed robbery on a payroll van, eventually leading to his arrest.

Wonderfully lurid British film, with Richard Burton's vicious Vic Dakin bearing uncanny resemblance to Ronnie Kray.

Setting the tone for the British gangster film, along with Mike Hodges' *Get Carter* (*qv*), for the post-*Bonnie and Clyde* (*qv*) generation, the film opens with Vic carving up an informer, then stringing him from the window of his fifth-storey flat. Ducking and diving through London's seedy Soho locations, the film also prefigured Neil Jordan's *Mona Lisa* (*qv*).

Insecure, jealous, psychotic and kind to his mother, Vic is a gangster of the old school; strictly small-time, governing his manor and looking after his own, he is polite enough to inform fellow boss Frank Fletcher that he was planning a robbery on his turf. While he hardly controls an empire, he views himself as King of his Castle, and expects nothing less than respect, screaming the word in the denouement at his captors, adding 'You don't know what it is unless you're Vic Dakin!'

Class aspirations are sketched in Dakin's character: spurning poached eggs in favour of the French menu is not the only air he puts on. Upon surveying the factory his men are to knock-off, he makes a disparaging statement towards the workers and their way of life: 'Telly all week. Screw the wife on Saturday.' Add to this factory strikes and his disgust with the youth of today – 'Drugs, demonstrations... should never have abolished National Service' – and the script becomes a diatribe on the State of the Nation, with Donald Sinden's kinky MP indicating that sleaze is not a new Tory policy.

Violent Cop (So No Otoko, Kyobo Ni Tsuki)

(Japan, Bandai, 1989, 103 mins)

Credits
Dir: Takeshi Kitano
Prod: Hisao Nabeshima, Takio Yoshida, Shozo Ichiyama
Scr: Hisashi Nozawa
DOP: Yasushi Sakakibara
Ed: Nobutake Kamiya
Music: Daisaku Kume, Eric Satie
Art Dir: Masuteru Mochizuki

Cast: Takeshi Kitano (Det. Azuma), Maiko Kawakami (Akari), Makoto Ashigawa (Kikuchi, the rookie), Shiro Sano (Police Chief Yoshinari), Shigeru Hiraizumi (Det. Iwaki)

A misfit Homicide cop who believes in dispensing justice himself takes on a gangland drug dealer when he discovers that a colleague of his is involved in re-selling seized dope.

A direct descendant of Clint Eastwood's Harry Callaghan, and on a par with Harvey Keitel's role in Abel Ferarra's *Bad Lieutenant*, the so-called 'violently wild and stupid' Detective Azuma is a renegade gangster-cop, a relentless automaton making a mockery of the opening 'sacred vocation' claim for his profession. As he would in *Kids Return* (*qv*), Kitano, who rewrote the script having replaced Kinji Fukasaku as director, concentrates on outcasts; Azuma himself, his mentally-ill, drug-addicted sister (whom he looks out for only to kill eventually), and Kiyohiro (Ryu Haku), the psychotic gay hit-man all operate upon the fringes of society. By comparison, Kiyohiro's gangland boss Nito (Ittoku Kishibe) is as 'normal' as the office he runs his operation from. Using a restaurant as a front for the dope syndicate, the glimpses we get are limited but telling: 'It's you who's going to finish me... I want to kill you', he says to his hitman, repeatedly punching him. Kiyohiro in turn takes the blows without replying. This mark of respect depicts a society that has become segmented – each group existing by their own rules, in this case a code of honour stretching back to feudal times. Kitano (as director) depicts a modern malady; a 'madness' that permits cops to beat up teenagers in their own homes and innocent bystanders to be blown away by the law. As Nito's No.2 says in the downbeat ending (Azuma is killed by him, and another 'much smarter' cop drafted into Iwaki's position) 'Everybody's crazy'. Kitano's perspective (as actor and director) is both observer and participator; he is not fool enough to exempt either himself or his character from the problems he sees – a complex haze of overlapping boundaries, between the law and the lawless. Iwaki's dope-peddling, Nito's 'respectability' as a businessman and the violent cop straddling the two, highlight that it is no longer a question of 'right' or 'wrong', merely an endless, and seemingly unbreakable, cycle of corruption.

See also: *Better Tomorrow, A*; *Bullitt*; *Hard Boiled*.

White Heat

(US, Warner Brothers, 1949, 114 mins)

'Made it Ma. Top of the world!'
(Cody Jarrett, *White Heat*)

Credits
Dir: Raoul Walsh
Prod: Louis Edelman
Scr: Ben Roberts, Ivan Goff,
based on an original story by Virginia Kellogg
DOP: Sid Hickox
Ed: Owen Marks
Music: Max Steiner
Art Dir: Edward Carrere

Cast: James Cagney (Cody Jarrett), Virginia Mayo (Verna Jarrett), Edmond O'Brien (Hank Fallon/Vic Pardo), Margaret Wycherly (Ma Jarrett), Steve Cochran (Big Ed Sommers), John Archer (Evans)

A notorious criminal pulls off a train robbery, but following his subsequent imprisonment undergoes humiliation as a rival usurps his position as gang leader, seduces his wife and kills his mother.

Considered by many as Cagney's masterpiece, Raoul Walsh's *White Heat* brought the psychotic (upon Cagney's insistence) to the gangster genre. Cagney's character – displaying the most explicit Oedipal complex in cinema – was his first gangster since *The Roaring Twenties* (qv), over a decade before. With

Walsh's film Cagney's first gangster picture since *Each Dawn I Die* (qv), having made a conscious decision to evade the tough-guy image in the 1940s, this stirring return broke all rules. Relying more on the Western than previous gangster pictures, the film spurns the traditional rise-and-fall route in favour of the usurpation of the old order by the new. Cagney's Jarrett and his mother perish in favour of the likes of undercover Fed Fallon and Jarrett's wife, Verna, seduced by Big Ed. Both are adaptable yet capable of duplicity. Jarrett's first name, Cody, suggests he, however, lives by a scheme of honour, ignored by his peers. Such an adherence eventually leads to his downfall, despite his unusually 'modern' representation. His pathological devotion to his mother, the searing stress-induced headaches he suffers, his random outbreaks of extreme violence all point away from the environment-driven gangsters of the thirties – while curiously displaying the fruit of seeds first planted in Paul Muni's portrayal of Tony Carmonte in *Scarface* (qv). By turns emotional (witness the discovery of his mother's death in the prison mess hall via a line of whispering inmates) and inhuman (Verna states as much), Cagney's gangster is a complex and worthy creation.

With the shadow of the mushroom cloud hanging over the final scene, the twin evils of technology and society eventually defeat Jarrett, his individualism consumed and violated. From the new police tracking technology on display to the opening scene, as Cody rides the great 'iron horse' only for the train to steam burn one of his men, Jarrett becomes dogged by developments that overtake him. As much an apocalyptic warning as anything, the film reinvents prohibition, gasoline replacing liquor just as cocaine would replace that come the 1970s.

The film also signalled the end for gangster pictures pitting the lone figure against forces beyond his control; the following decade would see films like Walsh's and Jacques Tourneur's *Out of the Past* (qv) replaced by those depicting the gangster as the businessman, part of a faceless syndicate. *White Heat* remains the last of the truly great black-and-white gangster films.

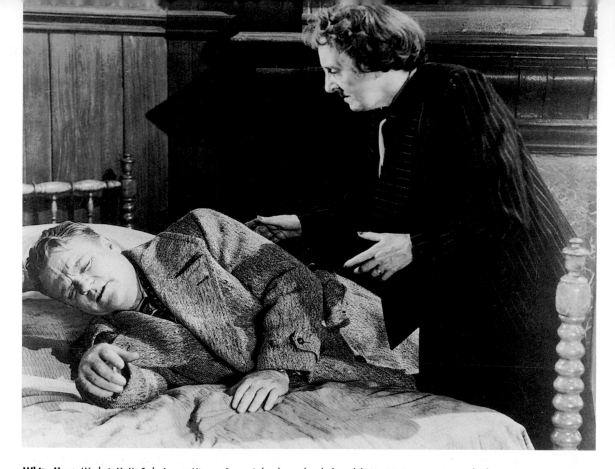

White Heat: 'Made it Ma!': Cody Jarrett (Jimmy Cagney) develops a headache, while Ma (Virginia Mayo) mops his brow.

Wise Guys

(US, MGM/UA, 1986, 91 mins)

'What's left is a limp, visually dull look at limp, mentally dull people.'

(Variety)

Credits
Dir: Brian De Palma
Prod: Aaron Russo
Scr: George Gallo
DOP: Fred Schuler
Ed: Jerry Greenberg
Music: Ira Newborn
Prod Des: Edward Pisoni

Cast: Danny DeVito (Harry Valentini), Joe Piscopo (Moe Dickstein), Harvey Keitel (Bobby DiLea), Ray Sharkey (Marco), Dan Hedaya (Anthony Castelo)

Two inept hoods set out to rob their Mafia boss, only to be set up to kill each other.

The biggest claim to fame for Brian De Palma's insignificant comedy is that it prevented Martin Scorsese's *Goodfellas* (qv) from being called 'Wiseguys', the original title to Nicholas Pileggi's book. Its only other link with the work is the casting of Frank Vincent, who featured in Scorsese's *Raging Bull*, and went on to gain parts as crew members in *Goodfellas* and *Casino*, as well as *The Pope of Greenwich Village* (qqv). As for De Palma, low-brow satire, notwithstanding early indie films like *Greetings* and *Hi Mom!*, is not his genre. In comparison to the coke-fuelled, garish *Scarface* (qv) three years before, this, with its trite explorations of loyalty, is naive and adolescent.

See also: *Bugsy Malone*; *Freshman, The*; *I'm Gonna Git You, Sucka*; *Johnny Dangerously*.

Yakuza, The (aka Brotherhood of the Yakuza)

(US, Warner Brothers, 1974, 112 mins)

Credits
Dir/Prod: Sydney Pollack
Prod: Michael Hamilburg
Scr: Paul Schrader, Robert Towne
DOP: Kozo Okazaki, Duke Callaghan
Ed: Thomas Stanford, Don Guidice
Music: David Grusin
Prod. Des: Stephen Grimes

Cast: Robert Mitchum (Harry Kilmer), Ken Takakura (Tanaka Ken),

Brian Keith (George Tanner), Keiko Kishi (Tanaka Eiko), Okada Eiji (Tono Toshiro)

An American in Japan seeks his friend's kidnapped daughter, and comes to blows with the yakuza.

As elucidating as his essay on the genre, the Paul Schrader co-scripted work in some ways is definitive of the yakuza film. As he notes of this 'lone wolf in the clan of gangster films', begun in earnest with Shigehiro Ozawa's *Bakuto (Gambler)* in 1964, 'The yakuza-*eiga* bears little resemblance to its American or European counterparts. The yakuza film does not reflect the dilemma of social mobility seen in the thirties gangster films, nor does it reflect the despair of postwar *film noir*. It [instead] seeks to codify a positive workable morality. Like the Western, the yakuza-*eiga* chooses timelessness over relevance, myth over realism; it seeks not social commentary, but moral truth.' The yakuza figure, meaning 'good-for-nothing' or 'gambler' superseded the Samurai in Japan's ailing movie output. It was revitalized by Toei Studios in the 1960s with their clutch of cheaply made yakuza movies – with characters as interchangeable as plots. Common conflict would arise from the battle between duty and humanity, opening possibilities to what Schrader called 'old forms of fascism'. As he pointed out, both the new left (student radicals) and new right (Mishima's Self-Defence force) took the genre as their own. The radicals, for example, were known to sit for hours watching such films in preparation for a clash with police.

Such moral obligation – shown in Schrader and Towne's own script – was indeed the antithesis of the American gangster film. Personal motivations become subservient to duty. That the word yakuza is built, in the Japanese Kana, from the numbers eight, nine and three (totalling 20, a losing number in Japanese gambling) indicates a perverse streak, a recognition of failure. As we are told: 'When an American cracks up, he opens up the window and shoots a bunch of strangers. When a Japanese cracks up, he closes the window and kills himself.' One may argue this is Pollack and Warner Brothers' ultimate exploitation of the oriental action film, capitalising on local colour. But Schrader and Towne – using Robert Mitchum as their cipher –

The Yakuza: Tank Ken (Ken Takakura) performs his duty, while Harry Kilmer (Robert Mitchum) takes five.

explore the rich and complex web of moralities that motivate each character. Like the impassive Mitchum we are observers into another culture, a code of honour that rigorously demands that burdens must be carried, sacrifices must be made. Including some of what Schrader listed as the '20 or so basic yakuza set pieces' (the finger cutting, duel scene, final battle), *The Yakuza* follows the demands of the genre, while drawing back the curtain for the Western audiences to obtain the insider's view.

See also: *American Yakuza*; *American Yakuza II*; *Black Rain*; *Boiling Point*; *Kids Return*; *Sonatine*.

Yao A Yao Yao Dao Wai Pe Qiao: See Shanghai Triad.

Years Without Days: See Castle on the Hudson.

Young Dillinger

(US, Allied Artists, 1965, 99 mins)

'An uninspired piece of flotsam washed up by the success of Bonnie and Clyde... the script flounders along in an attempt at turning Dillinger from all-American boy into murderous thug and back again at the drop of a plea from his dewy-eyed sweetheart... It doesn't, in fact, even begin to challenge Max Nosseck's Dillinger on its own B-picture territory.'

(Monthly Film Bulletin, upon re-release of film)

Credits
Dir/Ed. Terry Morse
Prod: Al Zimbalist
Scr: Arthur Hoerl, Don Zimbalist
DOP: Stanley Cortez
Music: Shorty Rogers
Art Dir: Don Ament

Cast: Nick Adams (John Dillinger), Robert Conrad ('Pretty Boy' Floyd), John Ashey ('Baby Face' Nelson), Mary Ann Mobley (Elaine), Dan Terranova (Homer Van Meter)

Biopic of the bank robber.

Made upon the lowest of budgets (check out extras walking around in 1960s clothing), this exploitative effort offers a highly romanticised vision of the Dillinger myth, taking severe liberties with the facts – not least, the plastic surgery he undergoes subsequent to becoming Public Enemy No. 1. With the opening setting him alongside Tom Powers, as he and girlfriend Elaine go to watch *The Public Enemy* (qv) with young John impersonating his idol, the film is on a losing streak from the beginning. Such emulation automatically negates the force of his own criminal activities, reducing him to a mere silver-screen hero-worshiper. Viewing his life in terms of his love for Elaine, rather than his relationship with Nelson and Floyd (whom he meets with in prison), his crimes ensure he will never be domestically happy. To get married he needed money. Upon procuring some illegally, his reputation means he is unable to apply for a marriage licence (else run the risk of capture).
Dedicated to those who fight the Dillingers of this world, the film closes with a biblical quotation: 'They have sewn the wind, and they shall reap the whirlwind.' (Hosea VIII, 7). Set to a picture of Dillinger on the run, the crime doesn't pay message comes through a little too loud and clear.

See also: *Bonnie and Clyde*; *Bonnie Parker Story, The*; *Bullet For Pretty Boy, A*; *Dillinger*; *George Raft Story, The*; *Lepke*; *Lucky Luciano*; *Machine Gun Kelly*; *Rise and Fall of Legs Diamond, The*.

Young Scarface: See Brighton Rock.

SOLIHULL S.F.C.
LIBRARY

Selected Bibliography

Andrew, Geoff, 'Demme God', *Time Out*, 21 June 1989, pp 28-30

Biskind, Peter, 'Dick Tracy', *US Premiere*, June 1990, pp 86-88

'The politics of power in 'On the Waterfront', *Film Quarterly*, Autumn 1975, pp 25-38

Carney, Ray, *The Films of John Cassavetes: Pragmatism, Modernism and the Movies*, Cambridge University Press, 1994

Christie, Ian/DavidThompson, *Scorsese on Scorsese*, Faber & Faber, 1989

Combs, Richard, 'Perform and Tell', *Sight & Sound*, Autumn 1984, p 299

'Public Enemy', *Monthly Film Bulletin*, February 1976, pp 38-39

Cook, Jim, 'Bonnie and Clyde', *Screen*, July/October 1969, pp 101-114

Dargis, Manohla, 'Method and Madness', *Sight & Sound*, June 1995, pp 6-8

Darke, Chris, 'The Kubrick Connection', *Sight & Sound*, November 1995, pp 22-25

Dyson, Michael Eric, 'Out of the Ghetto', *Sight & Sound*, October 1992, pp 18-21

Hayman, Martin, 'Perry Henzell Interview', *Cinema Rising*, August 1972, p 3

Kay, Karyn, 'Sisters of the Night', *Velvet Light Trap*, Autumn 1972, pp 20-24

Kaminsky, Stuart M., 'The Killers', *Take One*, July/August 1973, pp 17-19

Kerr, Paul, 'Kiss of Death: Review', *Time Out*, 15 June 1979, p 46

Klady, Leonard, 'Hard Boiled', *Screen International*, 24 July 1992, p 16

Lipman, Amanda, 'Leon: Review', *Sight & Sound*, February 1995, pp 47-48

Lomenzo, Elaine, 'A Fable for Adults', *Film Comment*, July/August 1984, pp 21-23

Macnab, Geoffrey, 'The Infiltrator', *Sight & Sound*, May 1997, pp 6-9

Martin, James Michael, 'Point Blank', *Film Quarterly*, Summer 1968, pp 40-43

Maxwell, Howard, 'Call Sheet: Get Carter', *Film Review*, November 1996, pp 44-47

McCabe, Bob, 'East End Heat', *Sight & Sound*, October 1997, pp 10-12

McEntee, Joy, 'Ladies, Bring a Poisoned Plate', Media Information Australia, May 1994, pp 41-48

McDonagh, Maitland, 'Straight to Hell', *Film Comment*, Nov/Dec 1990, pp 30-31

McVicar, John, 'Flowers of Evil', *Time Out*, 14 March 1990, p 18

Mills, David, 'Funk in the Age of Rap', *Black Film Review*, 1991, pp 6-8, 25

Pechter, William, 'Abraham Polonsky and Force of Evil', *Film Quarterly*, 1962, pp 47-54

Pond, Steve, 'Babes in Gangland', *US Premiere*, August 1991, pp 68-74

Pym, John, 'Framed: Michael Cimino', *Sight and Sound*, Winter 1990/91, pp 30-31

Rayns, Tony, 'The Harder Way', *Sight & Sound*, June 1996, pp 24-27

'Poet of Time', *Sight & Sound*, September 1995, pp 12-15

Richardson, John H., 'The Joel and Ethan Story', *US Premiere*, October 1990, pp 94-101

Rosenbaum, Jonathan, 'Lucky Luciano', *Monthly Film Bulletin*, June 1975, pp 140

Rosow, Eugene, *Born to Lose: The gangster film in America*, Oxford University Press, 1978

Savage, Jon, 'Tuning into Wonders', *Sight & Sound*, September 1995, pp 24-25

Scher, Saul N., 'The Glass Key: The original and two copies', *Literature and Film Quarterly*, Vol.12, n.3, 1984, pp 147-159

Schrader, Paul, 'Notes on Film Noir', *Film Comment*, Spring 1972, pp 8-13,

'A Primer: We're outlaws but we're humane', *Film Comment*, January 1974, pp 10-17

Schruers, Fred, 'Brando Giveth Brando Taketh Away', *US Premiere*, September 1990, pp 39-43

Smith, Anna Deavere, 'Spike Lee: Clockers', *US Premiere*, October 1995, pp 105-108

Smith, Steve, 'Godard and Film Noir: A Reading of A Bout De Souffle', Nottingham French Studies, Spring 1993, pp 65-72

Stivers, Cyndi, 'Family Reunion', *US Premiere*, January 1991, pp 76-84, 106

Strick, Philip, 'Bugsy: Review', *Sight & Sound*, April 1992, pp 45-46

'Bloody Mama', *Monthly Film Bulletin*, May 1971, p 93

Stringer, Julian, 'Your Tender Smiles Give Me Strength: Paradigms of Masculinity in John Woo's A Better Tomorrow and The Killer', *Screen*, Spring 1997, pp 25-41

Taubin, Amy, 'Girl N The Hood', *Sight & Sound*, August 1993, pp 16-17

Thompson, David, 'A Cottage at Palos Verdes', *Film Comment*, May/June 1990, pp 16-21

Thomson, Patricia, 'James Gray Writer/Director: Little Odessa', *The Independent*, April 1995, p 15

Tunney, Tom, 'Hard Boiled', *Sight & Sound*, October 1993, p 47

Woo, John, 'Private View: Chinese Poetry in Motion', *Sight & Sound*, July 1994, p 61

Wood, Robin, *Hollywood from Vietnam to Reagan*, Columbia University Press, 1986